Troubleshooting Your Rifle and Shotgun

By
J. B. Wood

DBI BOOKS, INC./NORTHFIELD, ILLINOIS

STAFF

EDITOR
Robert S. L. Anderson

ART DIRECTION
Mary MacDonald

COVER PHOTOGRAPHY
John Hanusin

PRODUCTION MANAGER
Pamela J. Johnson

ASSOCIATE PUBLISHER
Sheldon L. Factor

This book is dedicated to my wife, Marijo

Acknowledgements:

In putting this book together, I received assistance from many different sources. I would like to express my appreciation to each of those who helped:

B&S Sporting Guns, Glenn Lancaster, Dr. Kenneth Eblen, Ken Reynolds, Chris Reynolds, Bob Guenther, Ron Lankford, Glenn Wilson, James R. Harris, Daniel M. Byrne, Robert L. Greenwell, Ray Diekmann, Klee Raleigh, Arch Lenighan, Jack Hogan, Don Leathers, Chuck Snyder, Clarence Tillerson, John R. Wilkinson, Homer Koon, Boyd Barber, Gene Wilson, Jack Lewis, Ken Warner, George Martin, and Frank de Haas.

J.B.W.

ISBN 0695–81198–3

Library of Congress Catalog Card Number 78–70510

Introduction

Those who have been reading the monthly firearms publications for around 10 years will recall seeing my Troubleshooting column, which appeared in most issues of *Gunfacts*, then ran for about 2 years in *Guns & Ammo*. More recently, it has made brief appearances in *Gun World* and *Gun Digest*, and is presently running in *The American Handgunner* and *Guns Magazine*. There is a companion volume to this book, titled *Troubleshooting Your Handgun;* and, of course, you should get that one to complete the set!

There is one point that I would like to emphasize very strongly: *Neither of the books is intended to be an instruction manual for the amateur gunsmith*. Although some elementary gunsmithing operations may occasionally be described, you will more often find the suggestion that you obtain the services of a competent professional.

You will find numerous references in this book to the relative fragility of flat springs, also called "blade" springs. It should be noted, though, that these are not inherently fragile. Their tendency toward breakage depends directly on the degree to which they are flexed in normal operation. A blade-type spring not flexed to its limit may last as long as a more modern round-wire type.

Even the best designs are, in some areas, a compromise. Even the best designs may have a point or two that can cause trouble, after years of hard use. It has not been my intention to imply that because of some small quirk, the subject gun is a poor one. Some of the trouble spots occur very infrequently, and these are so noted. Among the guns covered are several that I own and use regularly. If I thought they were mechanically deficient, I wouldn't be using them.

The concept of *troubleshooting* is a simple one: *Diagnosis*. On the gun you might own or consider buying, these things may never happen. However, here's what to watch for, and if it happens, here's what to do about it.

J.B. Wood
Raintree House
Corydon, Kentucky
October, 1978

In regard to the mechanical and safety aspects of the guns covered in this book, it is assumed that the guns are in factory original condition with the dimensions of all parts as made by the manufacturer. Since alteration of parts is a simple matter, the reader is strongly advised to have any gun checked by a competent gunsmith. Both the author and publisher disclaim responsibility for any accidents.

Table of Contents

The British Enfield shown is a late rifle, made in 1942. It's a No. 4 Mark I*, and is different from the original SMLE in certain small details.

British Enfield Rifle

From 1895 to 1951, the soldiers of the British Empire were armed with Lee-Enfield rifles. In a long and often confusing line of "Marks" and "Numbers," the one with which most people are familiar is the original SMLE (Short, Magazine, Lee-Enfield), which came along in 1903. All of the various models differed only in small details, and the only true mechanical difference was in the No. 4 Mark I* rifle, an example of which is shown in the photos. Otherwise, the feed and firing mechanisms are virtually identical throughout the entire group.

From Lawrence of Arabia to the beaches of Dunkirk, the Lee-Enfield has proven its ruggedness and reliability time after time. Its rear-locking bolt and the fact that it cocks on closing may be listed on the minus side, but its mechanical design is practically faultless. Several blade-type springs are used, but they seem to break very infrequently. In some cases, this is due to a lack of severe flexing. In others, it is a tribute to careful heat treatment by the arsenals

where the gun was produced. The two leaf-type springs that receive the most frequent compression are the ones powering the extractor and the magazine catch. The magazine spring might also be included in this list, but its length and double-V shape minimizes extreme stress, and breakage is quite rare. Both the extractor spring and the magazine catch spring are small V-types, and if one of these should eventually succumb to fatigue, replacement is simple and easy and can usually be done by the amateur. Parts are readily available from several of the surplus dealers, and if these should run out in time, any of the springs could be duplicated by making slightly redesigned versions in round spring wire.

It is fortunate that the firing pin of the Enfield is not prone to breakage, because removing it is *not* a simple matter, unless you have a special wrench which will reach its internal collar. Also, its design is not conducive to repointing; however, making an entire new firing pin is not a diffi-

cult operation. Again, this should not be necessary, as parts are abundant.

The manual safety, located at the left rear of the receiver, is of unusual design. Its pivot-shaft has a rapid helical thread which moves a steel lug inward as the lever is swung toward the rear, the lug effectively blocking both the striker and the bolt. The striker has an external knob, allowing the gun to be manually recocked in case of an insensitive primer.

Removal of the bolt is done quite easily, but may be baffling to those who are not familiar with this gun. In the earlier rifles, there is an access cut in the right-hand bolt rail immediately to the rear of the receiver bridge, and a small spring catch beside it. The bolt head is positioned in line with the cut, the catch depressed, and the bolt head pivoted upward to vertical position. In the later Mark I* rifles, the access cut is forward, near the chamber, and there is no spring catch. Otherwise, the operation is the same. In both cases, the rear sight must be raised to clear the bolt as it is withdrawn to the

rear. In the later rifles, positioning of the bolt head at the release cut is made easier if the striker is in the uncocked position.

Most "gun" people are thoroughly familiar with the .303 British military cartridge, a round which is also available in commercial loadings. For those who aren't as familiar with the cartridge, it might be wise to point out that there is another round with a .303 designation—the .303 Savage, a sporting cartridge with entirely different dimensions. It is, of course, *not* interchangeable with the British .303 round.

Enfield bolts were individually fitted to each rifle, and although interchangeability is possible, it should not be assumed. If there is any doubt about the gun having proper headspace, have it checked by a competent gunsmith before firing it. This is a good policy to follow with *any* military rifle.

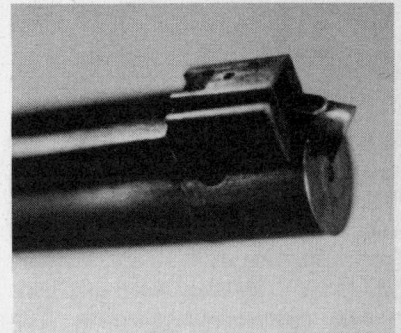

The Enfield has a large, heavy pivoting extractor, powered by a blade-type spring. Breakage of the extractor is very rare, and spring failure is uncommon. If it happens, replacement is not difficult.

On earlier guns, the bolt removal cut is at the rear, near the bolt handle position. On the No. 4 Mk. I* rifle (as shown in the photos) the removal cut (top) is near the chamber area (arrow). With the bolt at this point, the bolt head is pivoted (center) to the vertical position (bottom), and the bolt can be taken out.

Of unusual design is the safety catch (arrow). Its pivot shaft has a rapid helical thread, and when rotated to the on-safe position shown, it moves a heavy steel lug inward to lock both striker and bolt.

Bronco .410 Shotgun

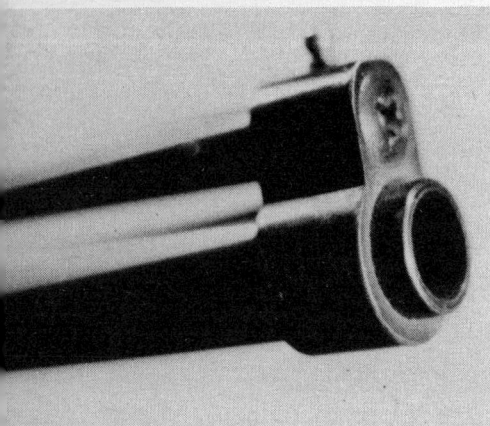

The Phillips-head screw at the muzzle should be checked occasionally for tightness.

Originally the Garcia Corporation offered this gun in two separate chamberings, .22 and .410, and both were intended for utility use. All-metal skeletonized construction made them lightweight, and they were good guns for the camper and fisherman, with other applications as a survival piece to be carried in autos and private aircraft. More recently, a combination version has been introduced, an over/under gun firing both the .22 and .410.

The Bronco achieves its light weight not only by its skeletonized design, but also by the use of non-ferrous alloy for the buttstock and receiver. In the .22, this caused no problems; however, the .410, being under somewhat more stress, has occasionally developed cracks in the handle which is used to pivot the barrel for loading. This ailment is not dangerous and seems to have no relation to the increased pressures of the shotgun. In the examples I've seen, the breakage seems to be due to the rougher handling that a shotgun might normally receive, in comparison to a .22 rifle. The base of the operating handle is deeply cut out to surround the barrel latch stud, leaving this alloy part fairly thin at that point—this is likely a contributing factor. Since the handle is an integral part of the sleeve which surrounds the rear of the barrel and its long pivot pin, the best break-age repair would require replacement of the entire sleeve. Parts are available, but the fitting of this one should best be left to a gunsmith.

It is possible to repair a cracked handle by drilling a slanted hole and cross-pinning the cracked parts in place, but this is not a job for the amateur, as the hole will come perilously close to the chamber area of the barrel. The gun shown in the photos has had this repair and has seen quite a bit of use since this was done. In some cases, though, this repair may not be possible, depending on the pattern of the break.

The Bronco is a true hammerless, striker-fired gun, and the trigger-shaped lever forward of the trigger guard not only releases the barrel to pivot, but also cocks the striker as it is pulled toward the rear. An oddly square-shaped cross-bolt safety directly blocks the trigger movement. The firing mechanism is well-designed, and no chronic breakage of any of its elements has been observed. The ejector is a manually-operated

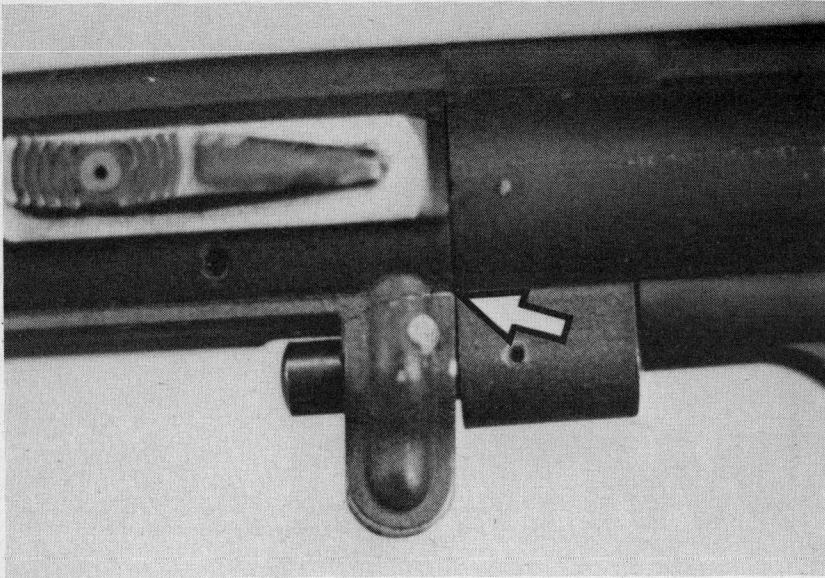

The barrel pivot-handle, which also serves as part of the barrel-latch system, tends to crack (arrow) with *rough* usage. Note the repair pin just below the crack.

sliding type, actuated by a large external thumb-piece on the left side of the barrel housing. It is of fairly sturdy construction, and does not break often.

The long barrel pivot-rod is secured at the muzzle by a counter-sunk Phillips-type screw, and this should be checked occasionally for tightness. The other components of the gun are retained by roll-type cross-pins, and the amateur is advised against complete disassembly. There are several unusual aspects of this design which can make amateur reassembly very interesting. Although the gun covered here is the .410 version, most of the remarks above could also be applied to the .22 gun. I have not had occasion to repair the more recent .22/.410 combination, and its barrel-locking design is different, so it should be considered separately.

As long as the relative fragility of the pivot handle is kept in mind, and this part treated accordingly, there is no reason why the Bronco, in either chambering, couldn't serve as a good camping, fishing, or survival gun for many years. It is otherwise quite durable, and its firing mechanism seems to be practically infallible.

With the barrel pivoted to loading position, the barrel latch plunger and stud can be seen. Note also the end of the repair pin, just below the pivot-handle.

Browning .22 Automatic Rifle

John Moses Browning designed this neat little rifle in 1913, and Fabrique Nationale of Belgium put it into production the following year. Remington leased the American production rights in 1922, made a few minor modifications in the design, and introduced the gun as their Model 24. A slightly redesigned version replaced this gun in 1936, this one designated the Model 241. It continued in production until 1951. Meanwhile, back at FN, the basic 1914 model was still in production. In 1956 their gun was altered to be very much like the final Remington version, and it is currently available. Throughout this 65-year period, Browning's original design has had only very minor changes.

As you might expect from a design that has lasted this long, there are few weak points. Almost all of the problems that occur in this gun are the result of improper disassembly and reassembly. The barrel adjustment is a prime example of this. This rifle is made with a quick-takedown feature, the barrel and forend separating easily

One of the Browning's unique characteristics is the fact that it can be broken down into dimensions that make it suitable for carrying by the backpacker or weekend hunter with limited space.

from the receiver and buttstock for convenient storage in backpack or suitcase, or for cleaning. One of the liabilities in rifles that have quick barrel removal of this sort is that they will often loosen up over the years, affecting both accuracy and feeding. With the Browning, this doesn't happen. At the threaded rear end of the barrel there is a lock ring, sliding in upper and lower tracks, and a knurled adjustment ring ahead of this, threaded onto the barrel shank, to snug barrel, lock ring and receiver together. The adjustment ring is held in tightened position by a spring-powered plunger which bears on the serrated edge of the ring. It's an excellent system and insures that the barrel is seated to its proper depth and tightness in the receiver. Over the years, I have seen so many of these in poor adjustment that I have concluded that barrel adjustment is best left to your gunsmith, unless you have had a lot of experience with this gun.

The latch which releases the barrel unit for takedown is located at the

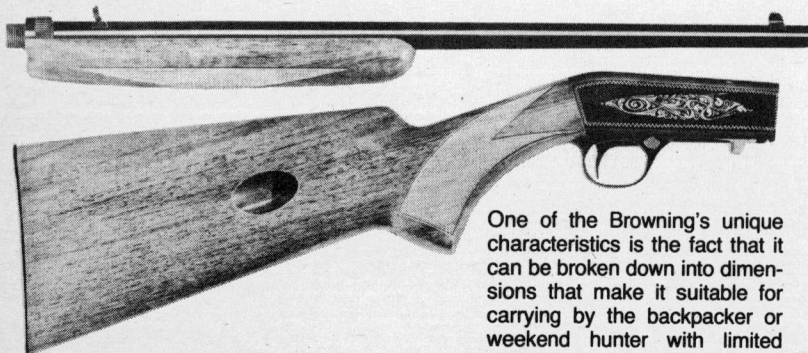

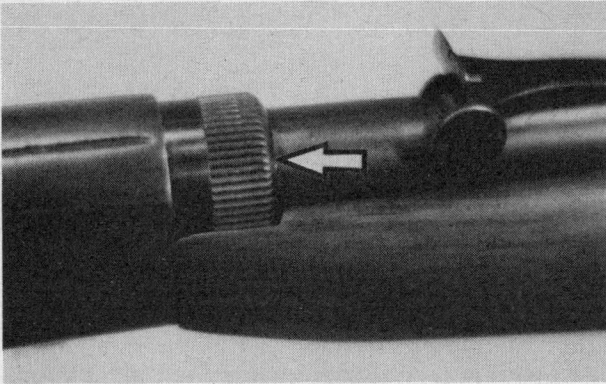

Arrow points to the barrel adjustment ring that maintains a snug fit of the barrel-to-receiver. This handy system eliminates the loosening up problem inherent in takedown rifles.

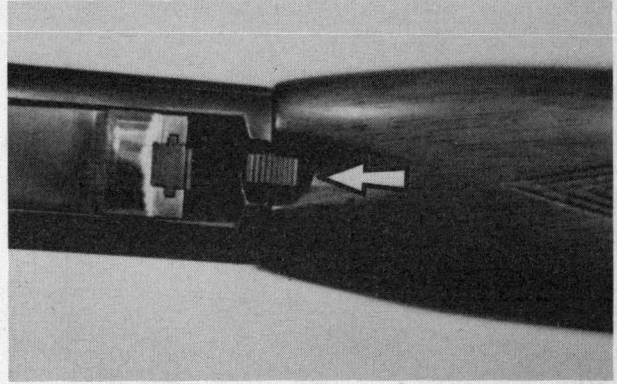

The takedown latch (arrow) is shown here in the locked position. To unlock, you move this latch in the opposite direction the arrow is pointing.

lower rear edge of the forend, and when pushed forward to release the barrel, the latch is stopped by the edge of the forend. If the forend is removed, however, there is nothing to stop the latch from being slid all the way out of its tracks in the underlug of the lock ring. When this is done, a small spring and plunger will depart and may never be seen again. These parts are essential, as they hold the barrel lock in position. Fortunately, all parts are readily available, and most of the larger gun shops will have them in stock. In this same area, if the lock ring is removed from the barrel shank, another spring-and-plunger set is likely to be lost, this one bearing on the adjustment ring.

It is fortunate that the internal parts of the rifle seldom break and that parts are easy to find, because this gun was designed in an era of meticulous handwork, and some of the parts have fairly intricate shapes, making shop reproduction difficult. The original striker, for example, is beautifully sculptured with a hollow, fluted body, tiny guide lug, and offset firing pin point. After 1972, when production of the gun was shifted from FN to Miroku of Japan, the striker was redesigned to simplify manufacturing.

On most models of this gun, the extractor assembly has four separate parts—the extractor itself, a spring, retainer, and cross-pin—and it is best left alone, unless removal is absolutely necessary. These parts fit together like a Chinese puzzle and are small and easily lost. When the trigger/bolt assembly is out of the re-

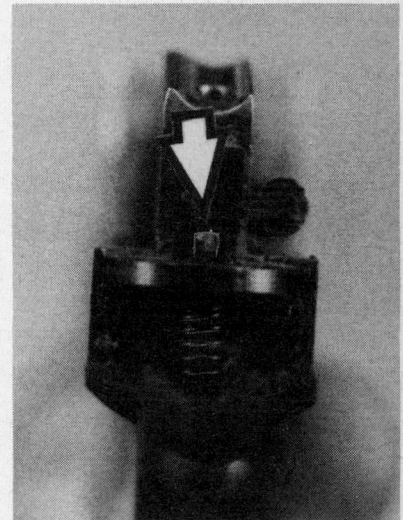

In this rear view of the trigger group, the arrow indicates the delicate engagement of the sear and disconnector.

CAUTION: When the forend is removed, the takedown latch (arrow) is easily slid forward out of its tracks in the barrel lock ring. When this happens, a small plunger and its spring are usually lost.

The twin-beaked extractor is mounted in vertical tracks in forward face of the bolt. There are four small parts in the extractor system, and, it should *not* be disassembled by the amateur.

ceiver, the cartridge stop can drop from the inside top of the receiver and be lost. Usually, this can only happen with older guns that have seen considerable use, as the stop has a very precise fit.

The engagement of the sear with the rear upper arm of the disconnector is fairly delicate, and with long use and extreme wear can begin to malfunction. This can usually be corrected by recutting or spring replacement, without installing new parts. Properly assembled and maintained, these guns seldom have problems.

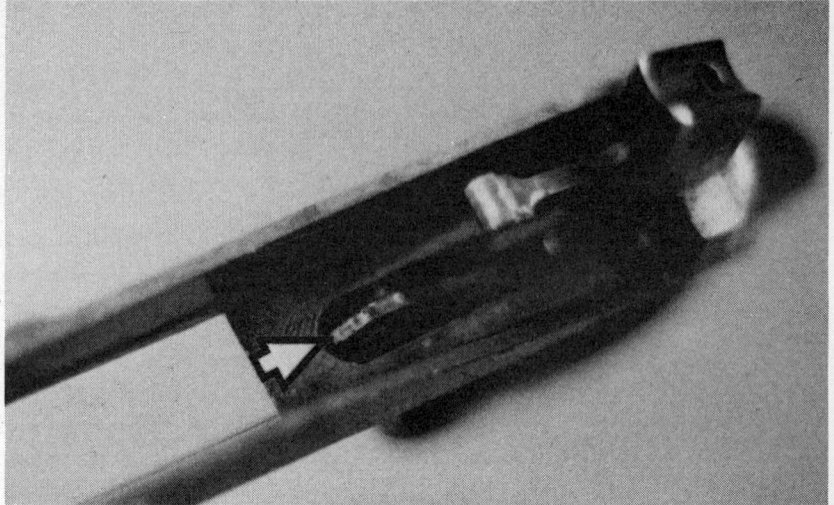

The long, curved disconnector (arrow) is mounted in the center of the trigger and contacts the underside of the breech block.

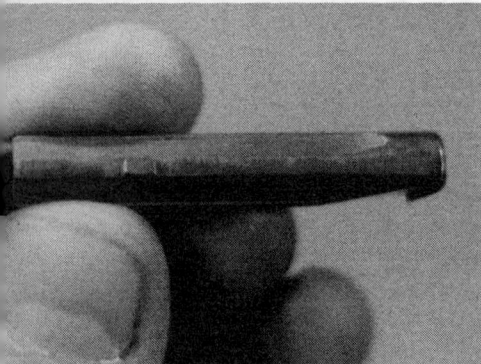

Replacement parts are available for the little Browning. The fact that parts *are* available is indeed fortunate as reproducing this hollow striker with fluted sides and offset firing pin would be time-consuming as well as expensive.

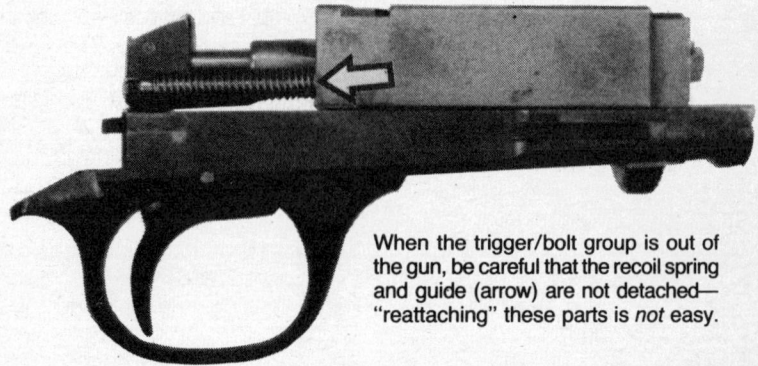

When the trigger/bolt group is out of the gun, be careful that the recoil spring and guide (arrow) are not detached— "reattaching" these parts is *not* easy.

Inside of the top of the receiver, the cartridge stop (left arrow) and the cartridge guide spring (right arrow) control the feeding.

12

Browning Lever-Action Rifle

In the coded Browning model designations, this gun is called the "BLR," meaning, of course, "Browning Lever Rifle." The gun was first offered in 1971 and is still in production. The early guns were made at the FN plant in Belgium, but since early 1974 the BLR has been made for Browning by Miroku of Japan. The internal mechanism of this gun is a brilliant piece of engineering. Unlike most lever-actions, the lever is not connected directly to the bolt. Instead, the upper portion of the lever contains a toothed track which contacts a circular gear, and the larger part of this gear mates with a toothed track on the underside of the bolt. The result is the smoothest lever-action yet made. There have been other gear-tooth applications in lever-action guns, such as the Sako and the Remington Nylon 76, but these did not have a fully circular gear acting directly on the bolt.

Because of the gear teeth on the underside of the bolt, the BLR has a very "early" cocking lobe for its ex-

The arrow indicates the "early" cocking lobe of the BLR bolt, necessitated by the gear teeth on the underside of the bolt.

With the action opened, the long row of gear teeth on the underside of the bolt can be seen. Note that the cocked hammer is well below the teeth.

13

The multiple lugs of the rotating bolt head and their lug recesses in the receiver should be kept clean and lightly oiled.

ternal hammer. When cocked, the hammer sets well below the gear teeth. Both lobe and hammer are of well-hardened steel, and there is ample allowance for any wear that might occur over the years. It should be noted, though, that any amateur attempt to "adjust" the trigger pull by altering the engagement of the hammer and sear can change the full-cock level of the hammer and cause it to contact the gear teeth on the bolt—a most undesirable situation.

The bolt has a rotating head with multiple locking lugs which mate with recesses inside the receiver. As with any locking system of this type, it is important that the lugs and recesses be kept clean and lightly oiled for continued smooth operation. The extractor is particularly strong and heavy, powered by a separate plunger and spring, and breakage is unlikely. The firing pin is of one-piece design, running the full length of the bolt and does not appear to be susceptible to breakage.

The lever latch, which keeps the lever snug when the action is closed, is located on the right side of the lever just above the trigger. This part is subject to considerable stress and wear each time the action is cycled, and I do know of one case in which the latch was broken at its narrowest point which is the cut for its retaining pin. The latch is well-supported in the lever, and I think breakage could be viewed as a freak occurrence. After many years of use, the lever latch might need to be replaced because of extreme wear, but I doubt that many of them will break.

The BLR has another feature that is odd in an outside-hammer lever action—a detachable box magazine with a four-round capacity. One could almost wish that they had made it for three rounds and kept it flush with the receiver. It protrudes slightly and in certain situations might be susceptible to damage. The complaint is mostly on the basis of appearance, though, as this magazine is of very sturdy construction.

The precise mating of the cocking gear with the lever and bolt, and other unusual aspects of the internal mechanism would suggest that complete disassembly for cleaning should be left to the gunsmith. The BLR is made with typical Browning precision, and I can detect nothing in the design that might cause any serious problems. It's one of the very good ones.

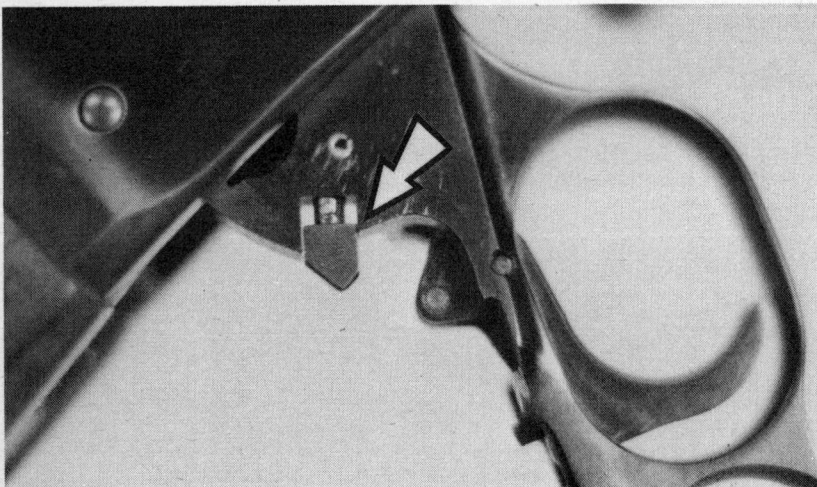

Arrow points to the lever latch, a part that is subject to considerable stress and wear.

Browning A-5 Shotgun

The old-timers can skip this introduction, as they will know the details well. For the newcomers, Browning patented the gun in 1900, and it was first produced by the Fabrique Nationale in Belgium, beginning in 1903. In 1905, the U.S. manufacturing rights were leased to Remington, and they made it from that date until 1948. As produced by Remington, there were several slight differences in the internal design, and while some of the parts of the two guns can be adapted, they are not freely interchangeable. After 75 years, the basic gun is still being made, the design virtually unchanged from John M. Browning's original specifications.

Its reliability is almost legendary, and most of the problems that arise are either from honest wear after many years of hard use, or from shooter error. In the latter category is the arrangement of the friction system. This gun operates on the long-recoil pattern, with the barrel and breech block traveling all the way to the rear, locked together, before unlocking. To reduce the rear impact of these heavy parts, there is a bronze friction piece in front of the recoil spring, surrounding the magazine tube, and the friction piece is compressed during recoil by a beveled surface inside the forward ring which supports the barrel. It is also compressed at the rear by a separate steel ring with a concave inner surface. After all this time, you would think that most shooters should have learned the proper way to assemble this system, however, failures to feed can often be directly traced to improper positioning of these parts. The original instructions specify that for heavy loads, the ring should be in front of the recoil spring, with the concave surface toward the rear of the friction piece. For light loads, the ring is re-

Shown is the proper arrangement of the friction system for medium to heavy loads. The ring is in front of the spring, with its concave surface toward the bronze friction piece.

15

moved, and placed with flat surface forward, to the rear of the spring, next to the receiver. Ninety percent of the A-5's that I have examined have the ring (if it's there at all), in the light load position, and the shooters ask why the recoil is so sharp, and why the gun is throwing the empty cases into the next field.

In most cases, it would be better to just leave the system set up for medium to heavy loads, for several reasons. The recoil spring, over a period of years and with much use, will tend to take a slight ''set,'' and will lose some of its damping effect, even though it still works the action effici-

The ejector (arrow) is riveted to the barrel extension. In case of breakage, replacement is a job for your gunsmith.

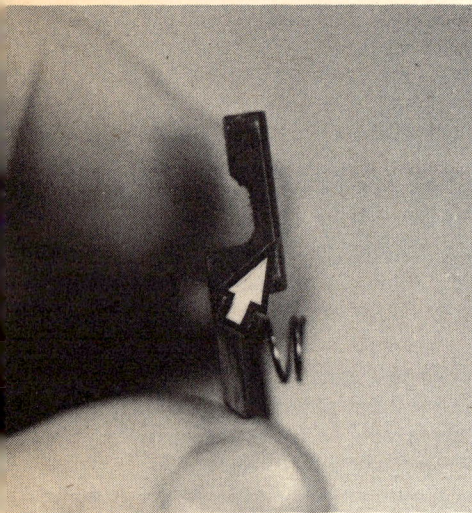

This is the cartridge stop. Its upper arm (arrow) is cammed outward by an incline on the barrel extension, and there is often wear at the contact point. This can usually be repaired without replacement.

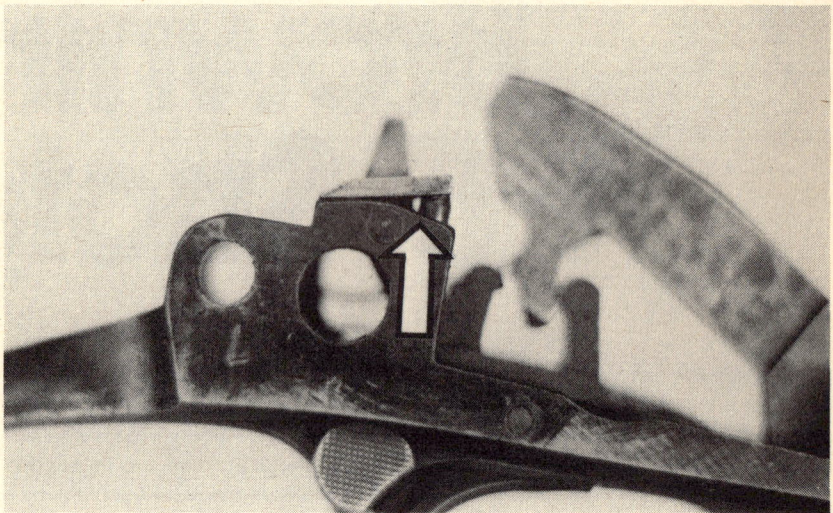

Arrow indicates the safety sear, a part that usually causes trouble only during amateur reassembly.

ently. Also, few shooters use shells that are loaded so light that the action would require removal of the compressor ring. On a very tight new gun, or one in which the recoil spring has just been replaced, it might be necessary to go to the light arrangement for some shells. While in the area of the friction system, it should be noted that the friction surface, the outside of the magazine tube, should be kept clean and oiled.

The ejector fits into a recess in the left side of the barrel extension and is riveted in place. It has two projections which contact the head of the shell and will often continue to work even if one

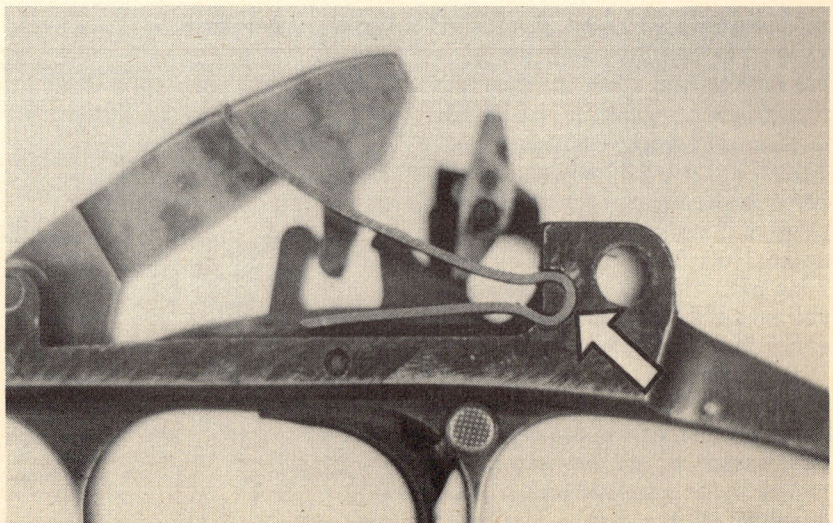

A blade-type carrier spring (arrow) is keyed into the trigger housing. These do not break often, but are susceptible to weakening.

of these is broken. If this part does require replacement, it's best to leave the job to your gunsmith. This is one of those things that looks simple—but it isn't.

The internal mechanism includes a safety sear, a device that prevents movement of the trigger until the breech is fully closed. This part causes no trouble in the normal operation, but it is the nemesis of the amateur reassembler. Unless he knows that the upper arm of the safety sear must be tipped into its track inside the bolt link bar, he'll never get the trigger housing back into place in the receiver. I have observed one case in which the safety sear pin was broken because someone lost patience and used force.

The forward edge of the carrier latch acts as a primary shell stop, and the secondary shell stop is a separate part, operated by its upper arm contacting an inclined surface on the barrel extension. This contact point will occasionally wear to such an extent that feeding will be affected. The shell stop can be replaced, of course, as all parts are readily available, but this is usually not necessary. The upper arm of the shell stop can be heated and reshaped slightly inward, to restore the proper reach.

The carrier spring is a flat type, V-shaped, with a keyhole-bend designed to fit over a stud in the receiver on the older guns, and into a recess in the trigger housing on later pieces. The carrier itself is also different on early and late models, being a single part on the older guns, and a two-part assembly on late ones. The spring occasionally breaks, but more often, on very old guns, it loses some of its tension, failing to return the carrier with sufficient snap for rapid feeding. Replacement of this spring is extremely simple.

The hammer spring seldom breaks, and if it should, almost any gun shop will have a replacement. This is fortunate on both counts, as this is a heavy blade-type spring with an open-

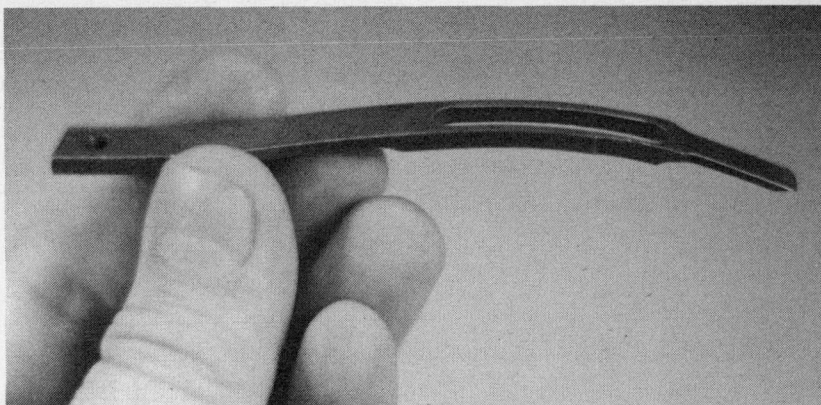

A typical A-5 spring is a heavy blade-type, with an opening in its forward position for the upper arms of the trigger. Reproduction would be difficult.

ing in its forward portion for the upper arms of the trigger, and reproduction would be difficult. The installation of a replacement should be done by a gunsmith. These same remarks could also apply to the combination trigger and safety spring, though this one could be made a bit more easily.

The carrier pivots on the blank tips of two screws which enter the receiver on each side, and it should be noted that these are individually fitted, especially on the older guns, and should

not be switched during complete disassembly and reassembly. In some cases, changing these from one side to the other will cause binding of the carrier which in turn may cause a failure to feed.

In addition to the Browning and Remington versions of this gun, the Savage company also made a series of very similar autoloaders from 1930 to 1958. Here, again, there were mechanical differences, and parts will *not* interchange.

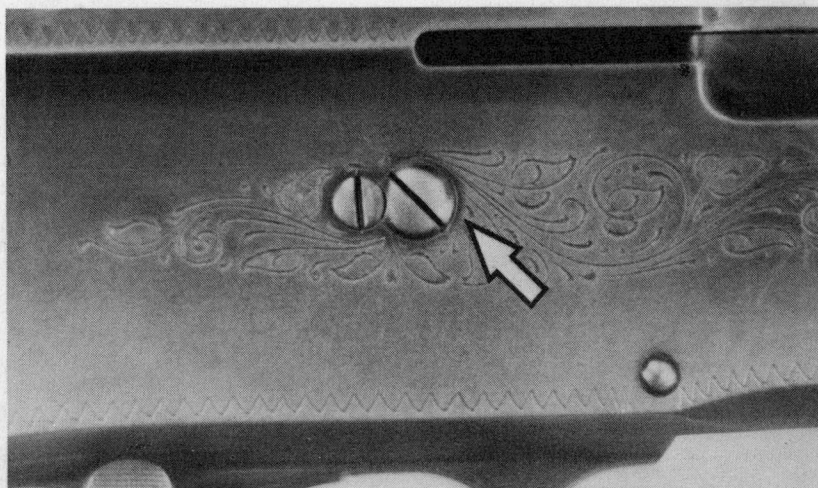

The arrow points to the right carrier pivot screw, which has a counterpart on the other side of the receiver. These are usually fitted exactly to each side, and if taken out, they should not be switched.

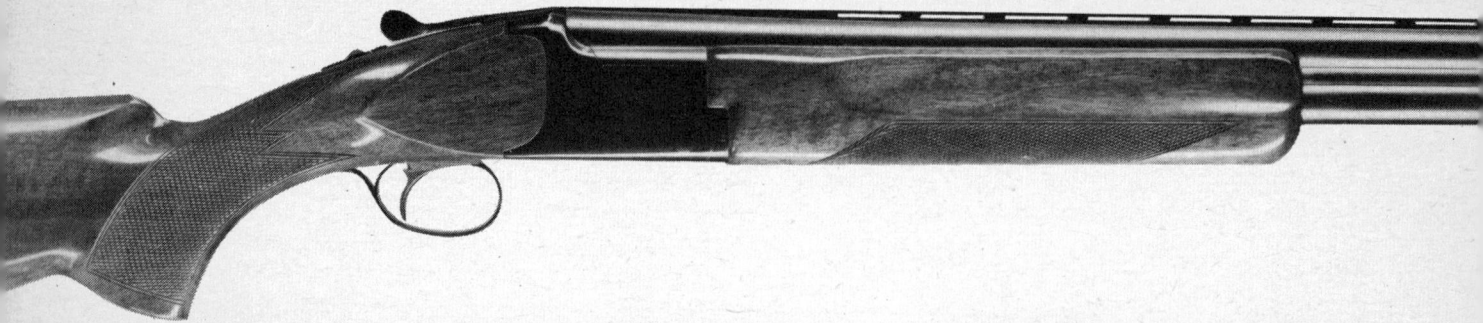

Browning Citori Over/Under Shotgun

For the many shotgunners who had long admired the elegant—and expensive—Browning Superposed over/under, there was welcome news in 1974 when a lower-priced model called the Liege was introduced. Just a year later, an even more economical version was offered, and named the Citori. By the following year, the Liege was discontinued, and the Citori continues in production today. To say that it has been enthusiastically received by the shooters would be an understatement. The price of the basic gun is only about one-sixth the cost of the Superposed, yet the Citori has many of the same features.

One of the differences is in the takedown procedure. On the Citori, the forend must be removed before the barrels can be separated from the receiver. The forend is retained by a lifter-type latch, and there is a beaked lug on the lower barrel which mates with the hook of the latch. After many takedowns, over a number of years, the beak on the lug will eventually sustain some wear. When this occurs, and the forend loosens, any tightening operation should be done to the latch in the forend, not the lug on the barrel. When replacing the forend on the assembled gun, the small pivoted part at the rear of the forend (the cocking lever lifter) must be carefully inserted into its T-slot between the front underlugs of the barrel unit before swinging the forend up into place.

The forend is retained by a lifter-latch, and wear may eventually occur on the beak of the latch lug on the lower barrel at the point indicated by the arrow.

During replacement of the forend assembly, the cocking lever lifter (arrow) must be carefully reinserted into its T-slot between the front underlugs of the barrel unit.

The key to the operation of the single trigger is the inertia block, operated by the recoil of the first shot, which switches the trigger into contact with the other sear. The inertia block is also connected to the safety system, and the safety button is also a selector, being moved from one side to the other, determining the barrel to be fired first. The weight, spring ten-

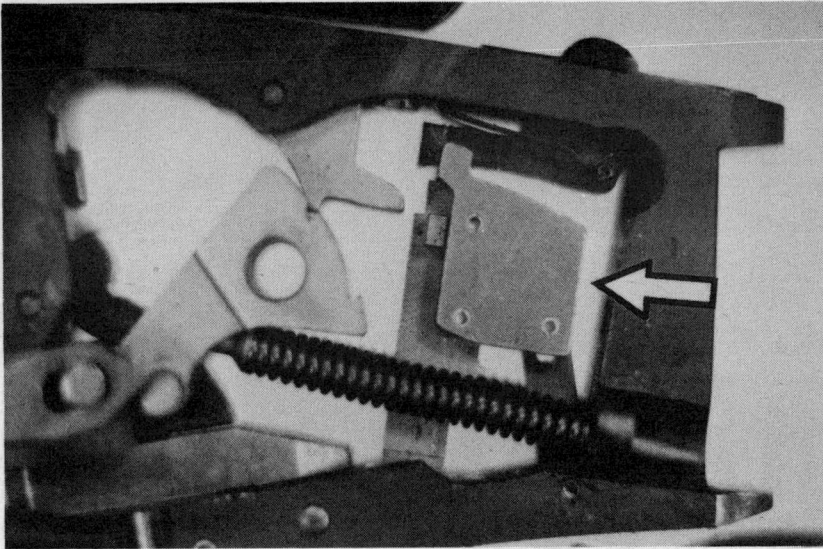

The arrow indicates the inertia block (operated by recoil) which switches the single trigger into contact with the other sear after one barrel has been fired. It is also connected to the safety and is shown in the on-safe position.

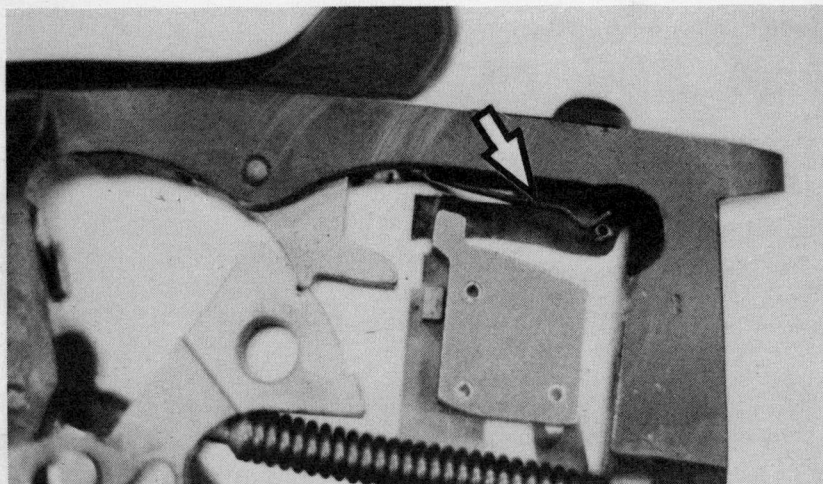

The safety positioning spring (arrow) is formed from flat stock. Breakage is rare, but they do occasionally weaken.

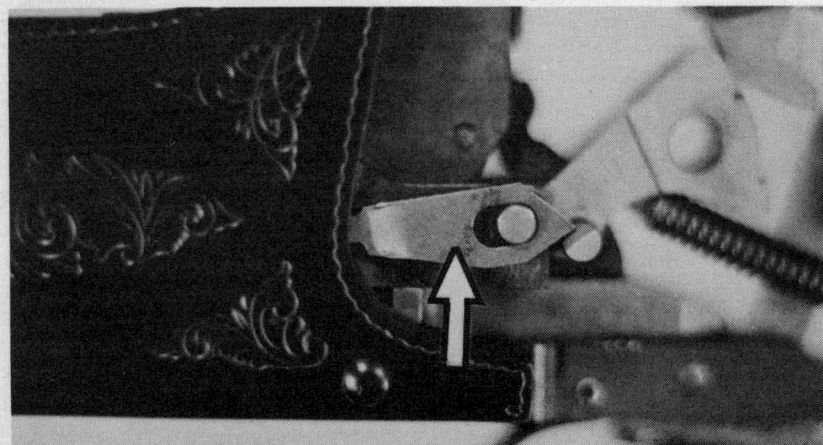

Here, the arrow points to the head of the left ejector trip rod, one of a pair. A stud on the hammer, seen just to the rear, alternately springs the rod outward or cams it forward.

sion, and free movement of the inertia block are essential to the proper operation of the single-trigger system, and the takedown and repair of this unit are definitely not in the realm of the amateur. Under normal circumstances, the inertia system requires no adjustment or special maintenance, and rarely needs attention. The only thing in this area that might require repair is the twin-armed safety positioning spring. It is a formed flat type, and since it is not severely flexed in normal operation, breakage is rare. These springs do occasionally weaken, but they can usually be reshaped to restore proper tension. Replacements are also available, of course.

The only other parts that may require occasional repair are the ejector trip rods, the devices that control the ejector hammers in the forend. These tempered rods extend back through the receiver to the hammers, and a side stud on the hammers alternately cams them forward, or springs them outward. If the spade-like rear heads of the rods or the main shafts become deformed (or lose some of their tension) the automatic portion of the ejector system will fail to function. This can often be repaired without replacement of parts, but it's a job for a professional.

Other than the two items mentioned above, the only repairs I have done on the Citori have been the replacement of an occasional broken firing pin—a thing that can eventually happen to any gun. Like most Browning products, the Citori has no chronic ailments, and with routine care should go on working almost indefinitely.

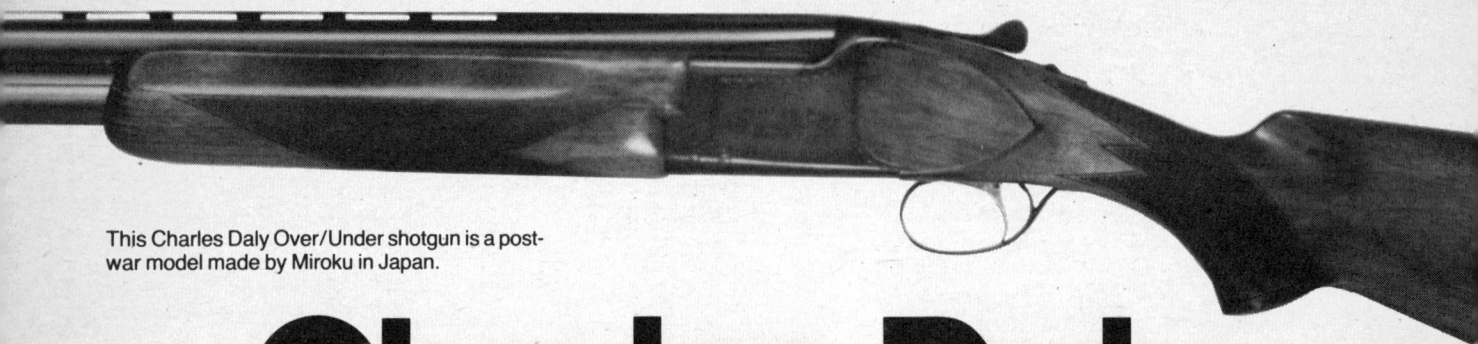
This Charles Daly Over/Under shotgun is a post-war model made by Miroku in Japan.

Charles Daly Over/Under Shotgun

The firm of Shoverling and Daly was in business as early as 1873, when they obtained manufacturing rights to the Marlin-Ballard rifle. Shoverling later left the partnership, and by 1920 the company, now under the Charles Daly name, was marketing a line of fine quality shotguns made exclusively for them in Suhl, Germany. From 1933 to 1939, some of the Daly guns were also made in Liege, Belgium. After WWII, production of the Charles Daly line was by Miroku of Kochi, Japan, and the guns were offered in this country until around 1976.

The last gun made, the Daly Over/Under, was of excellent quality in both materials and workmanship and had several good points in its design.

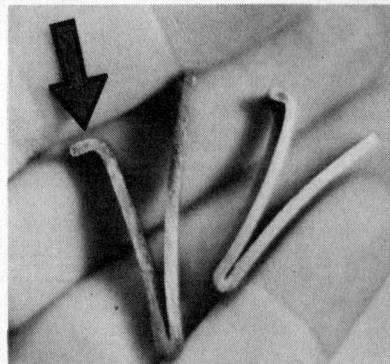
Occasionally, the right-angled tip of the hammer springs will snap off, at the point indicated by the arrow. Note that the two springs are not of equal size, and are not interchangeable.

Here, the arrow points to the engagement of the top hammer with the right sear. Note that the hammer, which fires the lower barrel, is pivoted in the top of the receiver.

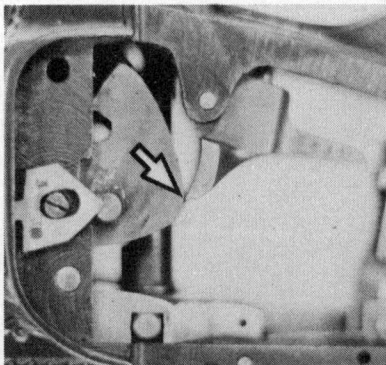
The left hammer, which fires the upper barrel, is pivoted at the center of the receiver. The arrow indicates its contact point with the left sear.

One of these was the arrangement of the hammers; the one for the lower barrel being pivoted near the top of the receiver on the right side, and the upper barrel hammer mounted at center on the left side. This gave both hammers a full arc, and eliminated the possiblity of a light strike from a shorter hammer that often occurs in

On the postwar Charles Daly, the only repeated breakage I have observed is the upper arm of the hammer cocking lever. The one shown here has been repaired by welding, and is not yet fully reshaped or rehardened.

guns that have both hammers mounted on the same pivot. In spite of the good points, though, the internal mechanism of the Miroku/Daly had elements of design that were, by today's standards, outdated. The hammers are rather intricately shaped, and although I have never seen one broken, the right one has an offset striking face that seems destined to eventually fracture. Some parts are still available from the last importer, Sloan's, but when the last hammers are gone, the reproduction of these will be difficult. If the hammer parts are saved when breakage occurs, it would be possible to make repairs by welding, then restoring the heat treatment.

The hammer springs are the older V-blade type, with a right-angled tip

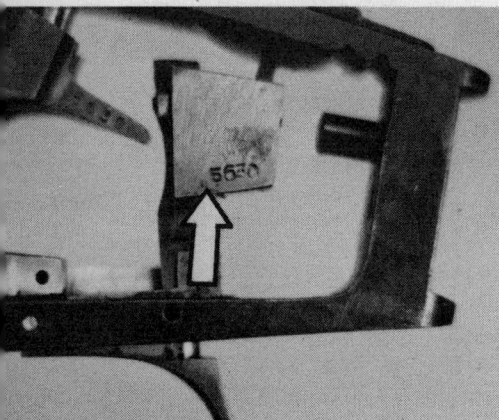

Here, the arrow points to the inertia block which switches trigger contact to the other sear after the first shot is fired.

which contacts a groove in the hammer, and this tip is prone to breakage. This type of spring will also weaken if the gun is left cocked for long periods of time. Commercially-made general replacements for these springs are available, but they require some fitting; and, installation is defintely a job for your gunsmith (and not an easy one!). When ordering a replacement for one of these springs, it should be noted that they are not of equal size and are not interchangeable, so you must specify which of the two is needed.

The vertical pivot-shaft of the barrel latch lever is extensively cut away to accommodate other internal parts and at one point is rather thin. I have seen no breakage of this part, but if it should happen, it could be repaired by welding. In the same area, the only repeated breakage I have observed is in the upper arm of the cocking lever, a part that is under considerable stress in cocking both hammers when the action is opened. Here, again, I have repaired these by welding, reshaping, and restoring the hardness. In regard to the latter, I bring the degree of hardness to a level slightly less than the factory original, as over-hardening is usually the cause of the breakage.

As in most over/under guns, the automatic ejector system is controlled by ejector trip rods, one on each side, and the spade-like heads of these are alternately cammed forward and sprung outward by studs on the side of each hammer. The rods rarely break, but if they lose temper, or are deformed by amateur tinkering, the automatic ejectors will stop working. The rods are easily repaired, but this is a job for a professional.

The safety catch is also the barrel selector, being moved from side to side to expose a small "U" and "O" on the upper tang—it controls which barrel is fired first. After the first shot, an internal inertia block, operated by recoil, automatically switches the trigger contact to the sear for the other barrel. The inertia system is balanced by the weight of the block and the tension of its spring, and normally requires no adjustment. If repair or adjustment is ever required, a com-

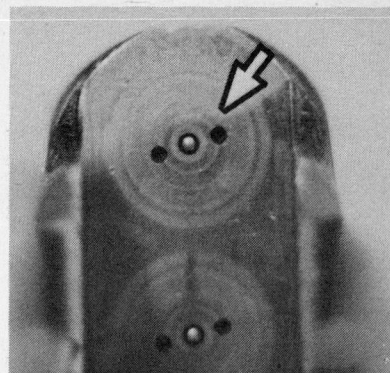

For firing pin removal, the bushing (arrow) must be unscrewed, using a special wrench.

petent professional should be consulted.

At some point in time, you will be faced with a broken firing pin—it can happen, eventually, to even the finest gun. In the Daly these are retained by bushings that are removable from the front of the breech face. Removal requires the use of a special two-pronged spanner; and, these bushings should never be removed by makeshift means, because it will usually result in damage to the bushing or breech face. If a gunsmith does not have the specific wrench to fit the Daly bushing, an excellent and relatively inexpensive wrench is available from Dan Bechtel's B-Square Company. If original replacement firing pins are not available, they are of simple design, and are not difficult to make.

Charter Arms Model AR-7 "Explorer" Carbine

First produced by the Armalite Division of Fairchild Industries, this handy little gun is now made by the Charter Arms Corporation, with the Model designation remaining the same. It is a camper's and backpacker's "survival" type arm. The main feature of this .22 semiauto is that its plastic (Cycolac) stock has compartments for the barrel, receiver and magazine, and when the rubber buttcover is snapped in place, it will even float in water. The whole thing weighs only 2¾ pounds.

The bolt cocking handle of the gun is designed to be pushed in when the receiver is stored in the buttstock case and pulled out for better leverage when cocking the bolt system before the first shot. The handle is allowed to move freely between the two posi-

(Far left) The bolt cocking handle of the AR-7 shown in it's "recessed" position. (Left) The same handle in its "extended" position. The "recessing" of the bolt handle allows the receiver assembly of the AR-7 to be stored in the AR-7's buttstock.

tions with no detent to hold it in either of them. Under normal circumstances this causes no difficulty. In an emergency or survival situation, however, if you had a dead primer or a jam and grabbed for the handle to feed a fresh round, fumbling to pull out the handle could cause a delay that might be embarrassing—or worse. I have a friend who takes this sort of thing seriously, and on his gun I installed a spring-and-plunger system to keep the handle in the extended position unless intentionally pushed in. The foregoing should not be interpreted as a serious criticism of the gun, as it works perfectly without this alteration.

Like the rest of the gun, the firing mechanism is very simple, with no weak points and no small complicated parts that might tend to break. The hammer is powered by a torsion-type round-wire spring, and one tail of this spring also returns the trigger. Removing a single screw and taking off a large sideplate on the left side of the receiver exposes all of the firing mechanism parts, and both the mainspring and the small coil which powers the magazine catch are easily detached when the plate is off, so proceed with care. The manual safety directly blocks the trigger movement and will reliably prevent accidental firing by a direct pull on the trigger. Since the trigger and hammer make direct contact, it can also be considered a sear-block type safety. It's a good, solid system.

The incidence of firing pin and extractor breakage is no more than with any other .22 semiauto gun with no inherent weaknesses. As a routine survival precaution, though, if this is your intended use, you should carry a few spares of these items and the principal springs. All parts are, of course, currently available from the Charter company, and they are interchangeable with the original Armalite parts.

One note on proper assembly: When installing the barrel, be sure that the little guide rib on top, just behind the rear collar, enters the corresponding slot in the top of the threaded section on the receiver before tightening the collar bushing to retain the barrel.

Left arrow points to the magazine catch spring, the right arrow indicates the combined hammer and trigger spring. The sideplate must be carefully removed as the above parts can easily become detached during normal disassembly.

When installing the barrel, be sure the guide rib on the barrel is aligned to enter the guide slot (arrow) on the receiver. If the rib is not aligned, you may damage the gun, severely.

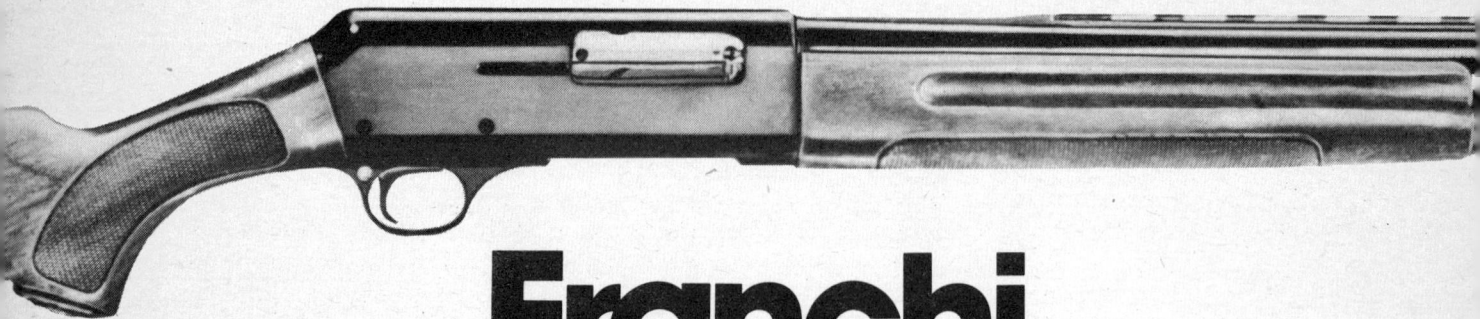

Franchi Automatic Shotgun

Made by Luigi Franchi in Brescia, Italy, and imported by Stoeger, this gun is a modern modification of Browning's original 1900 design and has several outstanding features. Both steel and alloy receivers were initially made, but most of the guns I've seen have the lightweight receiver. The Franchi has excellent handling qualities, weighing only 6 pounds, 4 ounces in 12 gauge, and 5 pounds, 2 ounces in 20 gauge. With these weights, you might expect it to have heavy recoil, especially in the larger bore, but its good balance and other design features distribute the kick so well that it's not noticeable.

The gun uses the Browning long recoil system, in which barrel and breech block travel to the rear together, the breech opening only after they have reached the full rear position. To retard the rear impact of these heavy parts, the usual friction system is used, and the arrangement of the compression ring for light and heavy loads is the same as described in the section on the Browning A-5 shotgun

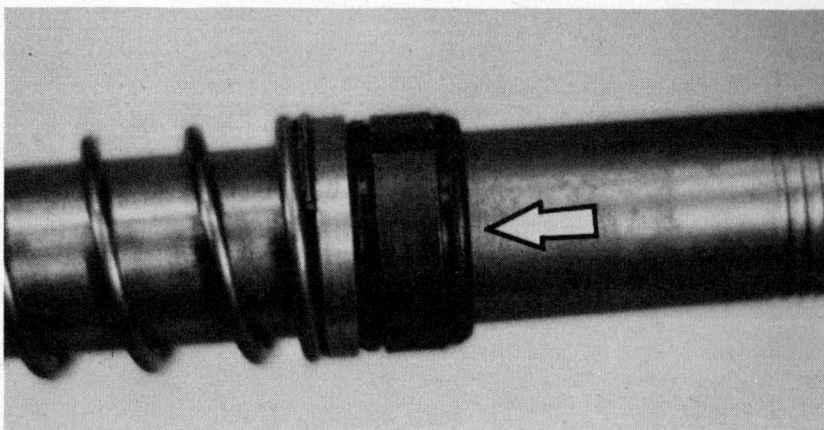

Just as in other long-recoil friction-retarded guns, the arrangement of the friction system is the same for medium to heavy loads, with the compression ring forward of the recoil spring and its concave surface toward the friction piece. In the Franchi, the friction piece (arrow) is of heavy plastic.

(q.v.). In late production Franchi guns, such as the one shown in the photos, the friction piece is not bronze, but heavy plastic. When I first saw one of these, I wondered if it might perhaps be the cause of some future trouble, as the friction heat acted on the plastic. I don't know what plastic they're using, but it must be the right one, as there have been no difficulties.

The only chronic ailment of the Franchi involves the carrier latch, and this appears only after several years of

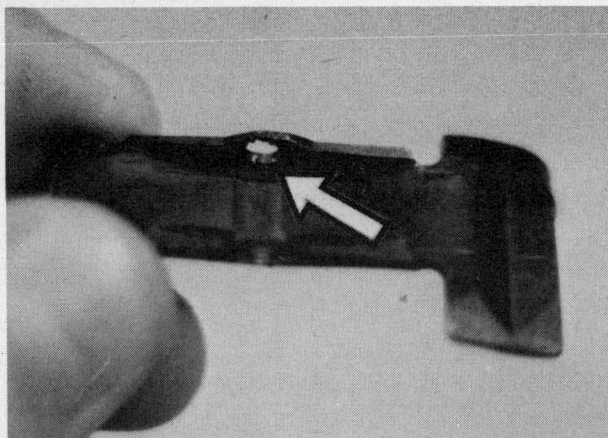

On this carrier latch, the lower pivot hole (arrow) is badly enlarged, the bridge of the loop is about to break.

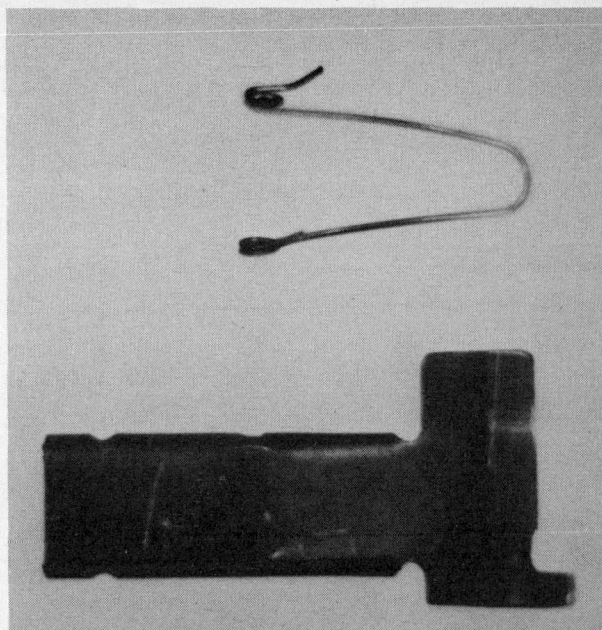

Here we see the carrier latch and its spring. The latch is made of formed sheet steel.

Arrows indicate the beveled camming lugs on the underside of the barrel, which operate the carrier latch and the shell stop during recoil.

constant use. The latch is made of formed sheet steel, its edges turned to form flanges which contain the opposed holes for its pivot pin. With referred pressure through the carrier from the bolt spring, the latch is under considerable repeated stress, and the outside loop of the pivot holes is fairly thin. The holes will eventually begin to enlarge, and finally the bridge of the loop will break. This will be immediately known, as the gun will begin to misfeed, a thing which otherwise just doesn't happen with a Franchi.

Replacement of the defective latch will correct this for a time, but there is a more permanent way. I usually raise a bead of steel weld at the pivot holes, leaving the walls of the latch thicker at that point, and then redrill the holes. If this is done in the right proportions, there is still room for the latch spring, and the problem is erased for a very long time.

The carrier latch and the secondary shell stop are operated during recoil by opposed camming lugs on the underside of the barrel, and on rare occasions I have known one of these to break or chip. Taking great care not to overheat the barrel, these can also be repaired by welding and recutting to shape. Needless to say, this should be done by a competent gunsmith.

Located on the rear arm of the carrier on the left side of the trigger housing, the carrier spring detent is a small semicircular piece of solid steel with a groove in its curved forward edge which fits against the arm of the carrier. This part is under heavy strain, and I have known them to break, but more often these are lost during amateur disassembly, as the spring can send them quite a distance when they are forced out of position. This part, and all others, are readily available

The carrier spring detent (arrow) is a semicircular piece of solid steel with a groove in its curved forward edge which fits the rear arm of the carrier. This part breaks occasionally and is frequently lost in disassembly.

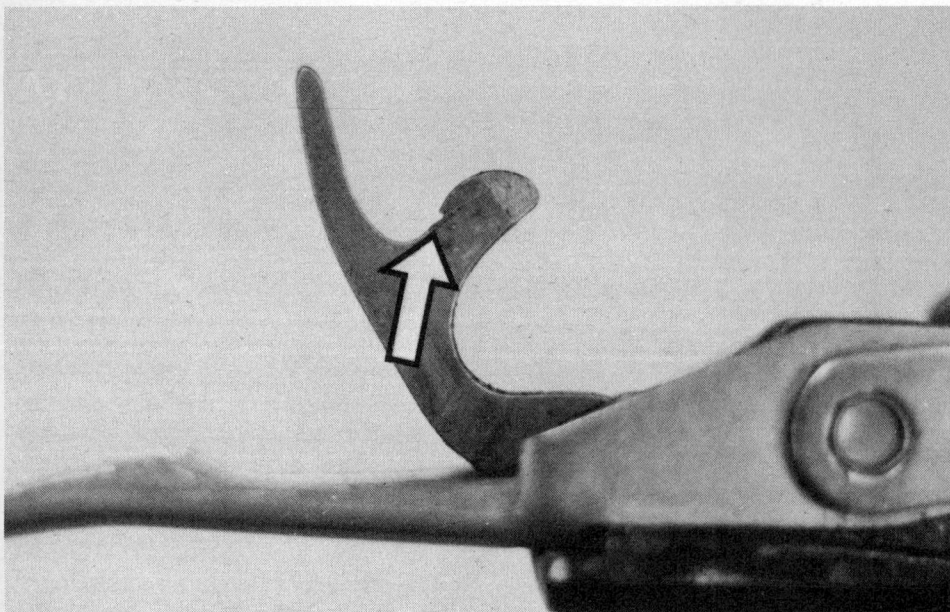

Engagement of the sear and the sear step on the hammer (arrow) is carefully engineered, and should not be altered.

from the importer, and most of the larger gun shops also keep a supply on hand.

Sear and the sear step engagement on the hammer is carefully engineered, and should not be altered by any attempted amateur "adjustment" of the trigger pull. Just as in other long-recoil guns, the recoil spring may begin to take a "set" after several thousand rounds and should be replaced. According to the Franchi factory, this should be done at somewhere between 4 and 5 thousand rounds, but your gunsmith can judge whether your gun needs this.

There is one operational feature of the Franchi which has caused some confusion for those not familiar with it. The gun does not feed the first shell from a full magazine by operation of the bolt handle, as in the Browning. When loading, the final shell is simply dropped in the ejection port onto the carrier, and the bolt release pressed to load it.

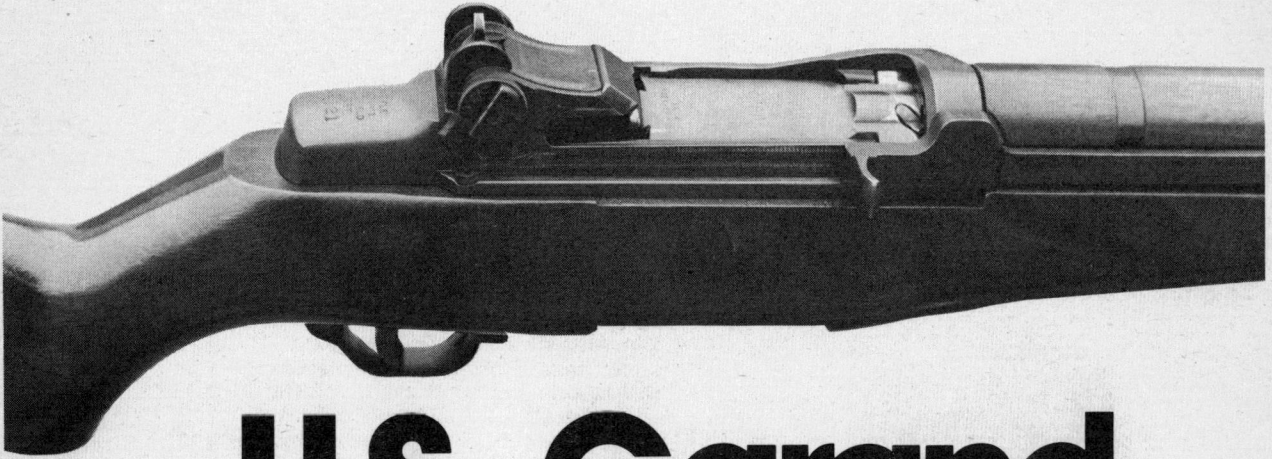

U.S. Garand Rifle

A few years ago, in a magazine article, I dissected the U.S. Rifle, Caliber .30, M-1, and listed its liabilities from a mechanical standpoint. The article contained one apocryphal story, one subjective opinion, and the rest of it consisted only of mechanical fact. It's unusual for a magazine article to generate a lot of reader response, but in this case I received a sackful of what could only be described as "hate mail." Obviously, a large number of WWII and Korean veterans feel very strongly about the old Garand.

The gun was adopted as U.S. Military Standard on January 9, 1936, and for its time, it was a remarkable achievement. John C. Garand's design became the first semi-automatic rifle officially used by a major power, and the gun does, of course, have its good points. The fully enclosed magazine system is less liable to external damage, and the cammed turning bolt allows a shorter receiver. The trigger group, containing the firing system, is a masterpiece of good engineering. Its anvil-like weight contributes to a steady hold and aids accuracy.

The weakest point in the design is the magazine system. The charger-clip loading limits the capacity to eight rounds, and reloading a partially-emptied magazine is not possible unless the clip is ejected and manually refilled—a tedious procedure. In hand-filling a clip, care must be taken that all rounds are seated fully to the rear of the clip, an endeavor that is unsuited to combat condi-

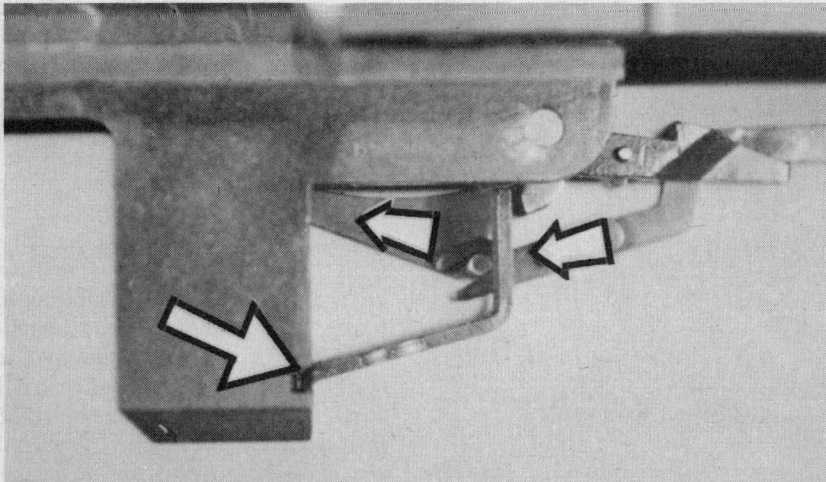

This photo will give you some idea as to the placement of some of the Garand's internal workings. The large arrow at the left points to the cartridge guide. The center arrow is on the follower arm, pointing toward the follower unit. The arrow to the right is on the follower rod and indicates the direction of the spring tension.

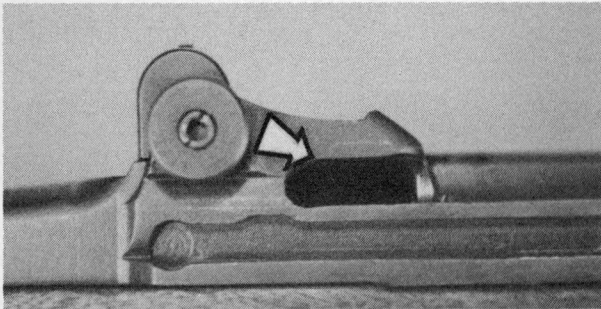

Even the good guns have faults: The gap in the receiver (arrow) behind the bolt allows free entry of dirt, sand and/or water.

The M-1 Garand's eight-round "en bloc" clip at the left, an empty clip is shown on the right. When the ammo is expended, the clip is mechanically tossed free of the action allowing for the insertion of a fresh clip full of ammo. Reloading the en bloc clip, by hand, can be tricky; and, from a combat or even "sporting-use" point of view, reloading a partially-emptied clip is not feasible.

Breakage and malfunction of the Garand's trigger group is almost nonexistent—it's a fine piece of engineering.

One potential problem is in the area of the upper rail of the receiver (both photos)—extensive wear may cause cracking.

tions. Aside from this, which is in the realm of practical use, the system is a mechanical nightmare. The magazine follower receives its spring tension from a pivoting follower arm, activated by a follower rod which receives its tension from the recoil spring. The front of the magazine well is closed by an angled plate of steel called the cartridge guide. With this system, the balance of recoil spring tension, pressure against cartridges, and the gas transference rate is fairly delicate. A slight weakness of the spring, a residue constriction of the gas port, an underpowered round, or any slight deformity of the cartridge guide, and you will have a jam. As with any mechanism, complication increases the possibility of malfunction. The feed system of the M-1 is complicated. Since any feeding problem can be due to one or more of the factors mentioned above, it will usually be necessary to consult a gunsmith who is familiar with this rifle.

Although the gas systems are quite different in the M-1 and the Carbine, their bolt locking arrangement is very

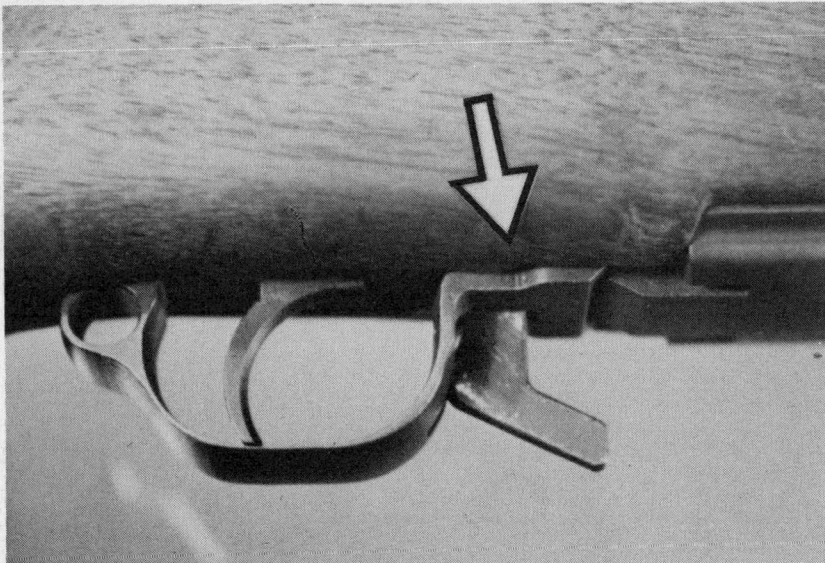

If your Garand has an "extended" safety like the one shown (arrow) don't go shopping for a new safety, it's just a "winter" safety that enables gloved hands to do the job a little easier. The normal safety doesn't project like this one, and, it has a hole in it to facilitate field-stripping.

The arrow points to the external portion of the action slide, or "operating rod," as the parts lists call it.

similar, and they share a quirk in this area. The right upper rail of the receiver is slanted inward for travel of the right lug of the bolt, and the outside edge is recessed for the lug of the operating slide. This makes the rail rather thin at one point in its cross-section, and many rifles, after long use, tend to develop cracks in the rail. In this case, replacement of the receiver is best, but I have rejoined these with weld, taking *great* care to avoid overheating the rest of the receiver.

The operating slide is exposed for nearly half its length on the right side of the gun, and I have seen several cases in which a M-1 had been dropped in a rocky area, bending the exposed portion of the operating slide inward, rendering it inoperative. This part can be easily replaced, as all parts are very much available. The operating rod can also be reshaped, but this should be done by a gunsmith.

The gas system should, of course, be kept absolutely clean and dry. Any type of oil or grease is death to a gas-transfer mechanism, as the heat from the powder gases will instantly bake the lubricant into a hard scale—this scale will build up to a point where it will constrict the gas port and all action is stopped.

There is one final thing that should be mentioned—the classic ailment wryly called "M-1 Thumb." The bolt remains open after the last shot is fired, and the insertion of a loaded clip depresses the bolt catch, *instantly* releasing the bolt, which is driven forward by the compressed recoil spring. If the thumb pushing the clip into place is still there, the bolt will close on it like a bear trap. All those who trained with the rifle know that the proper method of loading is to restrain the operating rod handle with the heel of the right hand while pressing the clip into place with the thumb of the same hand. The thumb is removed, then the hand whipped away to let the bolt go. This is awkward, and requires taking the rifle down from firing position, but if this procedure is followed, your thumb will remain intact.

And now, to those who may be reaching for pen and paper with vituperative intent, let me say that I am aware of the heroic service of this gun in two wars, from Remagen Bridgehead to Inchon, and nothing I've said about it can detract from that history.

German Gewehr 88 Rifle

That ungainly desert beast, the camel, was once described as a horse designed by a committee. Anything that is put together by a group, rather than the genius of one man, usually turns out badly. The German military rifle of 1888 was designed by an Ordnance Commission at Spandau Arsenal and had features of both the Mauser and Mannlicher systems. They really didn't do too badly, but within 5 years the developments of Mauser made the gun obsolete. Even so, quantities of the Model 88 continued in German service for quite a few years, and many were used as late as WWI. In 1905, the German military cartridge was increased in power, and the bullet diameter changed from .318 to .323, with the shape also being altered to a pointed or Spitzer type. A number of the Model 88 guns were altered to fire the new round, and these were stamped with an "S" on the receiver ring. In spite of the marking, these guns are only marginally safe with modern 8mm loads, and their use in the Model 88 is *not* recommended.

Receiver ring marking shows that this gun was made at Amberg Arsenal in 1896. Note the "S" above the crown, indicating that this gun was later altered to use the redesigned 8mm cartridge of 1905. In spite of the marking, these guns are only marginally safe with modern 8mm rounds.

With its fully enclosed cartridge head recess and integral ejector and extractor, the bolt face of the Model 88 looks quite a bit like those in several modern sporting rifles. The appearance is deceiving, though, as it does not have the strength associated with modern arms. The bolt has a separate head which is easily removable, giving access to the extractor and the ejector, but further disassembly of the bolt is best left to a professional. When the bolt head is removed, the tiny ejector can easily fall out, so take care that it isn't lost.

The extractor is tempered to be its own spring, but it is well-designed and does not break often. Except for the rear sight spring and the lower barrel band retainer, all of the other springs in the gun are helical coil, an unusual thing in a gun of this period. In its day, the Model 88 was a successful military rifle. In addition to being the standard German Infantry weapon for 10 years, the gun was also made on a contract basis for several other European nations, for Peru and

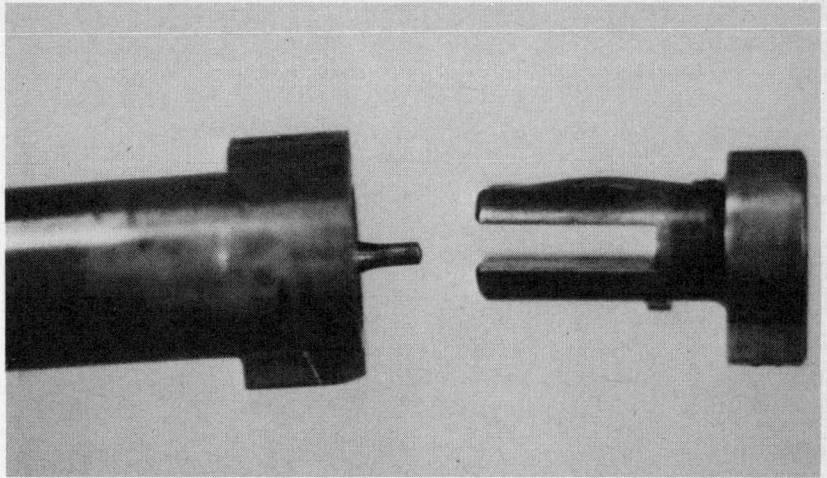

With its fully enclosed cartridge head recess and integral ejector and extractor, the bolt face of the Model 88 looks much like those in several modern sporting rifles.

The separate bolt head is easily removable, but further disassembly of the bolt is best left to a professional.

Brazil in South America, and for China. The basic action, much improved and strengthened, is echoed today in the fine Mannlicher-Schoenauer rifles.

At the time this is written, there is no great problem finding replacements for a broken or missing part. The guns were sold in quantity as surplus prior to 1968, and the used-parts dealers can usually supply whatever you might need. Several of the surplus dealers are still selling some of these guns, and are advertising them as safe with present-day 8mm Mauser rounds, basing this on the "S" marking. Once again, shooting even the relatively mild U.S. commercial load in the Model 88 is risky. Feeding one of these a warmed-up 8mm handload could create some interesting problems for your hospital.

If you want to safely shoot the Model 88, there are two ways: Either obtain the proper dies and carefully handload your cartridges down to the early pressure level, or have one of the custom loaders, such as Ballistek, make them for you. Otherwise, the Model 88 should be used as a conversation piece on the wall of your den.

Separate bolt head, showing the extractor, which is tempered to be its own spring.

When the head is removed from the bolt, the tiny ejector can easily fall out and become lost.

H&R Model 360 Ultra Rifle

A purely subjective opinion, but the H&R Model 360 Ultra gets my vote as the best-looking centerfire semi-auto currently made. It is also one of the best mechanically, with a simplicity of design that makes operational problems practically nonexistent. It is a gas-operated gun, and the piston system has no delicate parts, no complicated baffles or flanges to trap residue. All that is required to keep it in perfect working order is to occasionally wipe the normal accumulation from the smooth exterior of the piston, and, of course, never let any lubrication come near it.

The bolt tips upward at the rear to lock into the roof of the receiver, giving a much smoother action than the turn-bolt types. The trigger housing and magazine floorplate are made of alloy, but all other parts of this gun are machined steel. The extractor is large, heavy, and well-designed. Even though it is tempered to be its own spring, breakage is very unlikely.

Located on the left side of the trigger guard housing, the disconnector is also a large and heavy part and is retained at its center by a screw which is also its pivot. This screw should be checked occasionally for tightness. Considering its weight and good mechanical advantage, breakage of the disconnector is unlikely.

The Model 360 does not stay open when the last shot is fired, but there is a manual hold-open catch, which the factory calls the ''bolt stop,'' on the right side of the trigger housing at the lower edge of the stock. Pushing upward on this serrated latch while drawing back the bolt will lock it in the open position. The top of the hold-open catch, where it engages with a notch in the action bar, is sharp and narrow, but since this is a manual latch I doubt that this will ever cause

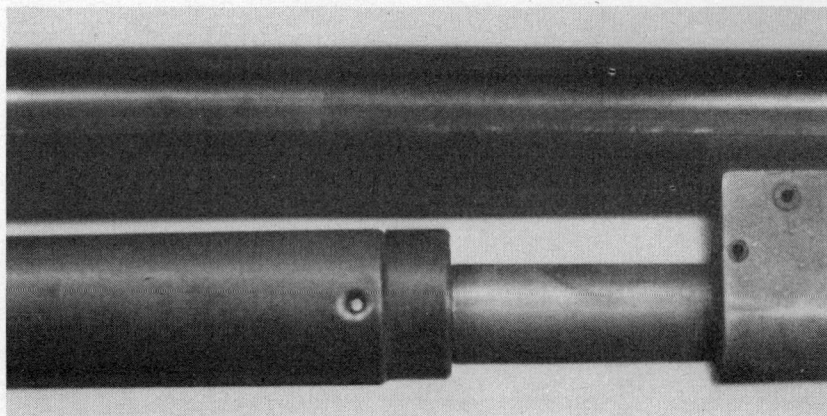

The gas piston and operating slide are shown in the pre-firing position. Note the clean, simple design of this system.

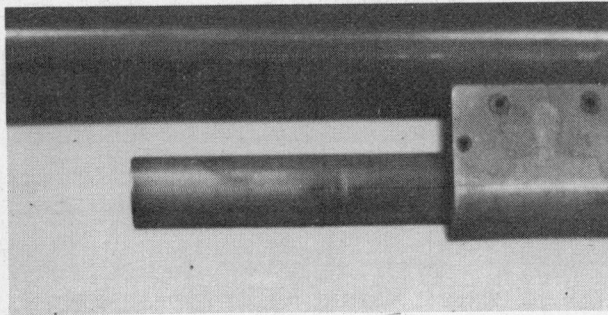

Arrow points to the forward end of the disconnector, the top of which contacts the action slide bar. Tightness of the combination pivot and mounting screw should be checked occasionally.

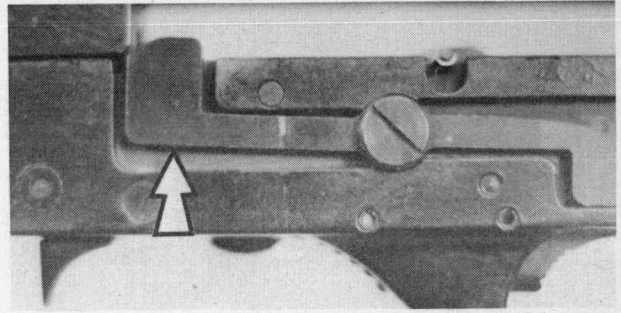

Here the gas piston is shown in the pre-firing (top) and extended (lower) positions. The system should be kept clean, and *never* lubricated.

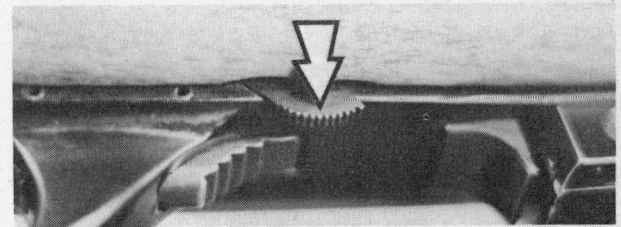

Arrow indicates the manual hold-open catch. To the left is the safety, shown in the off-safe position. To the right is the magazine catch, which is pushed forward to release.

any problem.

A sliding type, the manual safety is located in the forward base of the trigger guard and is similar in operation to the one found on early Browning A-5 shotguns. It is, however, much more positive than that on the Browning and does not act on the trigger but directly blocks the sear.

The magazine catch is located at the rear of the magazine and is pushed forward to release. The system is well-designed and does not appear susceptible to malfunction. The magazine is a single-line type, holding only three rounds, and this contributes to the flawless feeding of this rifle.

Takedown of the Model 360 has a few tricky points, and if you don't have an original owner's manual at hand, I'd advise that you leave the once-a-year cleaning to your gunsmith. If you do have the instructions and want to do this yourself, take care not to lose the little spacer of thin steel called the stock bedding plate, located between the front lug of the receiver and the stock. This little part is freed when the action is removed from the stock and is easily overlooked.

In the unlikely event that anything breaks, all parts are available. This, as you may have gathered by now, is one of the very good ones.

When the action is removed from the stock, take care not to lose this little spacer of thin steel, called the stock bedding plate. It goes between the front receiver lug and the interior of the stock.

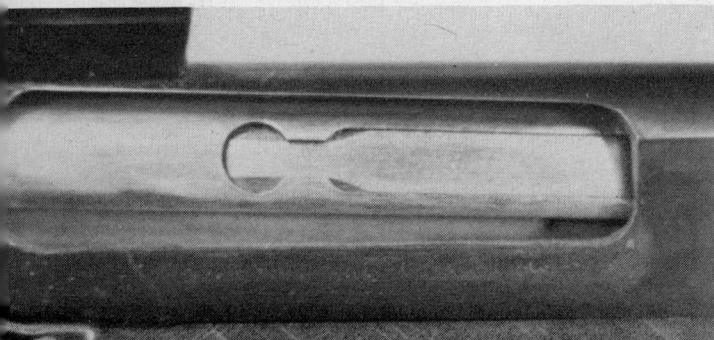

The bolt tips upward at the rear to lock into the roof of the receiver. Note the heavy, well-designed extractor, which is tempered to be its own spring.

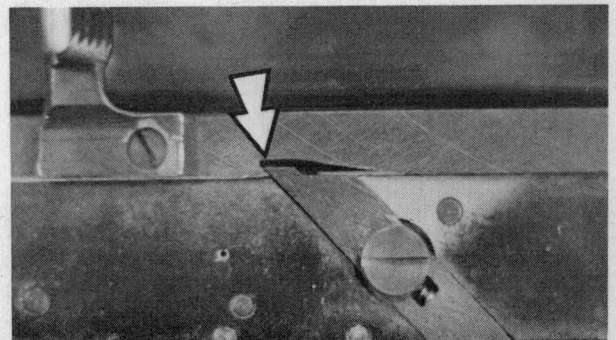

The arrow points to the engagement of the hold-open catch (bolt stop) with its notch in the action bar. The latch is not automatic, and breakage is unlikely.

H & R Model 760 Rifle

The action of this little rifle is very unusual—it's a single-shot semi-auto. The bolt is closed manually after loading a single round into the chamber. When the gun is fired, the bolt is blown open, and the cartridge case is ejected—the bolt remains open, ready for the insertion of the next round. The only other rifle made with a similar action was the Winchester Model 55, and, like the H&R, it soon vanished from the scene. It's a shame that neither of them lasted, as both made excellent guns for teaching youngsters to shoot. The H&R people may have had this in mind, as their guns in this series were made in small proportions, and they were a perfect size for young shooters.

The first rifle with this action was introduced in 1963 as the Model 755, also called the "Sahara." This one had a full Mannlicher-style stock, a barrel band, and a different front sight. Otherwise, it was identical to the Model 760, which came along in 1965. By 1971, both guns had been discontinued. This was apparently due to a lack of interest in this type of action, as the guns had no serious defects. I briefly owned a Model 760, mounted a small scope on it, and for a time used it to reduce the starling population of western Kentucky.

As indicated above, the guns have

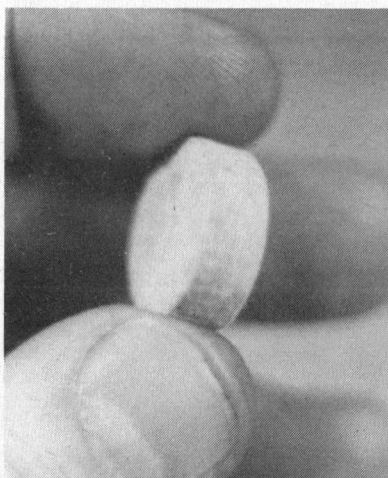

When the fiber buffer at the rear of the receiver deteriorates, it can be replaced with a 16-gauge shotshell wad. It's a perfect fit.

no chronic problems, but I have repaired them on occasion. I have noticed that the ones which required repair had seen long and hard use. At the rear of the receiver, inside, on the forward face of the receiver end piece, there is a fiber buffer which cushions the impact of the bolt as it is blown open. After several thousand rounds, the repeated compression will cause the fiber to break down, and replacement of the buffer will be necessary. As recently as a year ago, replacement parts for the 755 and 760 were still available from H&R, but few of the smaller gun shops carry parts for these short-production guns in stock. If the parts are not readily obtainable locally, there is a quick and easy way to replace the fiber buffer—a 16-gauge shotshell wad is a perfect fit inside the receiver. The wad will need to be holed at the center for the short rod on the receiver end piece, and its thickness may have to be adjusted slightly for the proper rear position of the bolt, but this is a job that even the amateur can do easily.

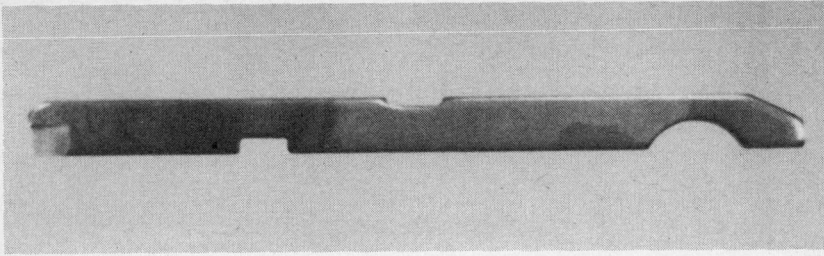

The firing pin of the Model 760 is made of flat steel stock and is not difficult to reproduce.

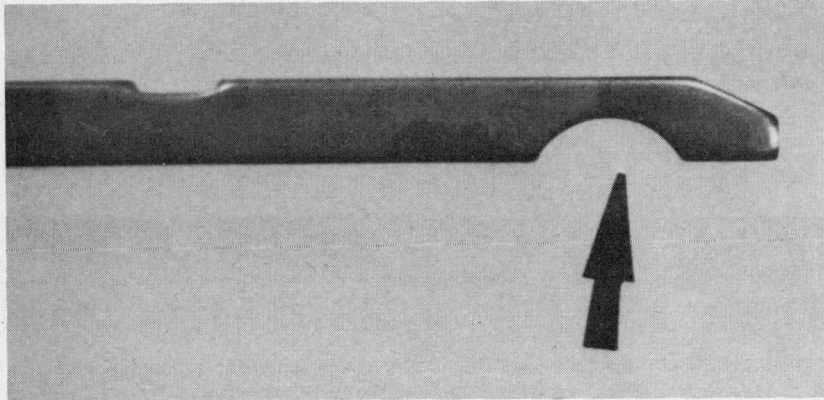

At the rear of the firing pin there is a semicircular cut to accommodate the bolt cocking handle. When the firing pin breaks, it is usually at this point.

The firing pin of the Model 760 has a deep semicircular cut at its rear to clear the bolt cocking handle, and the firing pin will occasionally break at this narrow point. The firing pin is stamped from flat steel, and I think that a few slipped into the production that were over-hardened, causing this breakage. It's not a common occurrence. If replacements are not readily available, making this firing pin is a simple matter for any good gunsmith.

The extractor has a fairly thin beak, but is not under the severe impact stress that is usually the case with a semi-auto, as the closing of the bolt is done by hand. I have replaced exactly two of these over the years; so, in spite of the thin beak, these must be quite durable. Here, again, if no new parts are at hand, making replacements will present no great difficulty.

The firing mechanism of the gun features a pivoting internal hammer and a separate sear. Achieving a respectably good trigger pull is not as touchy a job as with most semi-auto actions, since the bolt does not slam forward to disturb the engagement of a light pull. My own 760, when I obtained it, was unaltered and had a trigger pull that could charitably be described as somewhat heavy. Most of those I have examined were in the same category. With a good trigger job, though, these little guns have outstanding accuracy.

With the marvelous hindsight of the gun trader, I wish now that I hadn't let my 760 go. The next time a Model 755 or 760 comes along, I'm going to grab it.

The extractor has a fairly thin beak (arrow), and occasionally breaks at that point.

H & R "Topper" Shotgun

The Topper's ejector is a heavy, well-designed part—it rarely gives any trouble.

The Harrington & Richardson company has been making a good, moderately-priced single barrel shotgun since around 1908. The design evolved through a number of model numbers, and in 1946 the number 48 gun was named the "Topper," a designation still used today. Earlier guns had a conventional lateral-pivoting barrel latch on the upper tang of the receiver, but this was later changed to a vertical lever, located beside the hammer on the right of the receiver. The 16-gauge chambering was dropped a few years ago, and the gun is currently offered in .410, 20, 28, and 12 gauge in the standard models. A heavier 10-gauge gun, the Model 176, was recently introduced.

All parts of the Topper are heavy and well-designed, and breakage is unusual. Except for the occasional replacement of a firing pin, repair is not often necessary. The ejector, a frequent liability in this type of gun, is particularly sturdy and well-fitted. The hammer is a rebound type, returning after firing to a safety position, where it is blocked by a wide sear-surface on the trigger. A heavy blow on the hammer could fire the gun, but it would have to break one or more of the main parts to do it.

On late guns, the trigger guard and the spacer piece between the forend and the receiver are of plastic. The latter part is under no extreme stress, and the use of plastic material in this location causes no problem. The trigger guard, however, is subject to impact every so often, in normal use, and these do occasionally fracture. Replacement guards are not expensive, and all parts for the later guns are readily available. For the very early guns, some parts may have to be obtained from the used-parts dealers.

When a gun has seen long, hard use, and the barrel locking system has become loose, it can be repaired in the same manner as on most other single and double barrel guns. End play can be taken up by the installation of a steel pin at the center of the pivot recess on the underlug of the barrel. Vertical looseness can be corrected by peening the locking lug at its center, just below the lip, to raise the locking surface. It should be stressed that the impact point should be below the edge of the lug, as peening the edge itself

Left arrow points to the vertical barrel latch found on later models. The right arrow indicates the plastic forend base.

will do no good at all—the first shot afterwards will flatten it again.

Early guns had a pull-down type forend latch, but those of later manufacture have the forend retained by a single large screw. This screw, which is coin-slotted, should be checked occasionally for tightness. The action parts are mounted in the receiver by large cross-pins, and the amateur should not attempt disassembly. Re-installation of the trigger system requires the use of a separate slave pin, and there are other factors that can make the operation difficult.

The hammer on late guns is powered by a round-wire torsion-type spring, and although these seldom break, they have been known to weaken after long use. A new spring will cure this, of course, but it is often possible to reshape the two rear tails of the original to restore the tension. If this is done, care should be taken to see that the tension is not overdone, or the rebound system may be cancelled.

The single barrel shotgun is quite often used as a "first gun" for a youngster, and H&R offers a special youth model of the Topper, the Model 490, having a shorter stock to accommodate a child's reduced reach.

When extreme wear occurs in the locking-lug area, it can be remedied by installing a slack pin at the center of the pivot recess (left arrow), and by peening at the center of the locking lug (right arrow), just below the lip.

On late models, the forend is retained by a single large screw (arrow). This should be checked occasionally for tightness.

While the Ithaca Model 49 carbine is a single shot, it is offered in regular .22 and .22 WMR (Magnum) chamberings.

Ithaca Model 49 Carbine

The Model 49, based on a modified version of the old Martini action, was designed to resemble the familiar Winchester lever-action gun, including the "magazine tube" below the barrel. It was marketed as the "Saddlegun" by Ithaca and has also been recently offered by the Savage/Stevens company as the Model 89 and made for Western Auto Stores as the Model 103. These last two versions differ slightly from the original Ithaca gun, but several of the parts will interchange. From Ithaca, the gun is available with a shorter stock for young shooters, and its single-shot action and external hammer make it a good choice for the beginner.

On the Model 49 the receiver and lever are of alloy, while internal parts are of steel. The takedown is sufficiently complicated that it should not be tried by the amateur. Even routine removal of the breech block is a job for the gunsmith, as its large pivot pin is retained by a small spring-powered pin which rides in a groove in the pivot. Those who are unaware of this

arrangement will often try to drive the bolt pin out to one side or the other, shearing off the lock pin and deforming its tunnel in the bolt. Removing the lever first will take the tension off the lock pin, but even this will not guarantee easy removal, as the lock plunger is often reluctant to drop out of its groove, especially if there has been a previous attempt to drive out the pivot. The entire operation is best left to a gunsmith who is familiar with the Model 49.

Two of the weakest points in the design are the firing pin and the ejector system. In order to bypass the large pivot pin, the firing pin has a centrally positioned head which is offset to go down the left side of the breech block. Since the applied force from the hammer blow is not in a straight line, the offset portion of the

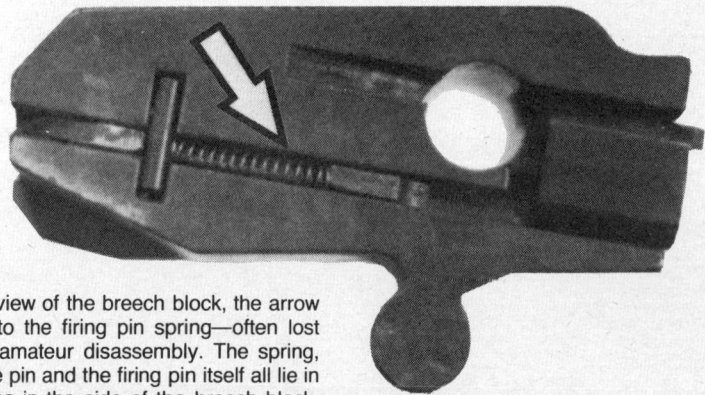

In this view of the breech block, the arrow points to the firing pin spring—often lost during amateur disassembly. The spring, its base pin and the firing pin itself all lie in recesses in the side of the breech block, retained only by the inside of the receiver.

firing pin is under heavy strain each time it is struck, and breakage is not unusual. Fortunately, replacements are readily available at most gunsmiths and from Ithaca. I once altered a Model 49 to use a straight, round-section firing pin which passed through the pivot, but considering the amount of work involved and the value of the gun, this is not really a feasible alteration.

The ejector is of the trip-type, being pushed in against spring tension and caught by a detent lever as a round is seated in the chamber. After firing, when the lever is swung down, the forward end of the breech block drops and the rear extension of the detent lever, or ejector trip, is struck by the front lower edge of the breech block. This action releases the ejector to snap backward, kicking out the fired case. Both the ejector and its trip are rather small and light, and breakage is not uncommon. The round body of the ejector has two deep recesses (one for the trip catch beak and the other for a retaining pin) and it will often break in one of those two places. The trip lever has a narrowed portion near its pivot point and will usually break there. Once again, both of these parts are

The older Model 49's combination front sight and magazine hanger (top) was made of alloy, retained by one screw, and tended to loosen. The later gun (below) has a much better arrangement.

quite easy to find, and they are inexpensive. Installing them, however, is another matter. Routine parts replacement on this gun is seldom a *routine* operation, and in this case the problem is frequently complicated by the combination of steel parts and an alloy receiver. The sear-trip plunger, for example, will usually refuse to drop out of its tunnel in the bottom of

the receiver, its sharp lower rim catching on the threads for the retaining screw.

Most of the problems mentioned above show up only after several years of hard use. If you start with a new gun, your youngster will have outgrown it by the time these troubles appear. If you're shopping for a used one, though, watch for these things.

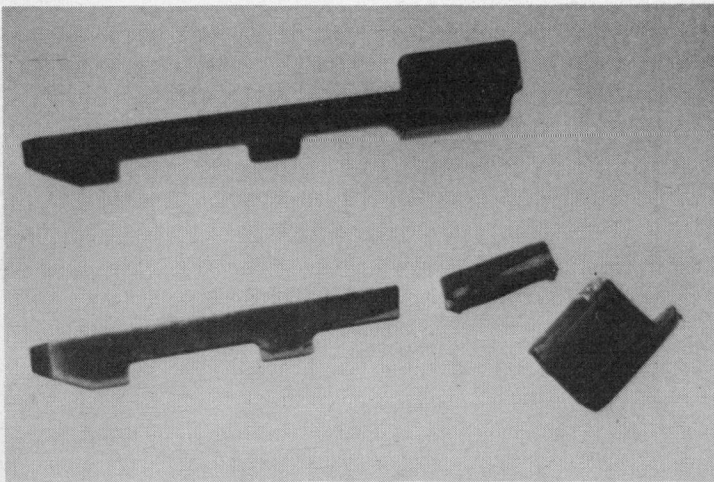

Because of its design, the firing pin breaks with some frequency. In this picture the firing pin on top is intact, while the one on the bottom is broken in two places.

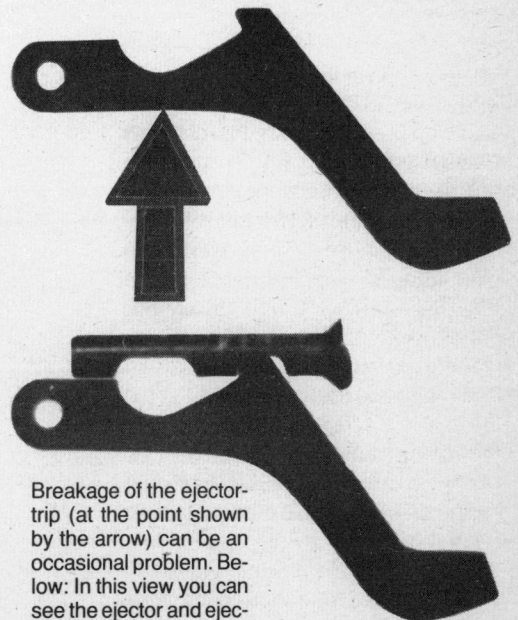

Breakage of the ejector-trip (at the point shown by the arrow) can be an occasional problem. Below: In this view you can see the ejector and ejector-trip in the position they occupy when assembled in the gun. (The ejector can be one of the most troublesome parts in the Model 49.)

Ithaca Model 72 Rifle

A few years back, the Ithaca company briefly made a .22 lever-action repeating rifle called the model 49-R. One unusual aspect of the design was the use of a vertically sliding carrier to move the cartridge from magazine level up to align with the chamber. The system was reminiscent of the one used in the old Winchester Model 73 guns. When the Model 49-R was discontinued, this feature was carried over into the early production of the gun that replaced it in the Ithaca line, the Model 72. The carrier was operated by a lever pivoted at the rear, and its lowered position was adjusted by a small Allen screw on the underside of the lower frame. The location of this screw, just forward of the trigger, led some shooters to assume that it was for adjustment of the trigger, and when they fooled around with it, the carrier ceased to function properly, failing to pick up the next round from the magazine. In extreme cases, this could even cause breakage of the carrier lever.

In guns of more recent production,

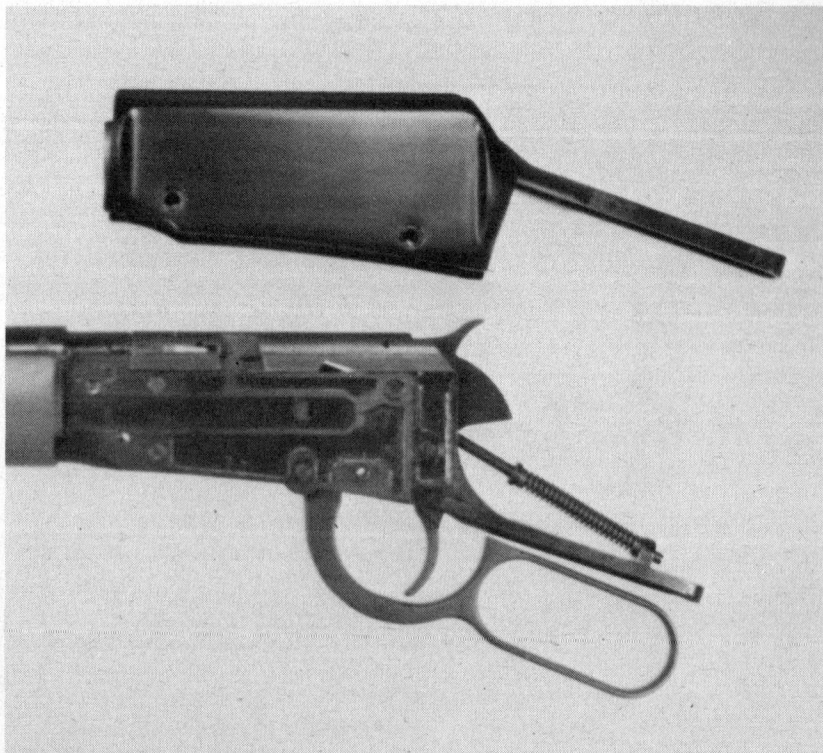

After the stock is taken off, removal of four side screws allows this unusual takedown of the receiver.

The bolt is of good, simple design. Note the twin extractors, visible at the right.

the vertically sliding carrier has been abandoned in favor of a fixed cartridge guide or feed throat, eliminating this problem. The left lip of the fixed guide has a heavy lug on top which serves as the ejector, and it has ample dimensions to preclude any difficulty from wear or breakage. The guide is similar to the conventional type found in several .22 semi-auto rifles, such as the Marlin Model 49, and uses a pivoting carrier which rises at its center.

Takedown of the Model 72 is, for a lever-action rifle, unique. After the stock is removed (by taking out the single bolt between the tangs), the removal of two screws on each side of

the receiver (four in all) allows the receiver and upper tang to be lifted off the main frame of the gun, exposing the bolt, which is easily taken off the top of the frame. The other parts are still inside the lower frame, and disassembly of this unit is not for the amateur. All of the internal parts have an ample strength allowance, and all springs are helical coil, so repair should not often be necessary.

The bolt is of good, simple design, and the firing pin is a plain, flat part that would be easy to duplicate if an original replacement were not immediately available. The factory can furnish all parts, of course, and most large gunshops will have them on

hand. The firing pin is not prone to breakage, but this can happen eventually to any gun. The early Model 72 guns had only a single extractor, but those of more recent production also have one on the left side of the bolt, a non-beak type to assure holding of the cartridge case until it strikes the ejector. Both are powered by coil springs, and neither causes any problem.

As now made, the Model 72 is a much simpler gun, and has no obvious weak points that will lead to future quirks. Since the design has been changed during its production, it would be advisable, when ordering parts, to give the serial number of the gun in question.

Ejector (arrow) is an integral part of the cartridge guide, and appears to be of ample dimensions to resist breakage and wear.

Ithaca Model 37 Shotgun

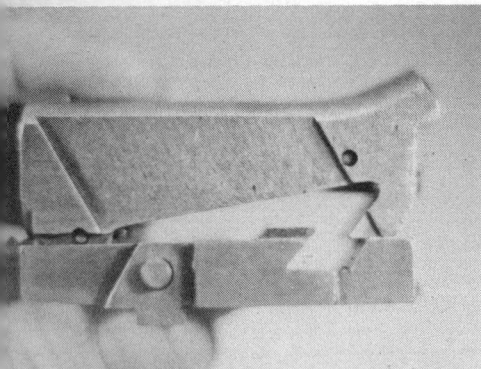

Here, the breech block and action slide are shown in the locked (above) and unlocked (below) positions.

In addition to its year/model designation, the Model 37 is also called the "Featherlight," in reference to its weight of only 5¾ to 6½ pounds, depending on the gauge. In most of today's lightweight guns, this is achieved by the use of alloy for certain major parts. In the Model 37, it was done by brilliant engineering. The design of the all-steel trigger housing and its mechanism is an excellent example of this. The number of parts was kept to a minimum, and the parts were made as light as possible without sacrificing strength. Another of the good features of this gun is that the receiver is completely closed at top and sides, with both loading and ejection through an opening at the bottom. Aside from keeping rain and dirt out of the receiver, this design also makes the gun an excellent choice for the left-handed shooter, and there is a left-hand safety available for it.

In the Model 37 the bolt locking system is a type often used in slide-actions, with a slide-piece which tips the breech block up at the rear to lock into a recess in the top of the receiver. In the Model 37, the slide-piece is particularly sturdy, and the mechanical advantage is good in both directions, either opening or closing the action. A well-broken-in Model 37 will fall open when the gun is pointed upward and the slide stop is pressed, so you can imagine how easily the action will function when on a level.

The action slide-piece is attached to the slide bar by a lateral spring-powered pin which locks into a hole in the bar—a very positive arrangement. In very old guns that have seen a lot of use, the slide pin spring can suffer from a loss of tension, and the pin will not have a firm engagement with the bar. The simple cure is replacement of the spring, and if the proper Ithaca part is temporarily unavailable, any small coil spring of the right strength and diameter will work perfectly.

Mounted at the top and bottom of the breech block face, the twin extractors are strongly made and seldom break. Both are powered by coil springs, with an ample allowance for

The all-steel trigger housing of the Model 37 is a masterpiece of good design—it won't give you any trouble.

Powered by a coil spring, the action slide pin (arrow) locks into a hole in the action slide bar—an excellent arrangement.

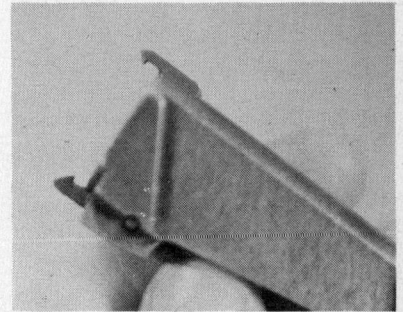

The twin extractors are powered by coil springs, and seldom need attention.

age weakening. In older guns, there may be some wear at the engagement of the stud on the right side of the hammer with the rear beak of the slide stop. If the wear is light, the parts can be recut to restore the proper meeting. If this is not possible, the hammer, slide stop, or both can be replaced—all parts are readily available.

One slightly negative point in the design of the Model 37 is that takedown for thorough cleaning of the interior of the receiver requires removal of the stock as the first step. On the other hand, this feature probably prevents a lot of amateur tinkering. When the trigger group is out of the gun, the right shell stop is free to fall out and care should be taken that it isn't lost. You may note that an edge view of this shell stop shows a slight curve, and this is not only normal, but essential to proper operation.

During its long period of manufacture, the Model 37 has had several very slight changes in design. One of these involves the magazine endpiece, the key to removal of the barrel. On guns made prior to 1955, this part (Ithaca calls it the "magazine nut") was supplied with a pull-out pin to give added leverage when loosening or tightening the endpiece. This was a help to those with weak hands, but it was noted that some hamhanded individuals were using the leverage pin to exert great force in tightening, bending the lug below the barrel. Guns made from 1955 to the present have a knurled magazine endpiece without the pin.

Another modification involved the interchangeability of barrels. On all guns currently made, barrels with different degrees of choke and other features can be easily switched without fitting. On Model 37 guns with serial numbers below 855000, however, the barrels are *not* interchangeable. If a new barrel is to be installed on one of these older guns, the gun must be returned to the factory for fitting. I have seen one amateur attempt at fitting a nonoriginal barrel to an older Model 37, and both receiver and barrel were ruined. Leave this operation to the factory.

Occasionally, in an older gun, a fired shell will be extracted from the chamber, but not completely ejected by the downstroke of the carrier arms. If this occurs, the carrier arms can be reshaped slightly to correct it, but this is a job for a gunsmith.

As a firearms writer, I try to maintain a generally objective viewpoint. Speaking as a gunsmith and shooter, though, I consider the Ithaca Model 37 to be the best slide-action shotgun ever made.

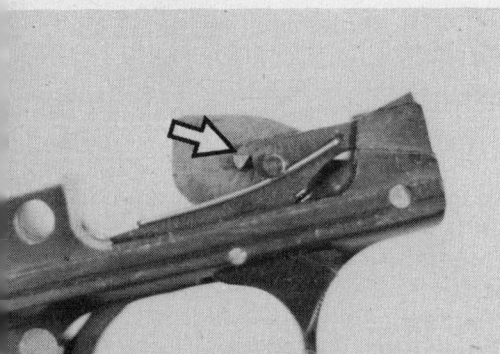

In older guns, there may be some wear at the engagement (arrow) of the hammer stud and the rear beak of the slide stop.

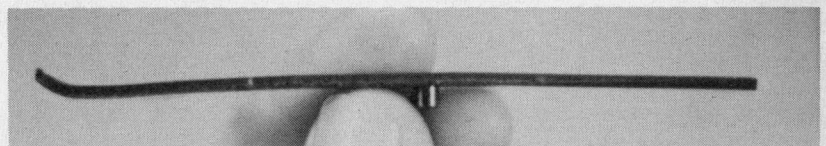

The slight bend along the length of the shell stop is essential to proper operation. It's not supposed to be straight.

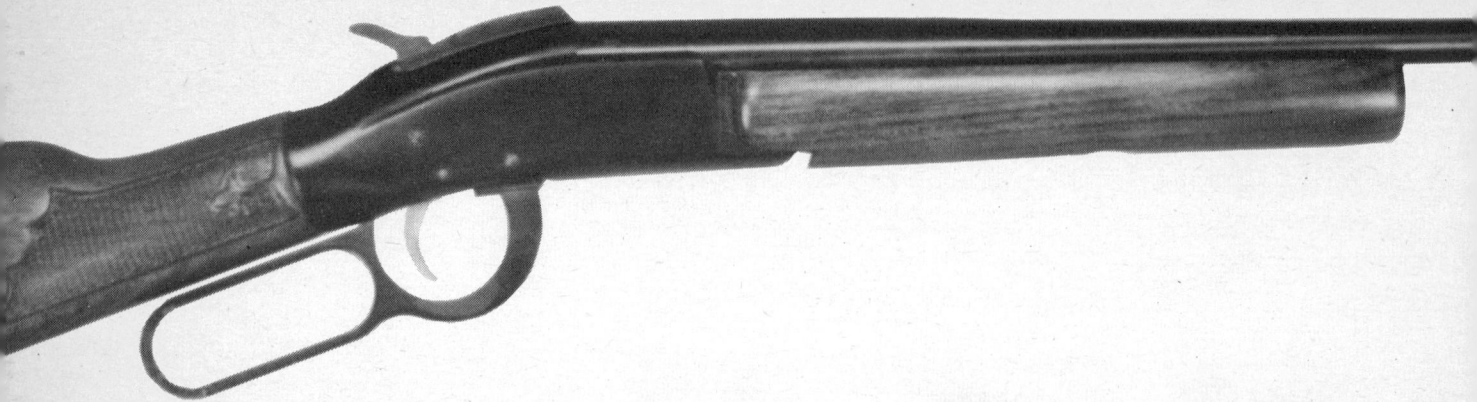

Ithaca Model 66 "Supersingle" Shotgun

The economy single-barrel of the Ithaca shotgun line is a rather odd-looking beast, in appearance a cross between a shotgun and a lever-action rifle. It was introduced in 1963, and in 1965 was also offered in a youth model, with a shorter stock and barrel and a factory-installed recoil pad. Its full-loop finger lever has a very short throw, just enough to operate the latch for its tip-down barrel. The receiver is an alloy casting; and, as in most single-shot guns, the internal mechanism is very simple.

All parts are powered by helical coil springs, and there is an ample allowance for age weakening. The hammer spring guide has a rebound cam which returns the hammer after its strike to safety position. The cam is held by a step on the hammer face resting on the sear, which is an integral part of the trigger. The trigger pin is of adequate size to support this if the hammer spur were struck accidentally.

The barrel is locked in place by a round bolt mounted in the lower part of the breech face, contacting a ledge on the underlug of the barrel. After several years of hard use, the round steel locking bolt may begin to wear its tunnel in the receiver, allowing the barrel latching system to loosen. If the wear is minimal, it can be tightened by judicious peening just below the edge of the shelf on the barrel underlug, to slightly raise the contact surface. If the wear is serious, though, this won't work, as a badly worn bolt tunnel will allow the locking bolt to be pushed down as the action is closed, and the bolt will fail to engage the

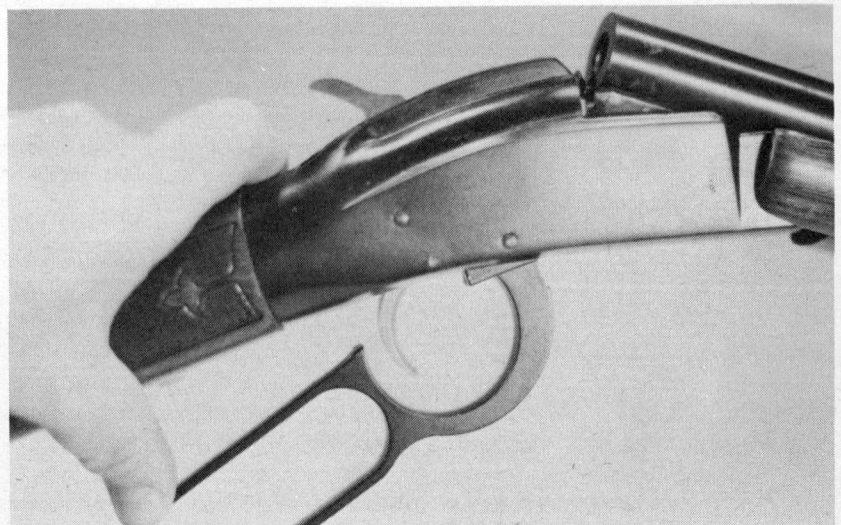

The Model 66 lever is moved only a short distance to release the barrel latch.

The forend is retained by a single large screw (arrow); and, this should be checked occasionally for tightness.

To remove the barrel from the receiver, the forend must first be removed, and then the large screw on the left side of the receiver. The barrel hinge is then pushed out to the right.

On the right side of the receiver, the barrel hinge pin is screw-slotted, and has a flat on the edge of its head (arrow) to stabilize it while the retaining screw is tightened.

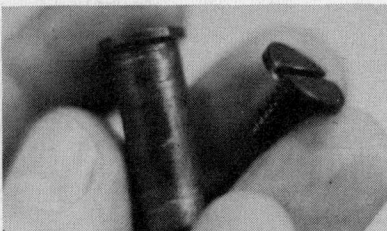

If the gun is taken down for transporting or storage, the barrel hinge pin and its retaining screw should be replaced in the receiver to prevent loss.

The ejector is somewhat similar to the one used in the Ithaca Model 49 rifle, but its size makes it less fragile.

tightened lug shelf. If this is the case, it's new-receiver time, and the gun must be returned to the factory.

As in most currently made single-shot guns, the forend is not a quick-detachable type. It is secured by a single large screw, and this should be checked every so often for tightness. To take the gun down for storage or transportation, the forend must first be removed to expose the barrel hinge and its retaining screw. The retaining screw is on the left side of the receiver, and after it is taken out the hinge pin can be pushed out to the right. On the right side, the hinge pin has a slotted screw-like head with a flat on one edge that fits a shoulder in its recess to stabilize the pin while the retaining screw (on the opposite side) is tightened or removed. When replacing the hinge pin, be sure that the edge flat is aligned properly, and the head of the pin fully into its recess in the frame. If the gun is to be apart for some time, as in storage or shipping, it's best to replace the barrel hinge pin and retaining screw in the receiver to prevent loss.

The ejector of this gun is somewhat similar to the one used in the Ithaca Model 49 .22 rifle, but in this case its larger size and non-trip action make it less susceptible to breakage. In the event that an ejector should chip, break or become worn, it is retained by a single cross-pin, and replacement is easy—it does not even require removal of the barrel. All parts are, of course, available, as this gun is still being made. It's currently offered in .410 or 20 gauge.

Ithaca's 500, 600, and 700 series over/under shotguns are mechanically identical, but feature differing grades of wood-and-metal embellishment.

Ithaca Model 600 Over/Under Shotgun

Made for Ithaca by the SKB company of Japan, the Model 600 over/under shotgun is one of a series, available in several grades, including the models 500 and 700. The SKB over/under has a box-lock action, and its internal mechanism is notably trouble-free. Although the two hammer springs and the barrel latch lever springs are all of V-blade type, they seem to be so well-made that the incidence of breakage should be very low. So far, since the introduction of this gun in 1967, I have not replaced a single one.

In fact, the only repair I have made on this gun, other than the routine replacement of an occasional broken firing pin, was one case in which the forend latch had become loose. The owner of the gun traveled to many Skeet and trap matches, and his gun was frequently taken down to be transported, causing wear in the forend latch system. The latch on this gun is the lifter type, with an inner beak on the lift-lever contacting a projection on the front of the lug mounted on the lower barrel. Since the heat of weld-ing would loosen the entire lug, it is not possible to add steel to the front projection. Instead, the beak of the latch lever is heated and bent slightly, to tighten its engagement with the lug.

The choice of which barrel will fire first is controlled by a selector button mounted in the top web of the trigger. Pushed to the left, the inner level which the button controls will cause the top barrel to fire first when the trigger is pulled. When the button is pushed to the right, the lower barrel is the first to fire. After the first shot, of course, the change to the other barrel is automatic, this function is accomplished by a recoil-operated inertia block. This mechanism contains no parts that are prone to malfunction, but if there ever is any trouble, repair

Looseness of the forend will be due to wear of the retaining lug on the lower barrel, at the point indicated by the arrow. Any repair should be done to the latch in the forend, not to the lug.

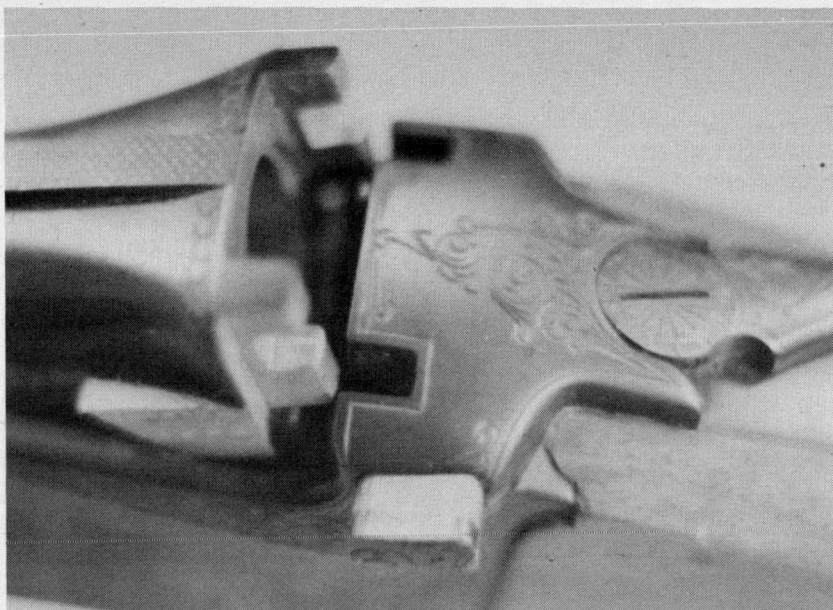

The Model 600 uses a variation of the Greener cross-bolt locking system, and any loosening will be after many years of hard use.

or adjustment should be left to a very experienced gunsmith.

The barrel latching system of the Model 600 is a variation of the Greener cross-bolt pattern, with the latch lever moving a heavy block of steel horizontally to the left, the beveled edges of the two notches in its forward surface contacting rectangular cuts at the center of twin projections from the rear of the barrel unit. Because of the excellent design of this system, it will be many years before any loosening from wear will occur. I have examined several of these guns which have seen a lot of use, and the breech still closes with the firmness of a bank vault.

The only real complaint I can make about the Model 600 is in regard to a routine repair, not the operation of the gun. Any gun, even the finest, will occasionally break a firing pin. Also, in many over/under guns, the firing pins are set in the breech block at an angle, and this can contribute to eventual deformation, after many rounds are fired over a period of years. The firing pins in the Model 600 are retained in the receiver by threaded bushings which require a special wrench. This can be obtained from the factory, or made in the shop with very little difficulty. The bad part comes when you start to use the wrench. In order to align the wrench with the firing pin

bushings, or retainers, it is first necessary to remove the stock, the hammer springs, and the hammers. Replacement of a broken or deformed firing pin should be done by a gunsmith, of course. All parts for this gun are readily available, and most large gun shops will have such things as firing pins on hand. (A short while back, SKB split away from Ithaca and currently sells their product under their own name. While Ithaca is still servicing "Ithaca/ SKB" guns the new SKB outfit advises they will provide parts and service for *all* shotguns made by them. SKB's new address: 190 Shepard Avenue, Wheeling, Illinois 60090.)

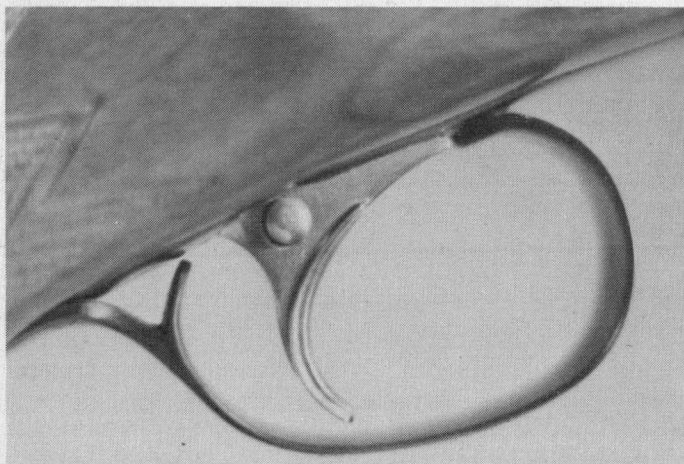

The choice of which barrel will fire first is controlled by a selector button on the trigger. Pushed to the left, the top barrel is first. To the right, the lower one. After the first shot, the change to the unfired barrel is internal and automatic.

Iver Johnson Champion Shotgun

The Champion has been around since 1909, and a slightly redesigned version is still in production today. This economical, single-barrel, outside-hammer shotgun has always been popular as a ''first gun'' for the young hunter. The outside hammer is a good safety factor, and the low cost allows shortening the stock to fit a younger shooter without the reluctance one might have with a more expensive gun.

As with most single-hammer shotguns, the Champion has a very simple mechanism, and all of the parts are of generous size with no tendency toward breakage. The hammer spring is a helical coil, and the springs powering the ejector, forend latch, and firing pin return are also of this type.

There are two flat springs which supply tension to the trigger and the barrel latch. The trigger spring is not severely flexed and rarely breaks. However, the large, curved barrel latch spring, which is screw-mounted in the forward floor of the receiver, is flexed to a greater extent each time the action is opened, and this spring will crack with some frequency. Replacements

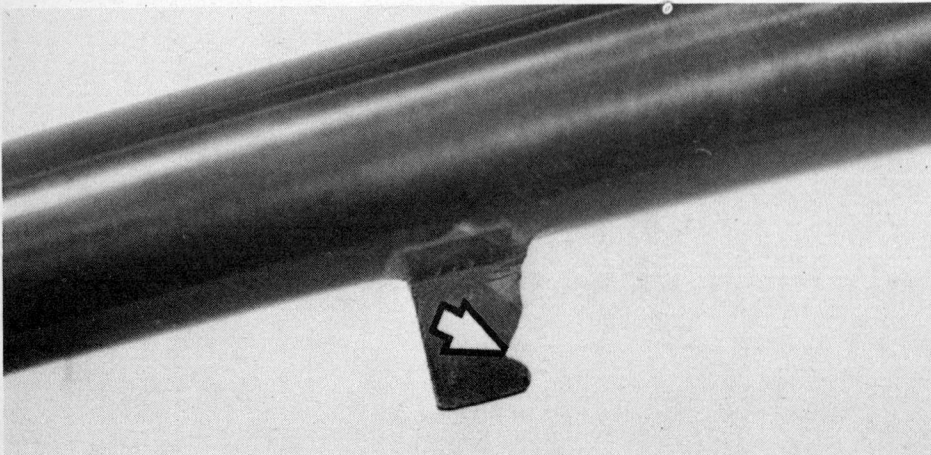

To correct a loose forend latch, the lug on the barrel can be drilled for a pin at the point indicated by the arrow. Weld should *not* be used, as this will often separate the lug from the barrel.

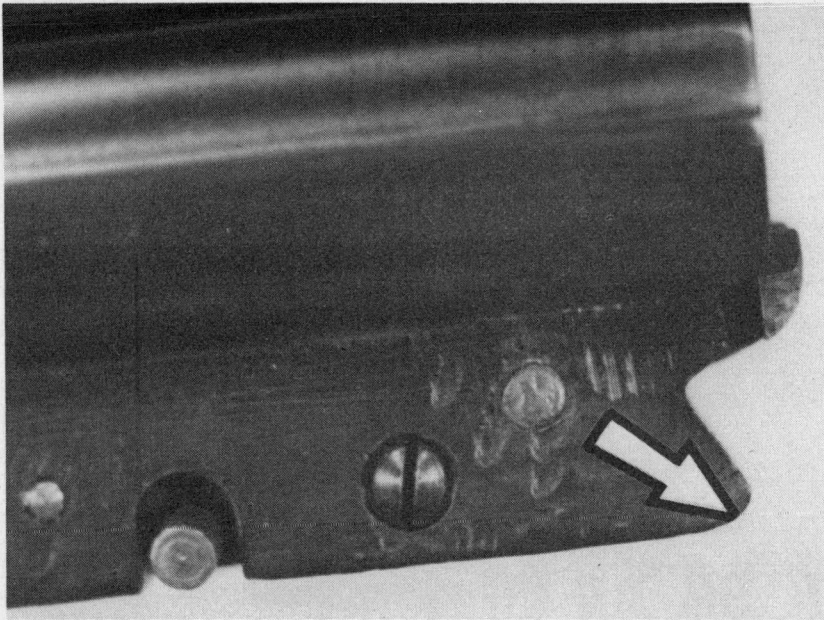

If the wear in the barrel latch system is not too excessive, it can be corrected (most of the time) by using a hammer and screwdriver blade to make a depression below the lip of the lug to raise its upper surface. The arrow shows the location, but this should be done at the center, *not* the edge.

are available for both of these springs, but installation is best left to your gunsmith. Amateurs attempting to install the barrel latch spring will often strip the threads of the mounting screw. If your local gun shop does not have replacements on hand, it is possible to make both of these out of doubled piano wire. In the case of the barrel latch spring, however, this will require a washer or some other sort of retainer at the mounting point and a longer mounting screw.

In the older guns, which have seen a lot of use, the barrel latching system will often become loose from wear. Aside from frequent misfires, there is some danger in this, as gas can escape at the breech. This situation is the result of wear at either the latching lug, the barrel pivot, or both. If the wear on the locking lug is extensive, its upper surface can be built up with weld and recut to shape. If the looseness is not as serious, the upper surface of the lug can be raised by peening a depression about 1/16-inch below its lower edge. Peening the edge

itself will do no good, as it will be flattened by the pressure of the first shot fired.

Wear in the barrel pivot can be corrected by drilling a 3/16-inch hole about ¼-inch deep at the center of the pivot curve in the barrel lug and installing a tapered pin, driving it into place. The head of this pin is then cut and polished to match the curvature of the receiver-mounted pivot rod, leaving enough protrusion to take up the slack.

The ejector on the Champion is of the trip-latch type, being released to kick the fired shell clear of the chamber as the barrel nears the full-open position. The detent surfaces on the ejector and its latch will sometimes wear to the extent that the system will no longer snap out. When this occurs, the ejector will usually still lift the fired shell sufficiently for it to be removed with the fingers, since the ejector spring will still be functioning when the gun is opened. Worn tripnotches can usually be recut without the necessity of replacing parts. Also, if the shell-contact portion of the ejector becomes worn, thus slipping past the rim as the gun is opened, this surface can be built up and recut to original shape. Again, this is a job for a gunsmith.

Many of the parts for the currently-made Champion will fit the older guns, though some will have to be adapted slightly. Your gunsmith, or the Iver Johnson Company, which is still very much in business, can advise you on this.

Japanese Arisaka Rifle

First of the modern small-caliber rifles adopted by Japan was the 6.5mm Type 30 of 1897, which replaced the obsolete Murata rifle. Like the guns which followed, the Type 30 was designed by an Imperial Commission headed by Colonel Nariaki Arisaka. The gun was redesigned in 1905 to become the Type 38, still in the 6.5 mm chambering. In 1939, a new 7.7 mm cartridge was adopted, and the Arisaka rifle was again redesigned to become the Type 99, and this is the gun most familiar to American shooters and collectors. The 6.5mm Type 38 rifles and the very early 7.7mm Type 99 rifles are well-made of good materials, but many late wartime Type 99 guns are quite rough, and of dubious quality in regard to materials. As with all military rifles, it's best to have any gun checked by a gunsmith before shooting it. Checking the headspace is of particular importance, as bolts were often switched. It should be noted, though, that when the bolt is original and the gun is one of the better-quality examples, the Arisaka is one of the strongest bolt-action rifles ever made, a fact proved by P.O. Ackley in extensive tests.

The basic design of the Arisaka shows definite Mauser influence, but there are several important differences. The bolt design is extremely simplified and uses a unique tubular striker with an integral firing pin. The firing pin portion is well-shaped, strong, and it rarely breaks. If it should break, the pin can be repointed easily. Also, at the time of this writing, parts are still generally available from several of the dealers who specialize in surplus military items.

The long, Mauser-type extractor is

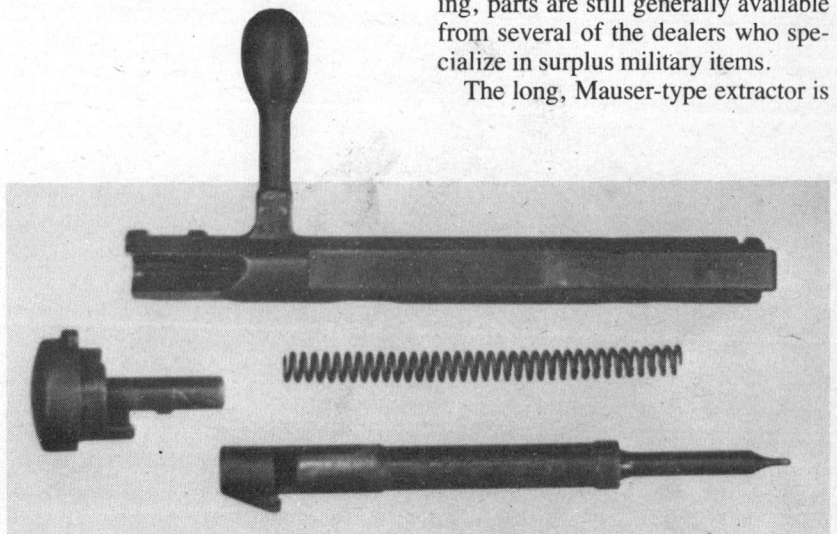

Here's the Arisaka bolt, field stripped with the extractor still in place. Note the tubular combination striker and firing pin.

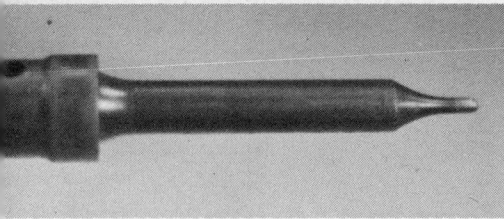

The firing pin portion of the long, tubular striker is well-shaped, strong and does not often break.

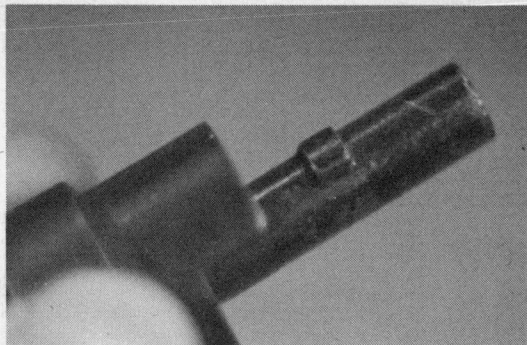

Combination safety catch and bolt end piece has a large lug on its internal shaft which mates with an open track in the tubular striker—a very secure system.

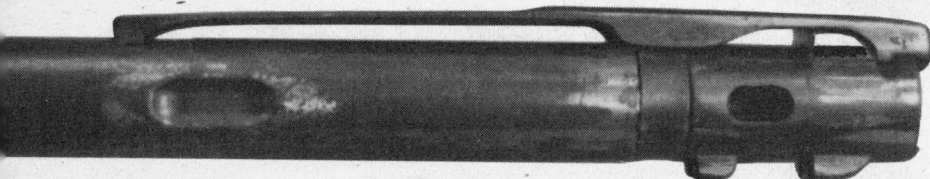

The long extractor is tempered to be its own spring, and is retained on the bolt by a Mauser-type ring. Note the large gas vent, and the small extra lug near the ring which operates the ejector.

tempered to be its own spring, and like most of those in this pattern it is more susceptible to weakening than breakage. A weak extractor tail can often be reshaped and retempered, but this is a job for the gunsmith. The combination safety catch and bolt end piece is retained on the bolt by internal recesses which mate with a large lug at the rear of the bolt, and no incidence of breakage has been seen. The inner shaft of the safety has a heavy lug which mates with an open track in the striker, a very secure safety system. The only times I have replaced the safety/end piece were in cases of loss. I can recall one incident in which an Arisaka owner was field-stripping his sporterized Type 99 on the shore of a lake, and during take-

down of the bolt (when the safety knob was turned to the dismounting position), his fingers slipped. Driven by the striker spring, the safety made a graceful arc into the waters of the lake, never to be seen again.

On the Arisaka the bolt stop greatly resembles the standard Mauser type, but there is an important difference. The outer blade spring of the Type 99 bolt stop powers only the stop itself. The ejector, which in the Mauser pattern is tensioned by a smaller inner arm of the bolt stop spring, is not spring-powered in the Arisaka. Instead, there is a small secondary lug on the bolt which strikes the ejector, camming it into action. This system works well and produces no problems. The large and heavy bolt stop

spring rarely breaks, but may weaken on occasion, especially on late wartime guns. It can usually be reshaped and retempered.

The Arisaka stock is usually made of two separate pieces of wood, and the joining seam is easily seen. This laminated construction not only made the stock stronger, but also allowed the use of narrower stock blanks during manufacture. When subjected to extremes of moisture or dryness, the stock pieces will occasionally separate, but they can easily be rejoined. For those who convert these guns into good sporting rifles, this point is not important, as both Bishop and Fajen offer excellent sporter stocks for the Arisaka.

In regard to sporterizing, it should be noted that the various models of the Arisaka are beginning to be noticed by the military rifle collectors, and any Japanese rifle in excellent original condition should not be altered in any way, as it may have collector value that is greater than its worth as a converted sporter.

A flat blade spring (arrow) powers the bolt stop. These will occasionally lose tension, but can usually be reshaped and restored.

An Arisaka stock is usually made of two separate pieces of wood, and the joining seam (arrow) is readily visible. When subjected to extremes of moisture or dryness, the two pieces will occasionally come apart.

Much to the chagrin of today's military rifle collectors, the Imperial chrysanthemum emblem was crudely removed from many of the Arisaka rifles. On this one, it is intact, hence it's more valuable.

51

Knickerbocker Double Shotgun

Back around the turn of the century, any hardware dealer or wholesaler who ordered a certain minimum number of shotguns from one of six or seven small factories in New England could have the guns marked with any name he chose. Because of this, the mailbag of today's firearms editor is usually filled with questions about such jewels as the "Essex," the "Long Tom," and the "White Powder Wonder." One of the firms producing this type of moderately-priced shotgun was the Crescent Fire Arms Company of Norwich, Connecticut, a subsidiary of the H.&D. Folsom Company, a large New York wholesale establishment. One of their principal "brand names" was "Knickerbocker," and these good old doubles were also usually marked "American Gun Company—New York," a firm which existed only in the advertising of H.&D. Folsom.

Some of the "brand name" guns of this period were of only fair quality, but the Knickerbocker double was somewhat better than most. A true sidelock, it had several of the features found on only the finer doubles today, such as a lift-lever forend latch and cocking indicators for the internal hammers. The stock was as weakly-mounted as most on the doubles of this time, but the action was well-made and strong. The barrel latch system featured a heavy underlug and an auxiliary latch in the top rear extension of the barrels. The sidelocks are easily removed, as are the simple, cylindrical firing pins, and the latter are easily reproduced if broken.

The hammers are powered by heavy helical coil springs, and these neither break nor weaken. The sear springs are flat, curved blades, and these do break somewhat more often. Replacements must be made and installed by a gunsmith, as parts for these old guns are not often available, and even when they are found, they are seldom interchangeable.

Many of these guns, especially those which have seen a lot of use, will be suffering from looseness of the barrel latching system and the barrel pivot. End play can be taken up by drilling a hole at the center of the barrel pivot curve in the underlug and installing a steel pin to make up for the wear. The barrel latch can be tightened by careful peening at the rear center of the locking lug on the barrels, just below the operating surface. The auxiliary lug at the top can be adjusted in the same way.

The forend latch lug below the barrels is also subject to wear on the inside of its locking beak, and welding here is risky, as the heat can separate the barrels and ribs into four useless pieces. It is sometimes possible to lightly peen the beak toward the barrels, but there is a chance of breakage when this is tried. The best way to tighten a loose forend is to heat and reshape the beak of the lifter-latch, which can easily be removed from the forend for this operation.

A broken stock is a real problem, as even the used-parts dealers will seldom have these on hand. Replacement stocks for *some* of these guns are available from Bishop and Fajen, but

On the left, the small arrow indicates the retaining screw for the left firing pin. The arrow at right points to the left hammer indicator, which protrudes slightly when the hammer is cocked.

Small arrow at top points to the left firing pin. The lower arrow indicates the cocking rod for the left hammer.

you'll have to inquire whether they can fit your particular model. If the original stock is just cracked, and not badly splintered, it can usually be repaired with a good epoxy glue, but this is not a job for the amateur.

One very important thing to remember about any of the older shotguns is to have your gunsmith check to see if the barrels are of laminated construction, also called "twist" or Damascus type. If your gun does have barrels of this type, retire it. Give it a place of honor over the fireplace. *Never shoot smokeless, modern shotshells in a gun with Damascus barrels.* Laminated barrels are unsafe with any modern smokeless load, no matter how light. Even with special blackpowder loads, they are not to be trusted. The Knickerbocker gun shown in the photos did not have twist barrels and proved to be quite safe with moderate modern loads, but each individual gun *must* be checked by a gunsmith.

Hammer springs on the Knickerbocker are heavy helical coils and seldom break or weaken. The sears are powered by a curved flat spring (arrow), and these do occasionally break. Replacements must be made and installed by a gunsmith.

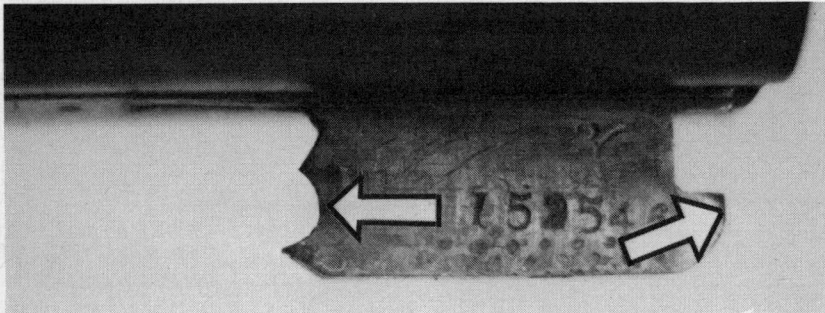

End play of the barrels can be taken up by installing a steel pin at the center of the barrel pivot recess on the underlug (left arrow). The latch itself can be tightened by peening at the rear center of the locking lug, just below the locking surface, at the point indicated by the right arrow.

There is an auxiliary latching lug on the rear upper extension of the barrels, and this tends to wear at the point indicated by the arrow.

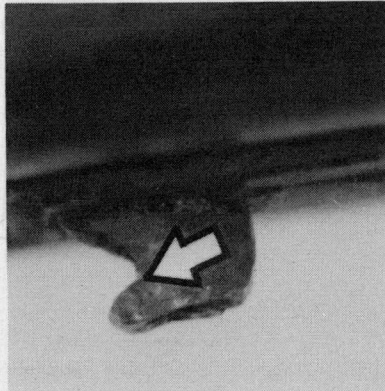

The forend latch lug below the barrels wears at the point indicated by the arrow and since heat cannot be safely applied to this area, tightening is best done by altering the beak of the latch lever in the forend.

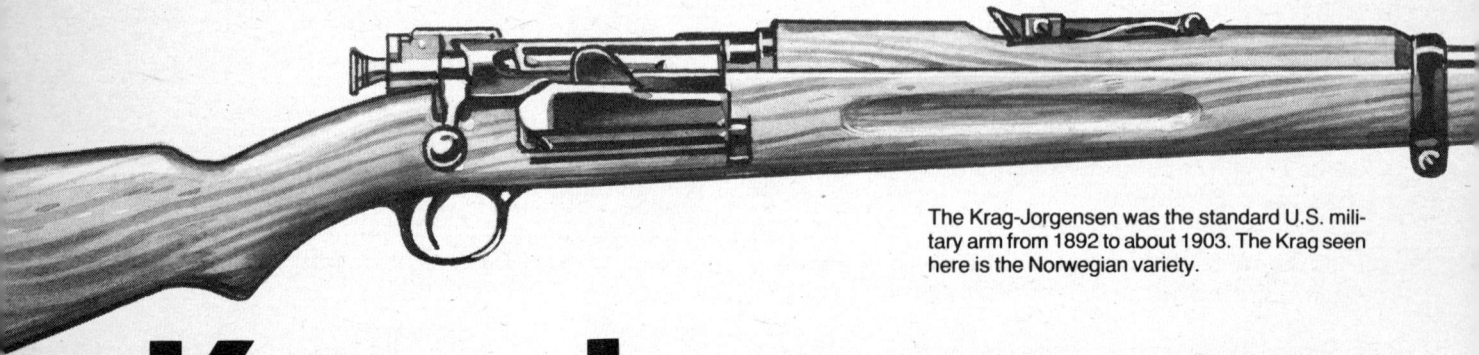

The Krag-Jorgensen was the standard U.S. military arm from 1892 to about 1903. The Krag seen here is the Norwegian variety.

Krag-Jorgensen Rifle

The .30-40 Krag was the standard U.S. Military rifle from 1892 to 1903, and in 1898 and 1899 saw action in the Spanish-American War, the Philippine Insurrection, and the Boxer Rebellion in China. Around 500,000 of these guns were made, a smaller portion of them in carbine style. The rifle was originally designed at Konigsberg Vapenfabrik in Norway between 1886 and 1889 by Ole Hermann Johannes Krag and Erik Jorgensen, and was adopted for military use by Denmark in 1889, chambered for the 8 × 58mm rimmed cartridge, and by Norway in 1894, chambered for the 6.5 × 55mm round, the same cartridge used by the Swedish military. The Danish version of the Krag is somewhat different in several details, the most obvious being that its magazine loading gate is pivoted at the front, rather than below as in the U.S. and Norwegian models.

The magazine system of the Krag is unique, being a horizontal integral box type with a Mannlicher-style feed arm which pushes the cartridges across the gun to the left side, then upward to be fed from the left side of the receiver. Since cartridges have to be loaded into the magazine individually, the system was eventually criticized by the military as being slow to reload, but it's an extremely reliable feeding arrangement. From a mechanical viewpoint, my only criticism is that the feed arm is powered by a blade-type spring. The spring, however, has good mechanical advantage and is not flexed too severely in normal operation. Also, this spring is of quite heavy stock, and breakage is rare. In the event of a broken magazine spring, if no original replacement can be found, it is fairly easy to make a spring from doubled round spring wire.

The attachment of the firing pin to the striker rod is rather complicated, involving a doll's head shape at the end of the rod, and a corresponding recess inside the body of the firing pin, which is cut away on one side to facilitate removal and attachment. It is fortunate that these firing pins don't

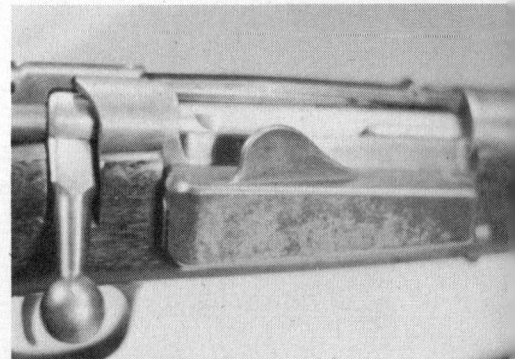

Here the unique Krag magazine is shown open (top) and closed (bottom).

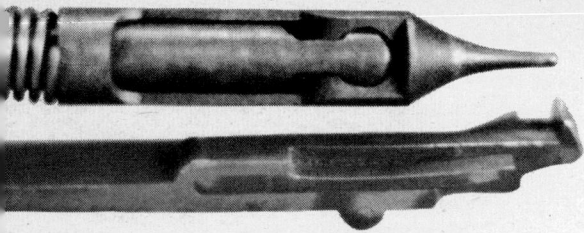

This close-up view of the firing pin shows its unique attachment to the striker rod. The part below is the extractor.

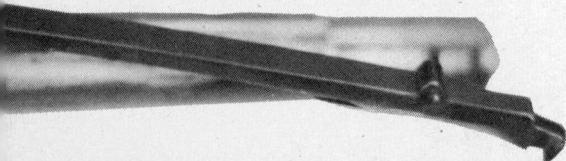

The extractor is heavy and well-shaped, and breakage is rare.

Here, the cartridge cutoff (arrow) is shown in the "up" position, allowing rounds to feed from the magazine.

break often, as replacement parts for the Krag are available only intermittently from the used-parts dealers, and making one of these firing pins in the shop would be time-consuming and comparatively expensive. I have, on occasion, repaired a broken tip by re-pointing.

Another unusual feature of the Krag is the extractor, which is attached to the striker assembly by a vertical hinge pin, and is also the key to bolt removal. To take out the bolt, you simply draw it all the way to the rear, and lift the front of the extractor upward while turning the bolt further to the left. When the bolt lug is aligned with the track in the top of the receiver, the bolt will come out easily. The extractor is tempered to be its own spring, but it is well-shaped and heavy, and it does not often break. Here, again, this is fortunate, as it would be difficult to reproduce.

On the left side of the receiver at the rear there is a feature common to military rifles of the time, a manual cutoff, allowing cartridges in the magazine to be held in reserve while the rifle is fired by single loading. For normal feeding, the cutoff is placed on the turned-up position. This part is of simple design, and is not subject to extreme stress that would lead to wear or breakage.

The ejector is pivot-mounted in the floor of the boltway, and is cammed upward by the bolt as it reaches full travel to strike the side of the cartridge case. Although it is under rather sharp stress at the moment of bolt impact, the part is so well-designed that it seldom will break. In fact, the only breakage I have seen in this area is one fracture of the ejector pivot pin, easily replaced with any pin turned to the right diameter.

The manual safety is a Mauser-type lever at the rear, on top of the striker assembly, and when turned over to the right locks both striker and bolt. The striker is equipped with an external knob, allowing the gun to be recocked without opening the bolt, in case of a hard-primer misfire.

Noting that the bolt has only a single forward locking lug, some have voiced concern about the strength of the locking system. Actually, the bolt has three locking points. There is a heavy guide rib on the right side which bears against a solid shoulder in the receiver, and the bolt handle base enters a deep cut in the heavy rear tang. It's not the bolt design that limits the Krag to moderate-level cartridges, but the primitive heat-treatment of the receiver. With regular loads in a gun in good condition, though, it is quite safe. Any rifle that has seen military use should, of course, be checked by a gunsmith before firing.

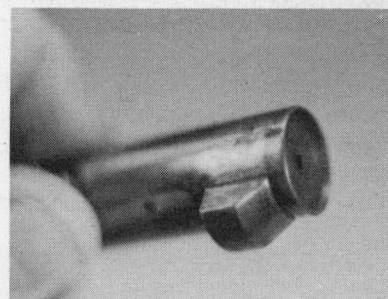

The bolt face of the Krag is recessed to enclose the entire rim of the cartridge. Note the single bolt locking lug.

L.C. Smith Hammerless Double Shotgun

The first of these guns was made around 1880 by the L.C. Smith Company of Syracuse, New York. Lyman Cornelius Smith established his firm in 1877, and about 30,000 guns were made before he sold the manufacturing rights in 1890 to the Hunter Arms Company of Fulton, New York. The L.C. Smith guns were made by Hunter Arms from 1890 to 1945, when the company was purchased by Marlin. Using the name "L.C. Smith Gun Company," Marlin produced the guns until 1950. For a short time thereafter they offered limited parts and service on these guns, but this has since been discontinued. Any parts needed will have to be found among the used-parts dealers, or made by a gunsmith.

In this country, most low to medium-priced double shotguns have been of the box-lock pattern, as this style is less expensive to manufacture. The L.C. Smith guns are in a separate class, as they are true sidelock guns, the hammer and sear mechanism being mounted on removable plates at each side of the receiver. The locks of this gun are of extremely simple design. Other than the bridle plate and mounting screws, the operating parts number only three—the hammer, sear, and mainspring. The spring is a V-blade type, supplying tension to both the hammer and sear, and is retained in the plate by a lug and small screw at the rear. This spring is flexed rather severely in normal operation, but is heavy and well-made, and does not break often. I have replaced these occasionally with torsion springs made of doubled round wire, but the spring shape must be changed because of the different stress pattern.

Other than the occasional breakage or weakening of one of the mainsprings, the only point in the locks that may need attention is the engagement of the hammer and sear. If there is extreme wear or chipped edges in the sear beak or the the sear step on the hammer, the hammer may fail to stay cocked when the action is closed. In some cases, the hammer may jar off as the gun is snapped shut, and if that chamber is loaded, the situation will be called to your attention in a very positive manner. The contact points can be recut, or built up with weld, recut and rehardened, by any good gunsmith. This will cure the problem

The L. C. Smith sidelock is of very simple design. A small screw (left arrow) retains the hammer spring. The only wear of any consequence will occur at the engagement of the sear and hammer (right arrow).

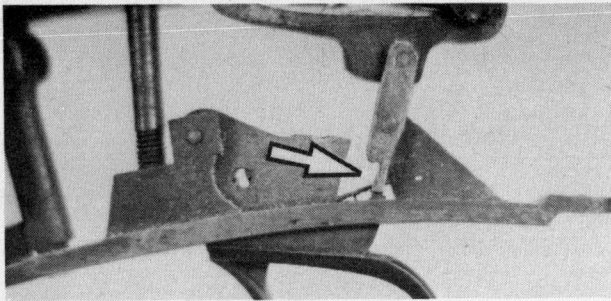

Here, the arrow points to the engagement of the safety block with the top rear of the two triggers. On some guns, there may be a different system.

The barrel latch spring (arrow) is a flat V-type, and weakness or breakage is not unusual.

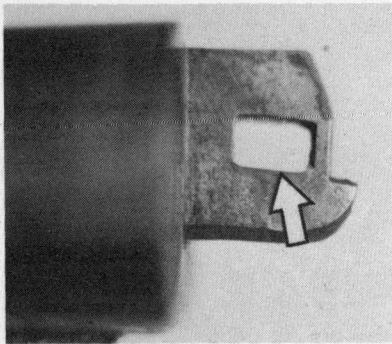

While the barrel latch system is designed to be self-adjusting, extreme wear may require some raising of the point on the barrel extension indicated by the arrow.

for many years. In some cases, shrinkage of the stock wood and overtightening of the tang screws can cause the triggers to bear against the sear tails, and this can produce the same symptoms. When this happens, either the triggers or sear tails can be relieved to give the proper clearance, or spacers can be made to restore the tangs to alignment.

Most "hammerless" shotguns use direct pushrods to cock the internal hammers, the rods cammed rearward by the downward movement of the forend iron as the action is opened. In the L.C. Smith, the cocking rods are not pushed. Instead, their forward ends have crank levers with studs that meet recesses in the rear base of the forend, and the rods are turned as the gun is opened. At the rear, the rods have a square shank which enters lifter lugs on each side; and, as the rods rotate the arm of the lug tips the hammer back. It's a strong system, and is smoother in operation than the pushrod type. The only trouble I have seen with these is an occasional breakage

of the lever studs at the front of the receiver, and this can usually be repaired by welding. In rare cases, the lifter or cocking cam at the rear may break, and in this event there is good news—Triple K has modern replacements for these, along with four types of L.C. Smith firing pins and both right and left ejector kickers, the latter having an offset arm which is subject to occasional breakage.

Both single trigger and double trigger models were made, and the safety systems are different. In the double trigger type, a projection at the top rear of the triggers is blocked by a pivoting lever, and the lower end of the lever is cut to a narrow projection which occasionally deforms or breaks off. In either case, the safety button on the upper tang will continue to work, but the trigger block will not function—a dangerous situation. On any L.C. Smith double trigger gun that you buy, it's a good idea to have a gunsmith check the engagement of the lever inside. A deformed lower end can often be straightened, but one with a broken tip may have to be replaced. It's not a difficult part to make, but the exact dimensions must be maintained for proper operation.

The barrel latch spring is a flat V-type, and weakness is found more often than breakage. It is possible to make a replacement from doubled round spring wire, and this will probably last longer than the original. The barrel latch itself is a rotary lug type that appeared first in the Baker gun, and was later used by Fox and Ithaca. Its upper arm enters a rectangular opening in a heavy rear projection of the barrels, and the design of the system makes it self-adjusting to com-

pensate for wear. Even so, if the wear is extreme enough, it may be beyond the adjustment qualities of the system. In that case, the lower edge of the opening can be carefully peened on its left side to raise the contact surface and tighten it. The extension must be well-supported while this is done. Adding steel by welding is out, as the heat could separate barrels and ribs.

On early guns, the forend is attached by a double latch. There is a conventional heavy curved blade spring which contacts a well on the lug below the barrels, and an additional set of spring leaves at the side, controlled by a button at the forward end of the forend. The spring leaves mate with notches on each side of the lug, and with this double system, looseness of the forend is unlikely. The heavy main latch spring is positioned by a lighter flat spring, screw-mounted inside the forend iron, which also powers the ejector lever at its other end. If this spring should break, a round-wire replacement can be made. In fact, in later guns, two separate round-wire torsion-type springs perform these two functions. Later guns also have only the single heavy blade latch, without the end button and side notch latches. In either type, breakage of the main latch spring can be repaired by making a round-wire replacement, but doubled wire of very heavy weight must be used.

As in most sidelock guns, the inletting for the locks tends to weaken the wrist area of the buttstock, and cracking is not unusual. If not too severe, this can be repaired with epoxy glue. If it's beyond repair, replacement stocks are available from the major commercial stockmakers.

Marlin Model 49 and Model 99 Rifles

The basic design of this .22 autoloader was introduced in 1959 as the Model 99. The original gun is no longer made, but later versions, the 99C and the 99M1, are still in production. A further modification was brought out in 1970, currently available as the Model 49DL, and this one is made in very similar form with other designations for Western Auto Stores (Model 150M), and for J.C. Penney (Model 2066). The 99 series guns are also made for several stores under their own names, and with the Glenfield marking. In all of these guns, the internal mechanism is practically identical, except for the changes necessary to adapt them for either box-type or tubular magazine systems.

As with most Marlin guns, these are well-made of good materials. The

The ejector (left arrow) is simply an extension of the cartridge lifter spring. The center arrow indicates the disconnector, and the arrow at right points to the nylon bolt buffer.

breech block (bolt) and cocking handle are particularly outstanding, being solid steel parts, machined to perfection. In this day of plastic and alloy, a welcome touch. It would have been nice if this could have been carried on into the feed and firing systems, as these contain some non-ferrous parts that cause occasional difficulties, especially after long use. The bolt buffer, for example, is made of nylon. The concept is a good one—it prevents the steel bolt, as it reaches full rearward travel, from battering the inside rear of the alloy receiver. The nylon material used, however, is fairly hard, and after several thousand rounds it will fracture. The part is quite inexpensive, and can be easily replaced by the non-professional. Keeping a spare on hand would be a good idea.

Made of plastic, the magazine follower seldom breaks in normal operation. It is easily damaged, though, when the magazine tube is out of the gun, since it protrudes about 1½ inches from the end of the tube.

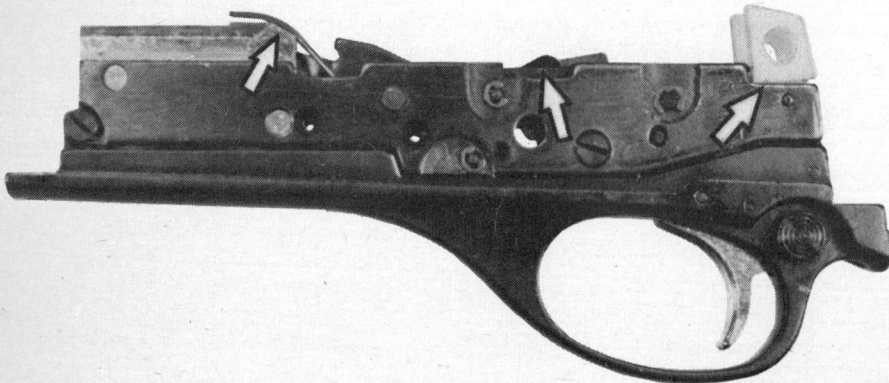

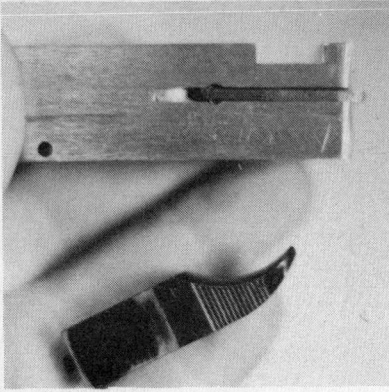

The breech block (bolt) and the cocking handle are solid steel parts, nicely machined.

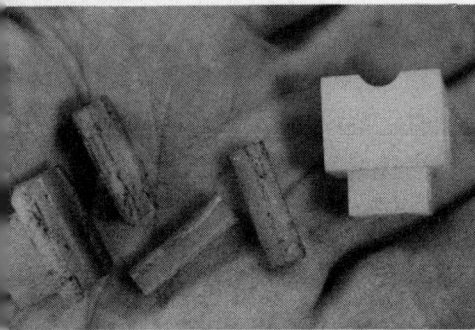

With long use, the nylon bolt buffer will eventually fracture, like the one shown at left. A new buffer is shown at the right.

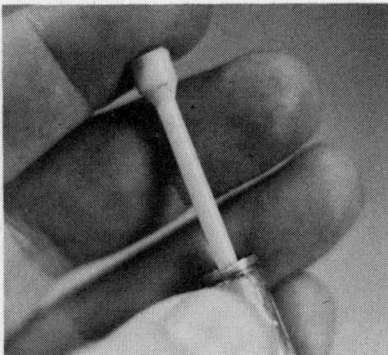

While the magazine follower is made of plastic, it seldom breaks in normal operation; however, it can be easily damaged when the magazine tube is out of the gun.

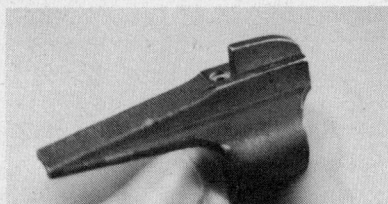

The cartridge guide, or feed throat, is made of alloy, and its surface is plated to increase smoothness and durability. With long use, the plating will wear through, and the feed lips will begin to deteriorate. As soon as this has reached a severe level, the gun will begin to misfeed. Again, this part is inexpensive, and readily available, but installation should be done by a gunsmith. The ejector is an extension of the cartridge lifter spring, positioned on the left side of the feed throat in a small groove. This seldom breaks, but occasionally it will get out of its groove and become deformed, especially with amateur tinkering. It can usually be reshaped and put back in place.

Another part often damaged during amateur disassembly or reassembly is the recoil spring (bolt spring) and its slim guide. With improper reassembly, and the use of force, it is easy to bend the guide and kink the spring, and when this happens, replacement is the only cure. The Model 49 and Model 99 break firing pins no more often than any other .22 autoloader, but if this should occur, the part is priced very low and is easy to replace. The firing pin is made of flat steel stock, and if a new pin should be temporarily unavailable, the part would be easy to make.

On the Model 99M1 rifle, and a few others in the line, the front sight is a ramp type with an integral barrel band, the entire assembly made of alloy, and secured by a single steel Allen screw. This screw should be checked frequently for tightness, to prevent loss of the sight. Overtightening, though, should be avoided, as the steel screw can strip out the alloy threads, and this will require either a new sight, or the making of a larger diameter screw.

The sear and disconnector engagement is of unusual design, and works perfectly, but is not tolerant of any tinkering, such as an amateur attempt to adjust the trigger pull. The small round-wire torsion-type spring that powers the disconnector is particularly susceptible to damage, as its stress direction is critical to proper operation. The entire firing mechanism, in fact, is one that should never be taken apart by the non-professional.

Bear in mind that the problems described above usually occur only after thousands of rounds, or from human error. The Model 49 and Model 99 are good, solid guns.

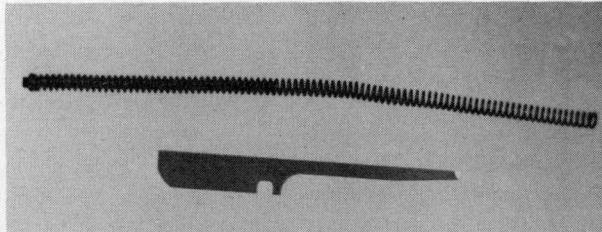

Often damaged during disassembly, the recoil spring and guide (top) should be handled with care. The firing pin, below, is made from flat steel stock and is easy to reproduce.

The cartridge guide, or feed throat, is made of alloy and is susceptible to wear. Note the severely worn feed lips on the one at far left, in comparison to the slightly used one at center, and the new one at the right. ➔

◄On the Model 99M1 rifle and several others, the alloy front sight is retained by a single Allen screw. This should be checked frequently for tightness.

Marlin Model 57M Rifle

In 1955, Marlin introduced a lever-action .22 rifle that was entirely different from their regular lever-operated guns. It was an enclosed-hammer design, and its most outstanding feature was a very short lever arc, only 25 degrees, in comparison with the usual 90 degree lever throw. It was actually possible to operate the lever by a flick of the fingers without

removing the hand from the stock. In reference to this, Marlin called it the "Levermatic," in addition to its designation as Model 56. This rifle had a detachable box magazine, and in 1959 a tube-magazine version was offered, and called the Model 57. In the same year, the basic design was altered to accommodate the .22 Magnum round, and this was the Model 57M, the gun

covered here. Between 1963 and 1969, a limited number of guns were offered in two centerfire chamberings, the .256 Winchester Magnum and the .30 Carbine, the Model 62 Marlin being the first rifle offered for the .256. The Model 56 and Model 57 ended production in 1964 and 1965 respectively, and the Model 57M and Model 62 were dropped in 1969, but

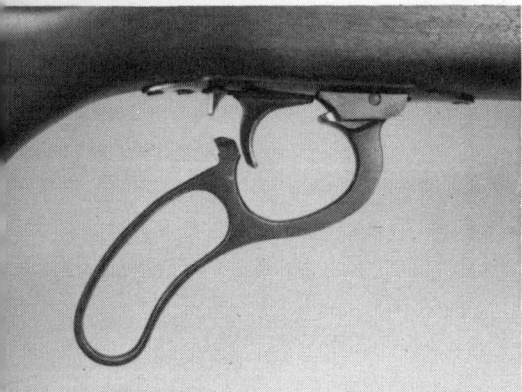

At full travel, the 57M's lever has an arc of only 25 degrees. This "short-throw" lever aids in fast operation.

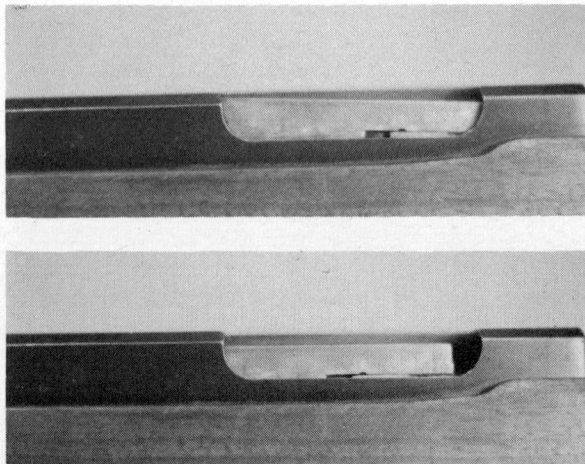

The breech block (bolt) is shown here in locked position (top) and partially opened (bottom).

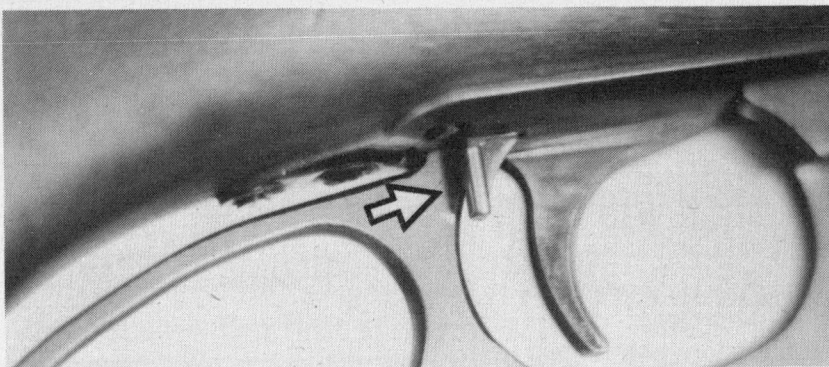

The safety catch (arrow) not only blocks the trigger movement, but also locks the lever in place.

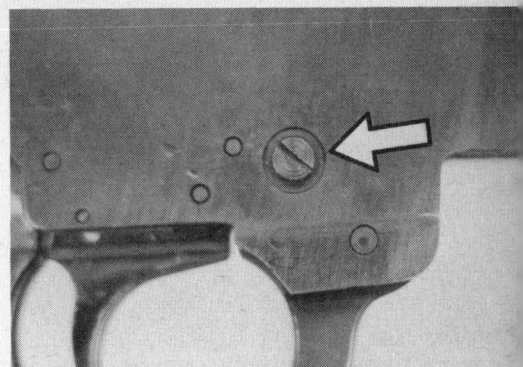

Arrow indicates the main sideplate screw, which should be checked occasionally for tightness. It should not be removed by the nonprofessional.

the factory still offers limited service on all four guns, as long as the remaining stock of parts lasts.

The breech block of the Model 57M tips up at the rear to lock against the top of the receiver and drops down to level as the action is opened. It's a very solid system, and it takes many years of heavy use before there is enough wear of the locking surfaces or the cam roller pin to allow loosening of the lockup. So far, I have not seen any of the rimfire guns that were loose enough to require attention. If this symptom should occur in the future, the linkage pin could be replaced, and a small amount of steel added to the locking surface at the rear of the bolt to restore tightness.

Located near the rear of the trigger on the right side, the manual safety not only blocks the trigger movement when applied, but also locks the lever. The safety is a formed-steel part, but it has ample bearing surfaces for the small amount of stress involved—it's not a source of any difficulty.

When the action is removed from the stock, the removal of a single large screw on the right sideplate will allow the sideplate to be taken off, exposing the entire firing mechanism. For the nonprofessional, the best advice is to check this screw occasionally for tightness, and otherwise *leave it alone*. Although the internal parts are mounted on fixed pins attached to the left sideplate, the interdependence of parts and the presence of several compressed torsion-type wire springs can make removal of that plate a nightmare for the amateur. If something in there needs attention, take it to a gunsmith.

The cartridge guide, or feed throat, of the Model 57M is a two-part unit, but its design and alloy construction make it very similar to the one used in the Marlin Model 49 and 99 rifles (q.v.), and it shares some of the same problems. The ejector, for example, is a raised lug at top left rear, and it is susceptible to both wear and breakage. If this is the only problem with the feed throat, there is, as the saying goes, good news and bad news. The two-piece construction allows replacement of only the left part, the one with the ejector, and Marlin still has this part. The installation, however, is best done by a gunsmith, as it requires removal of the sideplate mentioned above.

In the design of the Model 57M, as well as the other rifles in this group, the weakest point is the firing pin. These points break no more often than on any other gun, but at the rear they are cut diagonally, from the head forward, for clearance of the lever cam which moves the breech block. This leaves a wider section at the head, and a narrowed point partway up the body of the firing pin—the point at which they are prone to snap. The part is still available from Marlin for about $3, and wise owners of these rifles will keep a couple of spare firing pins on hand. Here, again, installation is not for the amateur, as it involves dealing with several small pinned parts.

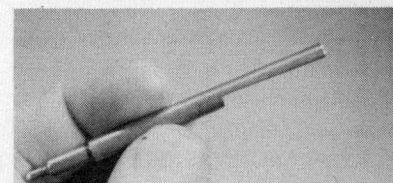

Here's the firing pin of the Model 57M, showing the diagonal cut at the rear for clearance of the upper arm of the lever.

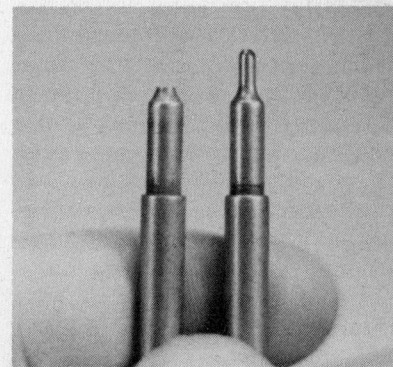

Broken firing pin points are not a chronic ailment with the Model 57M, but when it happens, and no replacement is available, the pin can be repointed by a gunsmith.

The cartridge guide (feed throat) of the Model 57M is very similar to the one used in the Marlin 49 and 99 rifles and shares some of the same problems.

Marlin Model 783 Rifle

Introduced about 6 years ago to replace their Model 980 rifle, the Marlin Model 783 is chambered for the .22 WMR cartridge, popularly known as the .22 Magnum. The Model 783 has a tubular magazine, but there is also a box magazine version, the Model 782, and the same basic design in regular .22 rimfire in the Models 780 and 781 rifles.

Earlier Marlin tube-fed bolt-actions had a cartridge carrier system of rather odd design which was susceptible to malfunction after a slight amount of wear occurred on critical operating surfaces. The Model 783 has a completely different system, with a large, heavy carrier that is a simple pivoting part, not dependent on meticulous fitting for proper operation. I doubt that this rifle will ever have any feeding problems which can be traced to the carrier.

The extractor is a spring-clip type, similar to those used in several other Marlin guns, and these are susceptible to occasional breakage. When it happens, though, it's not a serious prob-

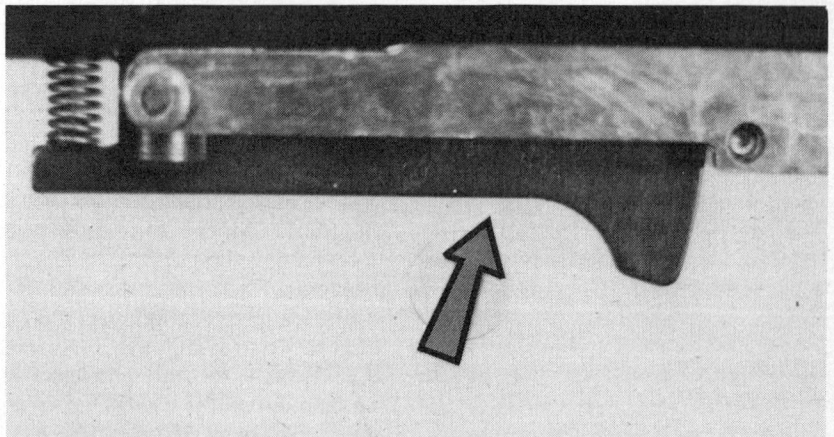

Cartridge carrier (arrow) is well-made, heavy, and practically immune to wear and breakage.

lem. All parts are readily available, the extractor quite inexpensive, and installation is not difficult. The two parts of the firing pin system are of simple cylindrical design, and the smaller tip of forward section may break on occasion, as can happen with any gun. Again, original replacements are inexpensive, but in this case the installation should be done by a

gunsmith. In the event that the firing pin is not immediately available in your locality, this part is easily made by any professional.

A trigger-block type, the safety system has a thumb-lever on the right side of the receiver moving a V-notched arm against a fixed pin on the right side of the trigger. The engagement is not susceptible to wear or

The extractor (top and bottom) is a spring-clip type, and breaks somewhat more often than those of machined steel design. The part is very inexpensive, and easily installed.

breakage, but the combination mounting and pivot screw of the safety should be checked occasionally for tightness. If it works loose, the safety arm could fail to engage properly with the block pin on the trigger.

Like those on several other Marlin .22 rifles, the magazine follower is made of plastic and does not often break in normal operation. However, when the magazine tube is removed from the gun, careless handling can break or deform the follower. The rear sight is of similar design to the one used on the Marlin 336 rifle, with a folding leaf retained by lateral spring tension of the rear arms of the sight base. The sight elevator in its slot at the center tends to keep these arms from being compressed, but care should be taken in heavy brush, as a sharp blow can cause the leaf and elevator to depart, leaving the base on the barrel.

The sear system is the prop-up type and causes no problems in normal use. With any sear system of this design, though, an amateur attempt to adjust the trigger pull would be unwise. The parts are well-hardened and can't be altered with an ordinary file. This could lead a tinkerer to try grinding, and the result would likely be the requirement of a new trigger and sear—parts which are sold only to qualified gunsmiths.

In the event that the magazine tube becomes badly dented or otherwise damaged in an accident, it should be noted that a slight change was made in the design of this system in June, 1975. So, if your gun was purchased new well after that date, it will require a different set of replacement parts. This applies only to the magazine assembly, as the other parts are unchanged.

The bolt is easily removed from the receiver by holding back the trigger, and the action is retained in the stock by a single coin-slotted screw. For routine cleaning, this is sufficient, further disassembly is not recommended for the nonprofessional. For example, amateur attempts at removal of the trigger pin will often break the trigger mounting stud away from the receiver, and replacement of this part requires return to the factory or the services of a very skillful welder.

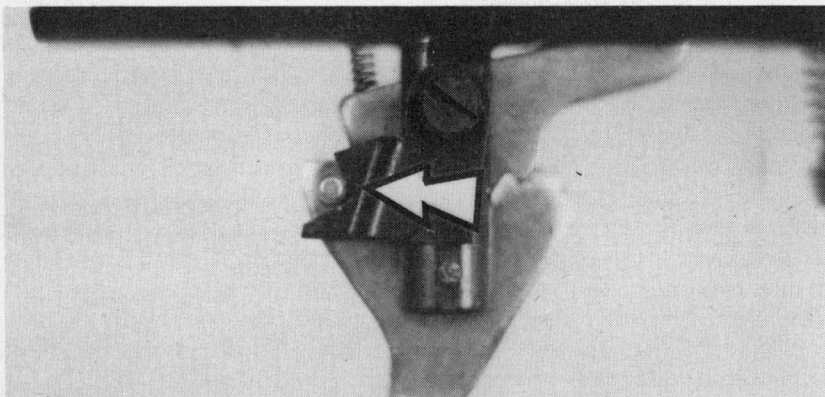

Here the arrow points to the engagement of the safety with the stop pin on the trigger. The on-safe position is shown.

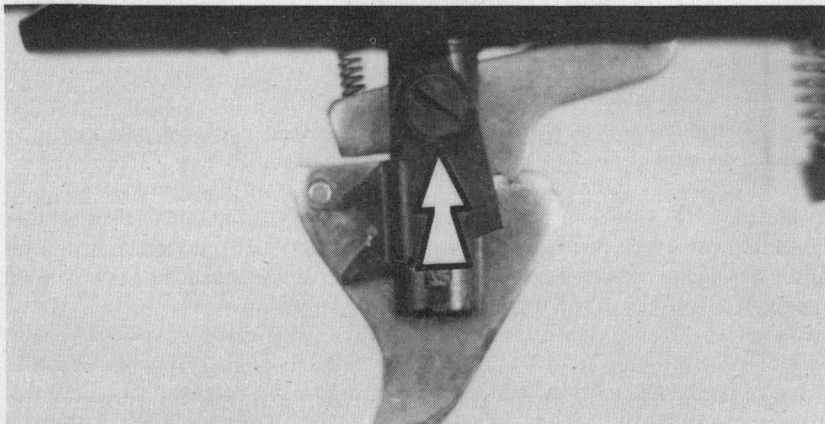

It's a good idea to occasionally check the safety pivot and mounting screw (arrow) for tightness.

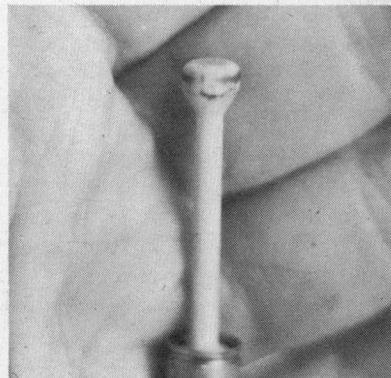

While it's not subject to breakage during normal operation, the plastic magazine follower can be damaged when it's out of the gun.

Marlin's Model 1894 rifle in .44 Magnum chambering is proving to be a highly popular lever-action rifle.

Marlin Model 1894 Rifle

The original Model 1894 rifle was made from that year to 1934, and certain elements of the design were quite different, so let's make it clear that the gun covered here is the *new* Model 1894, introduced in 1971, and based (in part) on the Model 336 action. Chambered for the .44 Magnum cartridge, this carbine is an excellent gun for hunting game up to deer-size, especially in the close-range situations that occur in heavy woods.

Although the bolt locking system and firing pin system are similar to the later Model 336 pattern, the breech block has a full-length external cover like the older gun—a feature which has the advantage of protecting the breech from any intrusion of dirt or small twigs. The loading gate is the type used on most lever-action rifles of this type, having a tempered internal tail to act as its spring. It is retained by a single screw just to the rear of the gate, and this screw should be checked occasionally to be sure that it hasn't loosened. The spring-tail of the gate is flexed rather severely in load-

The loading gate (right arrow) has a tempered tail which serves as its spring and is retained by a single small screw (left arrow). This should be occasionally checked for tightness.

ing, but this is a heavy part, and breakage is rare. This gun is still in production, and parts are readily available.

As in most lever-action guns, there is an automatic trigger-block which prevents movement of the trigger unless the lever is fully closed. This is a small stud protruding from the lower tang, just to the rear of the trigger, and it is depressed by an upper surface on the lever. Under ordinary circumstances, this system works perfectly.

Occasionally a lever will be sprung by accident, and a very slight deformation can cause a failure to depress the trigger-block. When this happens, the trigger cannot be moved. A bent lever can be straightened, but this is a job for a gunsmith.

The firing pin is a two-part system, with a short rear section which is spring-tipped downward as the action is cycled, taking it out of engagement with the forward section of the firing pin. The rising locking block tips the

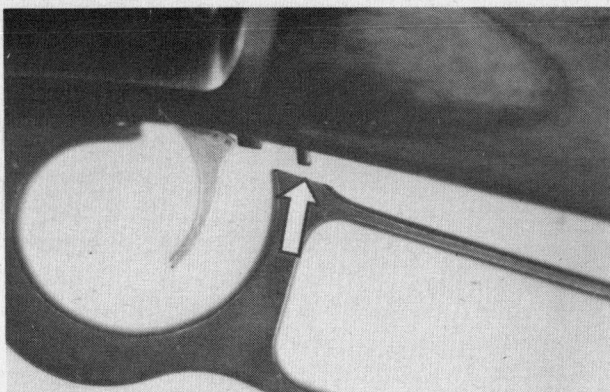

Arrow indicates the lever surface which depresses the trigger safety block (seen just above it) as the lever is closed.

Arrow indicates the locking recess in the breech block. Note the rear firing pin, tipped downward by its spring when the bolt is unlocked.

rear section back into place as the lever is closed. This insures that the gun cannot be fired unless the breech block is fully closed, serving much the same purpose as the trigger-block. The tipping of the rear firing pin section is powered by a small blade-type spring, and this is flexed each time the lever is operated. Breakage of this spring is not common, but they do occasionally let go. When they do, a replacement can be made without removal of the bolt, but when done this way there is a risk of warping the receiver, since driving out the retaining pin produces stress in a direction that is not normal. Removal of the breech block is not difficult, and in this case it should definitely be done.

Stud-mounted inside the left wall of the receiver, the ejector is also powered by a leaf-type spring. This one is longer, and flexing is less severe, making breakage very unusual. Again, replacement is not too diffi-

cult, but proper alignment with the ejector track in the breech block during replacement can be tricky. So unless you have some aptitude in this sort of thing, it might be best to have a gunsmith install this part.

The extractor is a formed flat steel clip-on type and is perhaps the single most-replaced part on the gun. This is not to say that it is chronically weak— it definitely isn't. These break with no more frequency than the same type of extractor in other guns, and in modern manufacture the guns using this type would make a long list. The balance of heat treatment in formed-steel parts of this type is more difficult to maintain, and occasionally one will slip through that is a little off, either too hard or too soft. When you replace one of these, the new one you put in may last forever. Extractor replacement should be handled by a professional, as it is easy to break the new part during amateur installation.

Also, slight fitting may be required for proper operation.

On late Marlin guns of this series, the rear sight is retained on its spring-leaf base by side projections on the leaf which fit into holes in the lower wings of the sight. Quite often, in brush country use, a swat from a small tree branch can spring one of the base lugs out of its hole in the sight, and the sight will depart, never to be seen again, along with its elevator. If your original sight is this type, it might be well to tuck a spare sight piece and elevator into your hunting pack, and take care to keep brush away from the top of the barrel. This, incidentally, is the only real criticism I can make on this good Marlin design, and it is easily corrected. If you ever lose the sight piece, just replace the whole thing with a Lyman # 16, and you won't be bothered by this again.

The rear sight is retained on its spring leaf by lateral projections that fit into holes in the base of the sight. A sharp blow can flex the spring, releasing the sight.

Marlin Model 336 Rifle

When Marlin's first lever-action rifle was patented in 1889, it had two important differences from the already-popular Winchester guns of similar pattern, and both were advantages. Ejection of cartridge cases to the right side rather than out the top may not have been as important in the early days, but now, with the universal popularity of scope sights, it has some real significance. The other difference is mechanical, and whether it's of great value is a matter of opinion. In

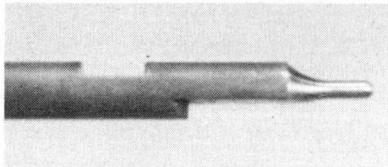

Here you can see that the forward end of the front firing pin is cut away to clear the upper extension of the lever. This gives a fragile appearance, but breakage is not common.

the Winchester rifle, the cartridge carrier is raised in the last small portion of forward movement of the lever, and when the lever is pulled back it is only closing the bolt. The forward movement of the Marlin lever only opens the bolt and extracts and ejects the fired case, the raising of the carrier being part of the beginning backstroke as the lever is closed. Some have observed that the closing of the lever is a stronger hand and arm movement, giving more positive carrier action and less chance of misfeeding because of operational error. I have done no research on this, but

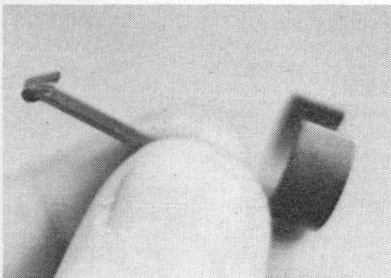

The extractor is the usual Marlin clip-on type, made of formed sheet steel. The beak occasionally breaks, but replacements are inexpensive.

from a logical view, they do seem to have a point.

Just as the Model 94 is the mainstay of Winchester, the Model 336 holds the same position for Marlin. The basic Marlin lever-action centerfire rifle was established in 1894, and the design was essentially unchanged until 1934. In that year, it was slightly changed to become the Model 36, and

Shown here is the contact of the hammer top and the cocking lug on the underside of the bolt. This hammer is equipped with an offset spur for use with a scope. Note the rear firing pin, automatically dropped out of alignment with the main firing pin.

A feature shared with the 94 Winchester (in the Model 336), is the trigger safety block (arrow) which prevents trigger movement unless the lever is fully closed.

was made in this form until 1948. At that time, an entirely new mechanism was introduced, closing the right rear portion of the receiver and changing the bolt shape from square to round, along with several other changes that were not as obvious. The model designation was also changed to 336.

The round breech bolt was fitted with the now-familiar clip-on extractor, a formed sheet steel part that might have been inspired by a pen or pencil pocket clip. Considering the difficulty of proper heat treatment of steel of this thickness, these extractors have a surprisingly long life. When they do let go, it is usually at the little folded beak—a tightly stuck cartridge case is death on these. The extractor is quite inexpensive, costing just $1.50 in a recent parts list, and installation is not difficult.

The forward portion of the firing pin is cut away on the left side to clear the upper arm of the lever, and this gives it the appearance of having a fragile tip. In actual use, this has proved to be a false impression, as the Model 336 breaks firing pins no more often than any other gun. The firing pin is in two parts, the main forward portion being struck by a very short rear firing pin, the latter being the part actually struck by the hammer. When the action is opened (and the locking block is lowered from its recess in the underside of the bolt), the rear firing pin is forced downward by a small flat spring, out of alignment with the head of the main firing pin. If the hammer should fall with the bolt partially opened, the main firing pin would not be hit. The little flat spring above the rear firing pin is flexed each time the action is cycled, and I have seen a few cases of breakage. In most cases, the firing pin will still drop down, impelled by gravity, but it would be a good idea to check it occasionally by pressing upward on the point while the bolt is open. The little spring costs 30¢, and installation is easy.

In older guns that have seen a lot of use, there may be wear at the top of the hammer, or the cocking lug on the underside of the bolt. If this becomes severe, the hammer will fail to stay cocked when the action is cycled. This can be corrected without replacement of parts by adding a small amount of weld to the top of the hammer and recutting to shape, but unless the entire hammer is rehardened afterward it will be softened by the welding heat, and will soon wear again. A better way is to drill the top of the hammer at its bolt contact point and install a driven hard steel pin, faced off to the proper cocking level.

The Model 336 has an automatic trigger safety block that functions when the lever is operated, preventing movement of the trigger until the lever is brought back to the lower tang, where it depresses a small stud behind the trigger. The combination spring which powers the safety block and the trigger-sear unit is a round-wire torsion type, and causes no difficulty. If one happens to be overly-strong or weak, it is easily adjusted.

The ejector is located in a recess in the left side of the bolt tunnel, and its mounting stud is visible on the outside of the receiver on the left side near the upper rear corner. The ejector is held in place by its track in the bolt, and is easily removed or may fall free when the bolt is removed. The ejector is powered by a flat curved spring, and these have sufficient leverage that keeps them from breaking often. When one does let go, they are available separately, but they are clinch-mounted on the ejector, and installation should be done by a gunsmith. The entire ejector with spring already mounted is also available at low cost, and this unit can be installed by any knowledgeable amateur.

The tail of the loading gate is tempered to be its spring, and the gate is mounted in the receiver by a single screw, located just to the rear of the gate on the right side. This screw should be checked occasionally for tightness. This advice applies, of course, to all of the externally visible screws.

The arrow points to the mounting stud of the ejector, held in place inside the receiver by its track in the bolt. The ejector is powered by a blade spring, but breakage is not common.

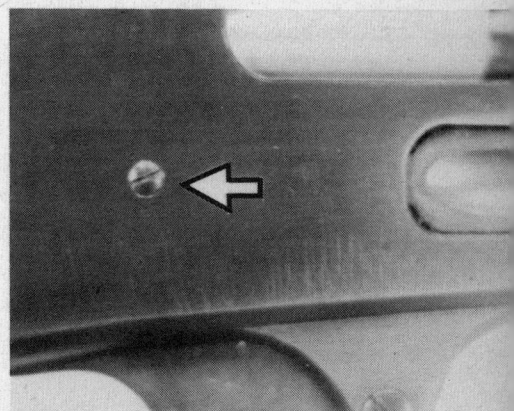

Here, the arrow indicates the loading gate screw, which should be checked occasionally for tightness. It threads directly into the spring-tempered tail of the loading gate.

Marlin Model 1889 Shotgun

Several years before Winchester scored with their Browning-designed Model 1893 and the very successful later version, the Model 1897, the Marlin Company had put on the market an excellent slide-action external hammer shotgun. Although it may border on blasphemy to say so, this gun, the Model 1889, was in some ways superior to the Winchester. Its breech block tracks and receiver support were better, and it was less likely to wear and become loose. The ejector was stronger, and the firing mechanism simpler and less susceptible to damage. Not having the massive carrier and poor mechanical advantage of the Model 97, the Marlin action was much smoother and easier to operate. The basic gun evolved into a series of numbered models, ending with the Model 42A, which went out of production in 1934.

As with most of the older guns, there were a number of blade-type springs in the design, and some of these will occasionally succumb to years of flexing. The hammer spring

is a heavy blade, and when it lets go it presents less of a problem than most of this type, as it lacks the hook-and-stirrup arrangement common to most of the mainsprings of its era. It is a simple blade, acting on a roller

The hammer is a massive piece of nicely machined solid steel. The sear steps, seen at lower right, are susceptible to wear and breakage, especially the safety step. Repair is not difficult.

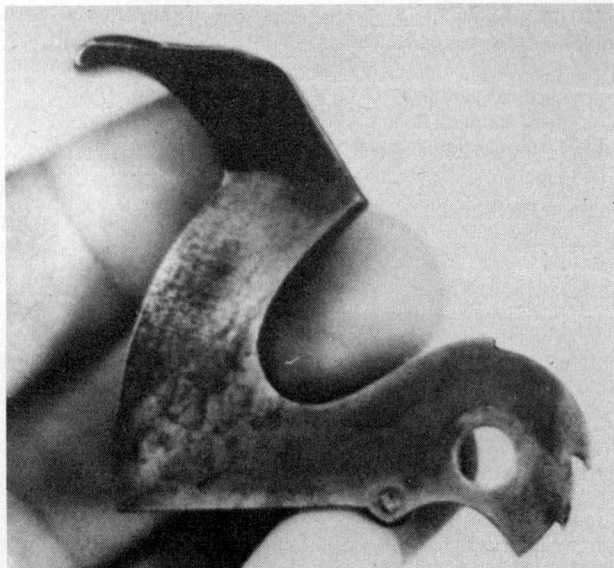

mounted in the hammer, and making a replacement is not difficult. A few of the used-parts dealers may occasionally have parts for these guns, but otherwise there are none available. The hammer is a massive piece of

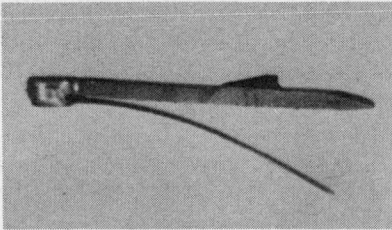

This is the ejector, which lies in a recess in the left inside wall of the receiver. It is powered by an attached blade-type spring, and these occasionally break. Fortunately, replacement is no great problem.

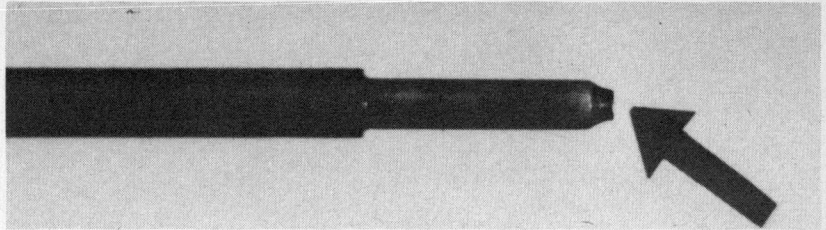

When a firing pin tip breaks, it's a serious problem, since the rear portion of the pin is rather intricately shaped, and *no* parts are available.

nicely-machined solid steel and gives no trouble other than wear or breakage of the sear steps on its front face, after years of hard use. The safety step breaks most often, as it is a deeper cut, with an overhanging flange. The steps can often be recut, or, if necessary, built up with weld, recut, and rehardened.

The ejector resembles the ones used in most Marlin guns, including some that are still in production. It is cammed into its recess in the left wall of the receiver by the closing bolt, and its small blade spring receives repeated compression. This is a simple, curved flat spring, and making a replacement is no problem for any gunsmith, or even the knowledgeable amateur. Breakage of the ejector itself is quite rare.

The tip of the firing pin breaks with some frequency, mostly because of age and crystallization. Considering the parts situation, this can be a serious problem for the non-gunsmith. Fortunately, these can be repaired. A hole is drilled in the end of the pin, and a new tip fitted to it, held in place either by silver solder or by cross-pinning. Making an entire new firing pin is impractical, as the rear portion of the pin is keyed into the bolt locking system, and its shape is rather intricate.

Inside the receiver, just forward of the trigger, there is a strangely-shaped little assembly of heavy steel consisting of two parts powered by blade springs. This is an inertia block, and its function is to prevent unlocking of the action slide until tipped by the recoil of a fired shell. In the early days of paper shells and uncertain primers, it was not unusual to have an occasional ''slow fire,'' a shell that did not have instant ignition, but might go off a second or two later, perhaps while the action was being opened. This little device insured that in case of a ''hang-fire,'' the shooter would have to manually unlock the action, allowing enough time for it to be safely opened. The inertia block is not essential to the operation of the action, and if one or both of its blade springs should break, the assembly can simply be removed from the gun. As an alternative, it is no problem to make replacements for these simple flat springs.

The Model 1889 has a good bolt locking system which features a heavy bar of steel within the breech block that tips downward at the rear to bear against the receiver. With all of these older guns, however, it would be wise to fire them only with light to medium loads, as the heat treatment of their receivers was not up to the modern level.

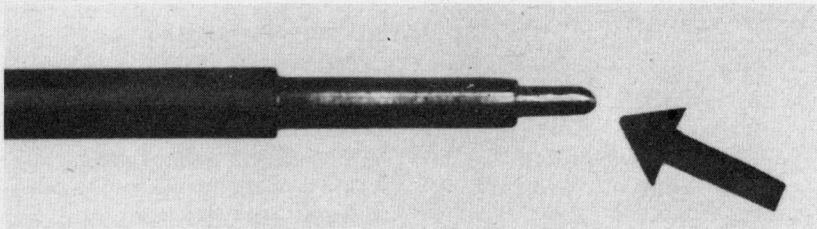

This broken firing pin was repointed by drilling a hole in the end and installing a new tip. This can be secured by either silver solder or cross-pinning.

This wierdly-shaped little assembly is the inertia block, designed to release the slide lock only when activated by the recoil of a fired shell. It contains two blade springs.

Marlin Model 55 "Goose Gun"

Among serious shotgunners, the bolt-action gets few votes as the ideal gun, and this is putting it mildly. It does, however, have its place. For very little more cost than a top-break single barrel, it offers the advantage of a three-shot repeater. And, there are those who actually prefer the handling qualities of a bolt-action. As an ex-

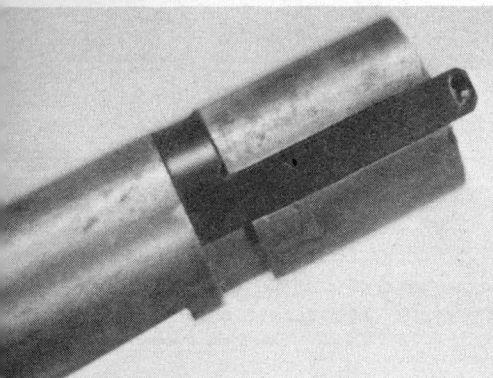

The Model 55 has the usual Marlin spring-clip type extractor. These break with some frequency, but are inexpensive and easily installed.

ample of the general type, I am including here the Marlin Model 55, also known as the "Goose Gun"—an advertising name which ascribes mythical qualities to its 36-inch barrel. Actually, the modern shotshell develops its maximum charge velocity in about 22 inches of barrel, and any length that is substantially beyond this can *reduce* the velocity by friction. Don't argue this with the old-timers, though. A stack of valid chronograph data wouldn't convince them. Still, if a shooter feels that he does better with one of these long tubes, why not?

The Model 55 has the usual Marlin spring-clip type of double extractor, and these break more often than those of solid machined stock with separate springs. The spring-clip type is quite inexpensive, though, and is easily installed on the bolt. A small screwdriver inserted under the broken extractor unit will flip it off, and the new one just pushes on and snaps into its recess in the bolt head.

On the Model 55 the combination

striker and firing pin is made of flat stock and breaks no more frequently than any other type. If the tip should break, it can't be repointed, but since the gun is still in current production, all parts are readily available. The sear system is the prop-up type, and there is a lug at the extreme lower rear of the striker which contacts the top of the sear. I have seen one case of breakage in this area, and one case of extreme wear due to insufficient hardening, but I think both of these could be considered isolated instances. It would be well, though, to occasionally check your gun for wear or signs of stress in that location.

The trigger housing has large holes in its sideplate which allow easy inspection of the engagement of the safety and trigger, and the trigger and sear. These should be checked occasionally by a gunsmith, to catch any signs of wear before they become serious. In both cases, steel can be added or the engagement recut, and parts replacement can usually be avoided.

The Model 55 has a detachable box

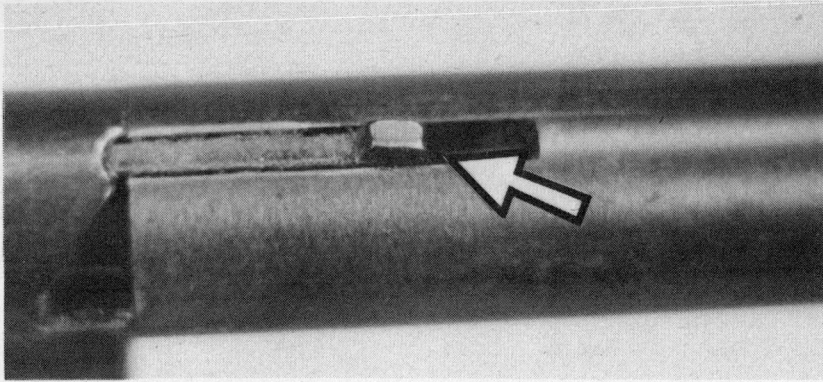

Arrow indicates the sear contact lug on the combination striker and firing pin, an area that should be checked occasionally for cracking or extreme wear.

magazine, and the magazine catch is of folded sheet steel construction, with an integral curved flat spring. If this spring breaks or weakens, a replacement can be made, but it may be more economical to just replace the entire catch, as the cost is less than $2.

This gun has a three-piece bolt, consisting of a front section, bolt handle, and rear section, and these are joined by a cross-pin which mates with a groove in the reduced-diameter rear projection of the front section. The groove is very near the rear edge of the projection, and breakage of the rear lip is not unknown. This can be repaired by welding, or the front section can just be replaced—it costs less than $7. It should be noted, though, that this part is supplied only to gunsmiths and is not available direct from the factory to individuals.

The Model 55 was introduced in 1964, and the basic gun is chambered for the 12-gauge 3-inch Magnum shell. A 10-gauge version called the "Supergoose" recently became available; and, except for changes necessary to accommodate the larger shell, it is mechanically identical.

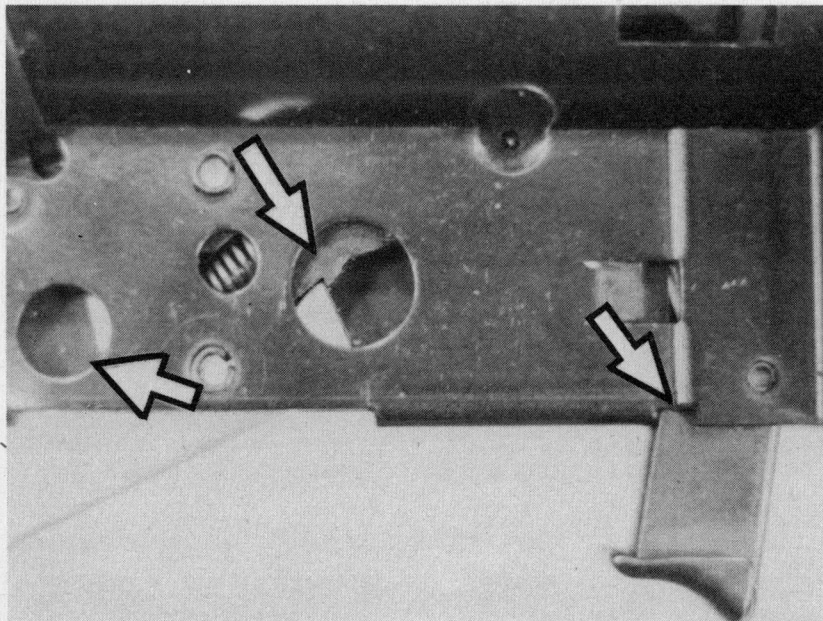

Inspection holes in the trigger housing allow checking of the engagement of the trigger and safety (left arrow), and the sear and trigger (upper arrow). The magazine catch (right arrow) has its own internal flat spring.

Marlin Model 39-A Rifle

The first Marlin lever-action .22 rifles were made in 1891 and 1892, and the gun was redesigned in 1897, this model being made until 1915. In 1915 during WWI, the Marlin company was sold and reorganized, and production of the gun was sporadic for a few years. Then, in 1922, a modified version of the original design was introduced as the Model 39, followed in 1939 by the Model 39-A. The older versions of the rifle are handsome guns with their octagonal barrels and slim stocks, but the modern gun is much better mechanically. This is mostly due to improvements in materials and heat treatment, as the internal design is basically the same as the original 1891 model. The principal changes have been in the stock and barrel shape, the magazine system, and the replacement of the flat hammer spring with a helical coil.

There are still several blade-type springs in the design, but most of these are not subjected to any severe flexing, and they seldom break. The occasional exceptions are the spring which powers the ejector, and the small cartridge guide spring above the chamber, inside the receiver.

Each time the action is cycled, the ejector spring is flexed and one of these will let go every so often. Replacement is not difficult, and all parts for the 39-A are readily available at most gunshops. The cartridge guide spring is mounted in the top of the receiver by a very small screw which enters from the outside and threads directly into the spring. This spring, also, is flexed upward each time the action is closed, and these will often break at the screw-hole. Replacement is not particularly difficult, but in most cases should be left to a gunsmith, as it is easy to cross-thread the tiny screw during installation.

The upper arm of the lever, which moves the breech block, also locks it firmly in place when the lever is fully closed. The top surface of the lever arm mates with a corresponding angled surface on a projection from the underside of the breech block, or bolt, camming it into position against the rear face of the barrel. It takes many thousands of rounds to wear these hardened surfaces, but when it happens, the breech will fail to close tightly. To correct this, the amateur will usually peen the upper end of the lever arm, raising a small hump of steel along both edges to take up the

Made from flat steel, the Model 39's firing pin is not as simple as it appears—the lower projections mate with other parts in the 39's breech block.

slack. The trouble with this is that these narrow peened-up edges will quickly wear off, leaving the situation where it was before, if not worse. The proper way is to add steel weld to the top of the lever arm, recut it to fit, and reharden the end.

Simply an upper projection of the trigger, the sear makes direct contact with the safety and full-cock steps on the hammer. This slim top part of the trigger occasionally snaps off, either from age, brittleness or from someone letting the hammer slip too many times when cocking. When this breakage occurs, the blunt end of the broken sear will no longer function with the safety step; and, depending on the nature of the break, it may fail to keep the hammer at full-cock. It is possible to build up and recut a broken sear, but it makes much more sense to simply replace the trigger. With the new part, some fitting may be necessary, and it's best for this to be done by a gunsmith.

The cartridge stop, or cartridge cut-off, as Marlin calls it, is screw-mounted on the left inside wall of the receiver, just below the ejector housing. Occasionally, when someone is checking for loose screws, they will give the screw, which mounts this part, a slight turn and move the part just enough to wedge it against the upper edge of its recess in the receiver. As a result, there is nothing to stop the next round in the magazine while the action is cycled, and there will be a spectacular jam. When tightening this particular screw, the cartridge stop should be carefully centered in its recess from within and held in this position with a thin-bladed tool (such as a knife) while the screw is set.

On earlier guns, the extractor was a solid, nicely-machined part, hand-fitted to the bolt. On current-production guns, it is a weirdly-shaped piece of formed flat spring steel. I have no mechanical complaint on these, as I haven't yet had to replace a single one, but it looks like a snake that's been run over. Fortunately, it can't be seen from outside the gun.

Made from flat steel stock, the firing pin looks deceptively simple. Actually, its several projections and

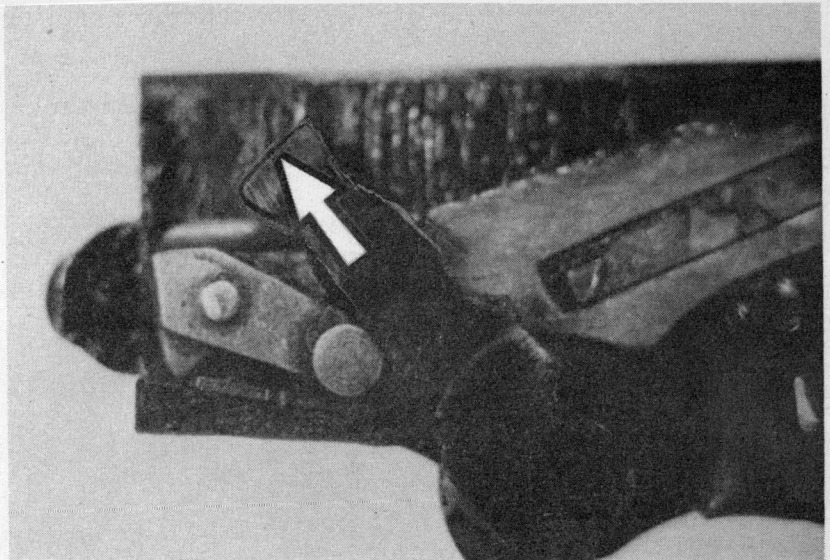

Arrow points to the upper surface of the lever arm which mates with a lower projection on the breech block. When properly joined (in normal operation) they lock the breech block in place.

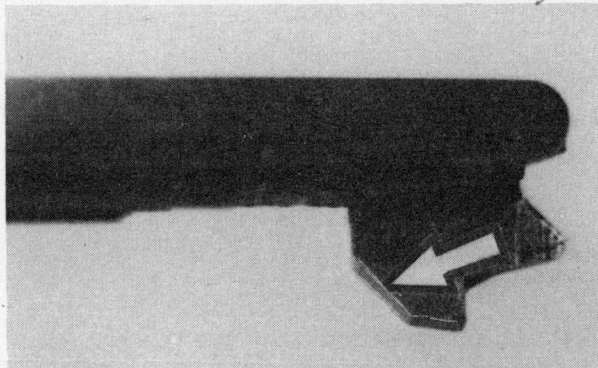

Extreme wear on the locking surface of the lower projection of the breech block (arrow) can prevent a firm lock-up of the 39's action.

This view provides us with a look at the 39's sear engagement (arrow). The "sear" itself is an upper projection of the trigger which fits into one of two recesses in the hammer. The upper "notch" (or recess) is the half-cock position—it serves as the safety.

planes are very precisely related to the lever and breech block, and the occasional broken firing pin should not be repaired, as the weld will likely affect the dimensions and make fitting difficult. Replacements are available everywhere and are not expensive. It might be well to note that the firing pins for the modern 39-A rifles are not interchangeable with those of the older guns, so if you have one of these, the pin may have to be repaired, or a new one made.

On later Model 39s, the extractor is formed of flat spring steel. They seldom break.

Arrow on the upper left points to the ejector while the arrow on the upper right points toward the cartridge guide spring, located directly above, and *slightly* to the rear of the chamber. Arrow at the lower right indicates the cartridge cutoff.

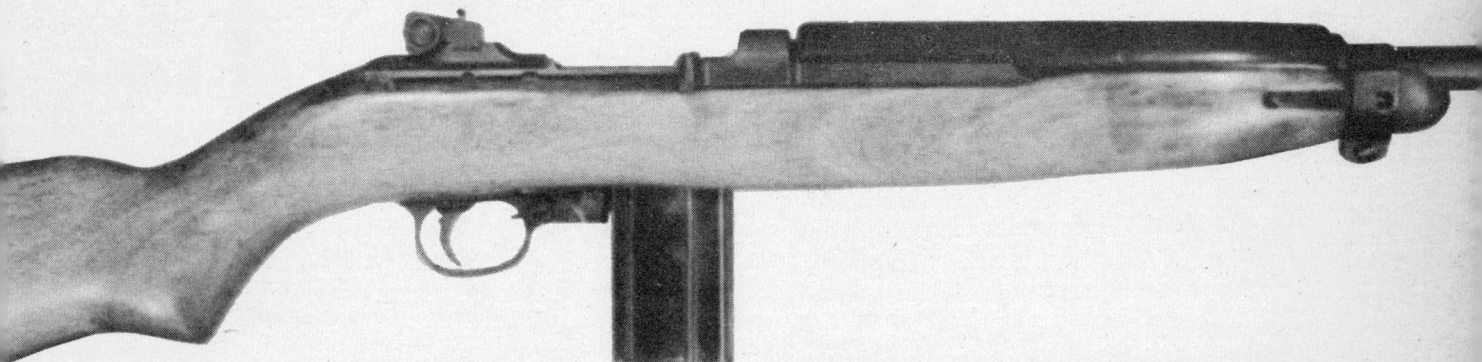

U.S. .30 M-1 Carbine

As almost everyone knows, the M-1 Carbine was designed by a team at Winchester and was adopted as a standard U.S. military arm in 1941. Light and handy, the M-1 Carbine has had a great deal of postwar popularity as a police weapon and also as a gun for home defense. It is not suitable for hunting because its cartridge lacks the impact energy for medium to large game and has too much power for small game.

The locking system utilizes a rotating bolt, unlocked by an angled track in the action slide. The slide is impelled by a gas-activated, short-stroke piston below the barrel. The proper mating of the camming surfaces of the right bolt lug and its recess in the action slide is of critical importance. These parts are normally well-hardened, and it will take many years of hard use before any problems develop due to wear in this area. If you close the bolt slowly by hand and feel a good deal of friction even though the parts are clean and lightly oiled, it may be that wear has caused a sharp edge to develop on the lug, and this is dragging inside the slide.

A simple answer to this, and to almost all other M-1 Carbine ills, is replacement of worn parts. There are almost countless sources of original military parts for this carbine, often brand new in the original military package, and they are usually inexpensive.

As with any gas-operated gun, oil and grease should be kept entirely away from the area of the gas piston. The hot powder gases will quickly bake any liquid lubricant into a glue-like substance that will stop the action

Proper mating of the surfaces of the right bolt lug and the internal areas of the action is critical on the M-1 Carbine.

With extreme wear, the dismounting cut (arrow) in the track for the action slide lug will enable the lug itself to literally jump out of the track during the firing cycle.

One of the Carbine's potential problems is the extractor (arrow) as it will occasionally break at its beak edge. Replacing an extractor can be difficult unless you possess, or have access to, a special ordnance bolt stripping tool.

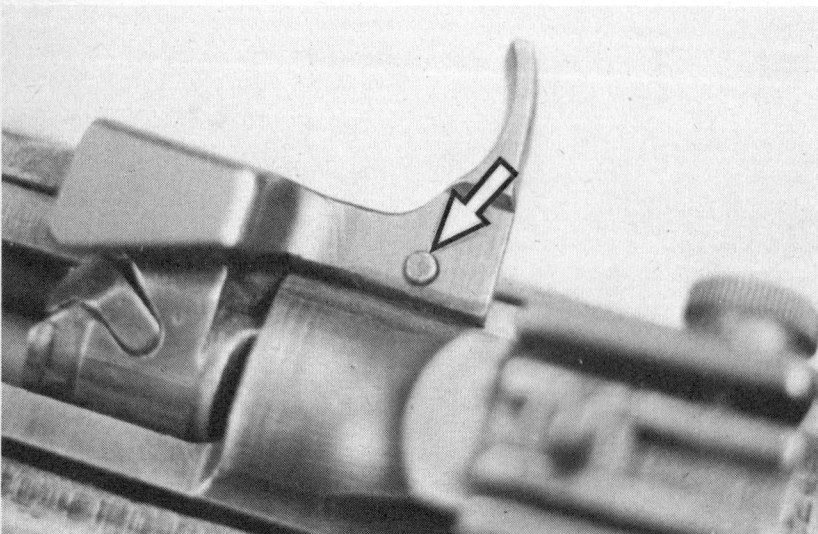

When the slide is removed from the action, take care that the operating slide stop pin (arrow) doesn't fall out and become lost—it's retained in the slide handle by only a small coil spring.

of the piston as if it were welded in place. On all guns of this type, the gas system should be kept clean and dry. In the Carbine, a tiny bit of oil is all right on the action slide tracks below the barrel, and on the recoil spring and guide. Otherwise, no oil forward of the receiver.

The right rail of the receiver, which contains the track for the rear lug of the action slide, is also curved inside to accommodate the bolt. During the recoil cycle, the underside of the right bolt lug slides on top of this rail. So, it receives wear in three areas, and in cross-section it is rather thin at some points. It is not unknown for the rail to crack. When this happens, an obvious cure would be to replace the receiver. I have, however, repaired this problem through careful welding and re-cutting. At the rear of the slide lug track is a dismounting cut, used during takedown to free the lug. When there is extreme wear in the forward rails of the action slide, the rear lug can occasionally jump out of the take-down cut during recoil—an occurrence which stops everything. Unless there is excessive wear in the tracks on the barrel and receiver, replacement of the action slide will usually cure this.

Since the breech face is recessed to completely encircle the head of the cartridge case, the extractor must climb over the case rim each time the bolt closes, and chipping of the extractor beak is an occasional problem. Extractors are plentiful and inexpensive, but installation is difficult without a special ordnance tool. This, too, is available, but it is *not* inexpensive. The major suppliers of surplus parts will usually have this tool, and if you plan to use an M-1 Carbine extensively, it would be advisable to get one, as the extractor pivot is also the retainer for the ejector and firing pin.

On top of the cocking handle, near the receiver, there is a small button which can be depressed when the slide is drawn back to hold it in the open position. This button, officially called the "operating slide stop pin," is controlled by a transverse coil spring which bears on a groove in the pin. When the action slide is removed from the gun, this little pin is retained

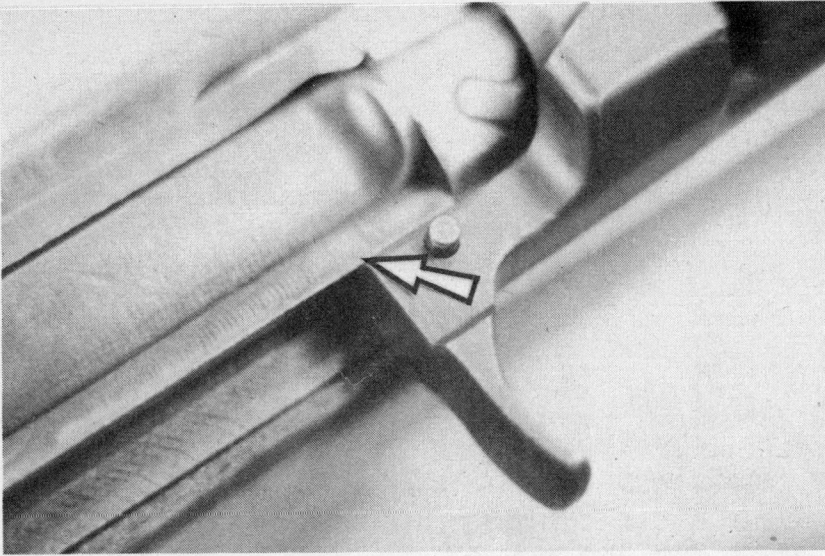

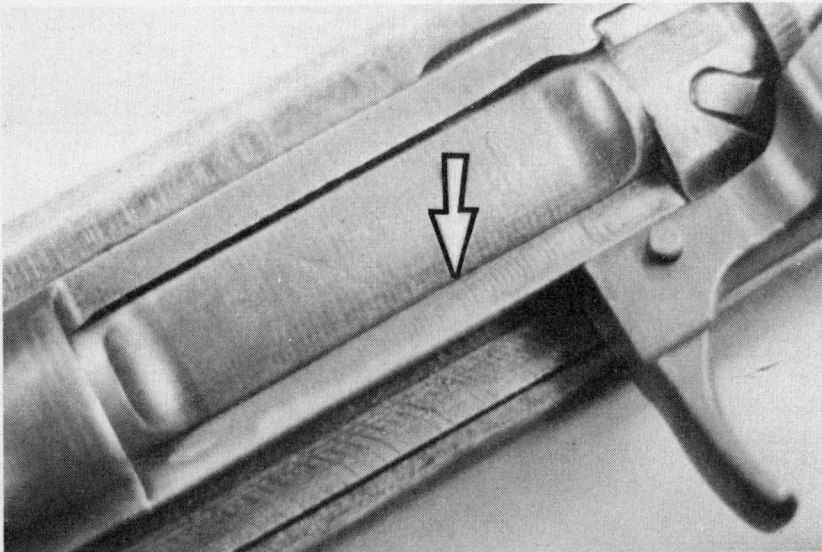

The right receiver rail, which contains the track for the action slide lug (top), is also internally curved to accommodate the bolt (bottom)—as a result, this section of the receiver is understandably quite thin and cracking in this area has been observed.

only by the pressure of this spring and can drop out the bottom of the slide and be lost. The gun will function without it, but there will be no way to lock open the action, other than using a magazine which has a bolt stop surface cut into the rear of the follower.

The trigger group of this gun is of excellent design, and breakage or other malfunction of the parts in the firing mechanism is quite rare. In the unlikely event that something does let go, all of these parts, too, are readily available.

In the years since WWII, there have been two major commercial makers of the Carbine, initially using quite a few surplus parts. These guns, made by Universal and Plainfield, are still in production, and they have slight mechanical differences from the original military M-1 Carbines.

Model 1891 Argentine Mauser Rifle

The immediate ancestors of the Argentine Mauser of 1891 were the Turkish Model of 1890 and the Belgian Model of 1889. These rifles were the first to introduce two important points of Mauser design—the box magazine, and the one-piece bolt with two opposed forward lugs. The Argentine Mauser was initially made on contract by Ludwig Loewe and Company of Berlin, and was used by the government of Argentina from 1891 to 1909. The gun was chambered for the Mauser 7.65 × 53mm cartridge, a round that was loaded commercially in the U.S. until around 1936. Norma still offers a sporting load, and cases can also be made by reforming empty .30-06 brass. The bolt of the Model 1891 rifle lacks the extra locking lug of the Model 98, but is quite safe as long as loads are kept to the level of the original cartridge.

The Model 1891 has a straight bolt handle that must be altered if a scope is to be mounted, and the safety is the now-familiar flip-over type, having only two positions. (Over to the left is the off-safe movement.) The action cocks as the bolt is closed, a feature not well-liked by most American shooters, but the operation is silky-smooth. This is due in part to the good design of the system, and partly to the German craftsmanship of that day. The bolt face features a full cartridge head recess, and the extractor, which is tempered to be its own spring, is T-slot mounted just above the right lug. Breakage of extractors does not seem to be a problem, but I have seen a few that had been deformed by amateur disassembly. Unless it is absolutely necessary for repair, the extractor should not be removed.

The firing pin has no particulr ten-

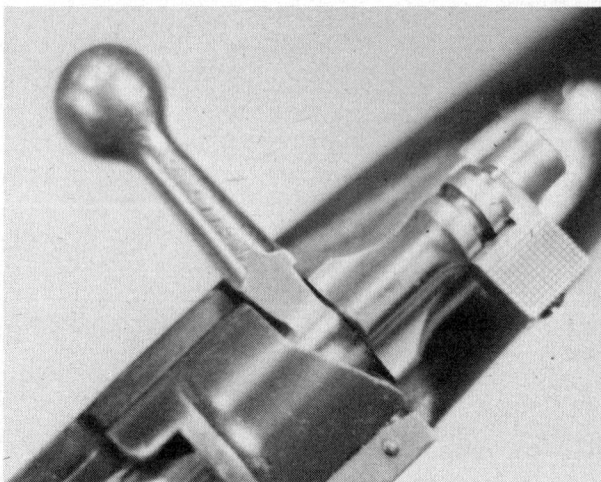

Shown in the off-safe position, the Argentine Mauser of 1891 had a straight bolt handle, and the familiar flip-over type safety.

Here's a close-up view of the bolt face, showing the slot in the left lug for the ejector. Note the full cartridge head recess.

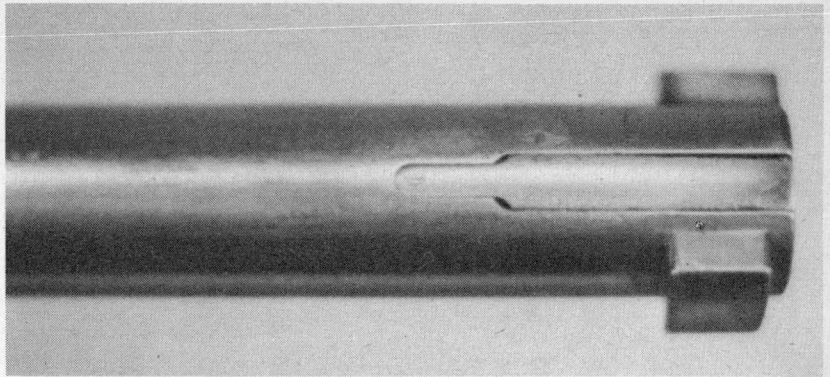

The extractor, tempered to be its own spring, is T-slot mounted. The two bolt lugs at the front were the only ones provided.

dency toward breakage, but if the tip should snap off, it can easily be re-pointed. The Model 1891 is full of blade-type springs, but these are heavy, and tempered by experts. Breakage is rare. If one does let go, it is often possible to make a round-wire replacement of slightly different design that will function perfectly. At the present time, replacement parts are usually available from several of the used-parts and surplus dealers, but certain items are in short supply.

The Model 1891 is designed to be loaded from the top with five-round charger clips, but single-loading the five cartridges is no problem. The magazine is not intended for removal in normal operation, but can easily be taken off for cleaning by turning the retainer at its lower front out of en-gagement with its slot in the front of the magazine housing. This single-line magazine is the bane of those who like to convert military rifles to sport-ers, as there is no practical way to eliminate its projection below the un-derline of the stock, and its position makes hand-carrying in the field some-what awkward. In military use, with the rifle slung on the shoulder, this was not an important consideration.

On the Model 1891, the serial num-ber appears on top of the bolt handle, and this should be checked against the number on the receiver. If they are not the same, be suspicious of the head-space. Even if the numbers match, it's a good idea to have any surplus mili-tary rifle checked by a gunsmith be-fore firing it. It should also be noted that the finely-made Model 1891 rifle is of interest to collectors of military rifles, and one in excellent original condition should not be altered in any way. These guns were sold here in quantity before 1968, and they are not rare, but those in really nice condition are worth a slight premium to the col-lector.

While the fixed magazine is not designed for removal in normal use, it can be taken off for cleaning by turning the retainer (arrow) out of its engagement slot in the front of the magazine housing.

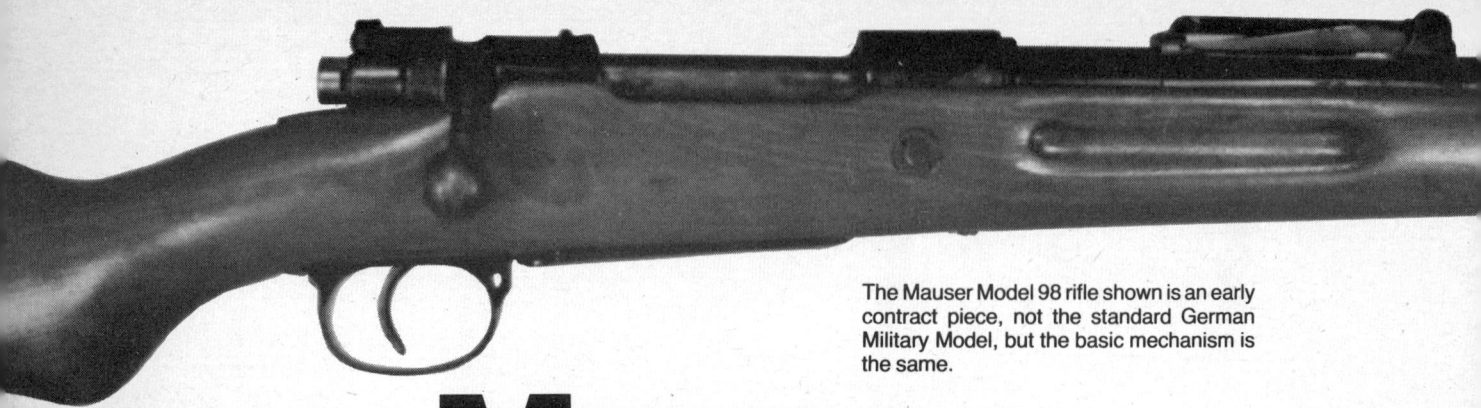

The Mauser Model 98 rifle shown is an early contract piece, not the standard German Military Model, but the basic mechanism is the same.

Mauser Model 98 Rifle

For anyone charting the development of the bolt-action rifle, the Mauser of 1898 would have to be the most prominent milestone. Even today, 80 years later, bolt-action rifles are still being made on the same basic pattern. The other Mauser turn-bolt designs which preceded the Model 98 were excellent guns, but the later rifle had several important improvements, the two most notable being the addition of a third locking lug and a gas shield on the bolt end piece.

The famous third lug is located at the rear of the bolt, locking into a recess in the bottom of the receiver when the bolt is turned down. The presence of this lug adds a margin of safety when using cartridges loaded much heavier than those of the other early bolt-action rifles. This third lug is the main reason that Mauser 98 actions are so sought after for conversion to modern magnum-level sporters. In this regard, it should be noted that any surplus or war-trophy action should be headspace-checked by a gunsmith, especially if the number on

the bolt does not match the one on the receiver. Even when the number is matching, it's a good idea to have any wartime action checked, as quality control was not as strict during the press of wartime production.

Tempered to be its own spring, the

familiar long Mauser extractor is retained on the bolt by a T-slot on its underside which mates with flanges on a split ring which encircles the bolt. Extractor breakage is rare in normal operation, but they are often damaged during amateur removal and re-

Arrow indicates the famous "third lug" or "safety lug" on the Model 98 bolt, a feature which allows the use of high pressure loads.

The serial number is often stamped on the bolt handle and should be checked against the number on the receiver. If it isn't the same, have the gun checked by a gunsmith before firing it.

While the slim firing pin point looks deceptively fragile, breakage is not common.

placement. The rear spring-tail will occasionally lose temper and weaken, especially on late wartime guns having less precise heat treatment, but the extractor can usually be reshaped and retempered by a gunsmith. Also, most parts for the Model 98 are usually available from the used-parts dealers.

The flip-over type Mauser safety acts directly on the striker head, and on the true Model 98 it has three positions. Off-safe position is over to the left. In vertical position, the safety locks the striker, but the bolt can still be opened. Over to the right, it locks both the striker and the bolt. The locking surfaces on the safety are subject to wear, but in most cases this part is well-hardened, and it takes many years of use before wear is apparent. Most of those that I have replaced were damaged by amateur gunsmithing. Each safety was factory or arsenal fitted to its individual cocking piece, and any replacement cocking piece (striker head) must be hand-fitted to the safety. Any alterations should be made to the striker head, *not* the safety.

When the bolt is disassembled, the slim firing pin point may appear fragile, but it isn't. The firing pin is an integral part of the striker, and there are flanges on each side at its base which prevent full travel of the striker unless the bolt is fully locked. On the rare occasion that a firing pin tip breaks, it can be repointed by a gunsmith. Replacement striker/firing pin units are usually available from the used-parts dealers.

The bolt stop is powered by a rather complex blade-type spring which has an integral smaller spring that tensions the ejector. The larger bolt stop portion rarely breaks or loses tension, but the smaller inner part is susceptible to both. These are often broken by attempts to remove the ejector without first driving out the slot-mounted spring. When a replacement is not available, it is possible to make and install a spring to power the

Here's the familiar long Mauser extractor, which is tempered to be its own spring, and is retained on the bolt by a T-slot which mates with flanges on a split ring which surrounds the bolt (arrow).

ejector alone, keeping the original large spring to power the bolt stop.

The ejector is a simple flat-steel part, and if broken or lost, a replacement can easily be made. Care must be taken, though, to make the new ejector to exactly the same dimensions for proper operation and to harden it to the right degree, as it takes quite an impact from each ejected shell case.

In addition to the standard German Army model, the Mauser 98 has been made on a contract basis for several other nations. Some of these contracts were for a relatively small number of rifles, and with certain markings these guns are desirable collector pieces. So, when considering a sporterizing job, it would be wise to check the collector value of the gun before you alter it.

The safety catch, shown in the full on-safe position, is susceptible to wear and damage in the area indicated by the arrow. In this case, it has been ruined by an amateur attempt at fitting a replacement striker head.

The bolt stop (arrow) is powered by a rather complex blade-type spring having a smaller inner leaf which tensions the ejector. The ejector portion of the spring occasionally breaks.

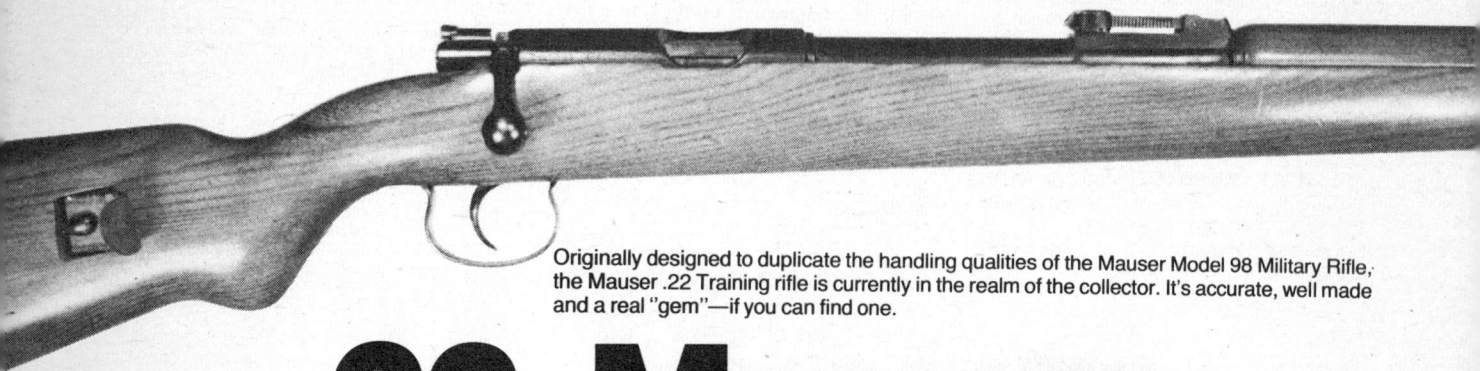

Originally designed to duplicate the handling qualities of the Mauser Model 98 Military Rifle, the Mauser .22 Training rifle is currently in the realm of the collector. It's accurate, well made and a real "gem"—if you can find one.

.22 Mauser Trainer

Most of these beautifully-made little guns were of pre-WWII manufacture, and because of their popular caliber, they were an especially prized trophy for the returning military personnel. They were made by several firms— Gustav Genschow, BSW and others —but the most wanted has the familiar square-ended oblong mark with the word "MAUSER" in the center. They were, after all, designed to be very much like the famed Model 98 Military Rifle and were often used to train both the *Jugend* and new members of the regular army in the use of that gun. The fact that most of them were also marked "DEUTSCHES SPORTMODELL" can, at this late date, be viewed with a certain wry amusement. Today, in the hands of many proud owners, these guns are finally seeing the true sporting use that their marking implies. Lamentably, some of these have been sporter-*ized,* a fact which causes much gnashing of teeth among the collectors.

Just as with any pre-war Mauser, the quality, fit and finish of these guns is outstanding. In a single-shot bolt-action gun, there is very little that can go wrong, and this mechanical fact is further enhanced by the excellence of the materials and the usual Mauser standards of heat treatment. The safety is the familiar flip-over lever at the rear of the bolt, directly blocking the head of the striker when turned up to the vertical position. When moved all the way over to the right side, it also locks the bolt. There is ample allowance for strength, and I've never heard of one of these breaking.

The firing pin at the forward end of the striker rod has a graceful sweep from collar to point, minimizing the crystallization factor, and it rarely breaks. In any rimfire gun, of course, *snapping-when-empty* should be avoided. When the rifle is being put away after use, with an empty chamber, holding the trigger back while closing the bolt and turning down the

One of the strong points of the Mauser Trainer is its firing pin that features a graceful taper from the collar to the point. The tapering minimizes crystallization and prevents breakage.

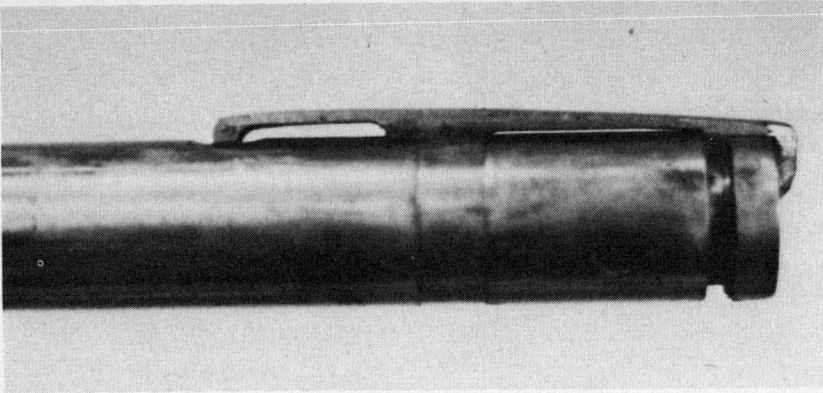

The extractor, a miniature of the one on the Model 98 military rifle, is tempered to be its own spring and is retained by a circular ring on the bolt.

handle will ease the striker down gently. In the event that you do have a gun that has been mistreated and has a broken firing pin point, any good gunsmith can repoint it. No replacement parts of any kind are available, as these guns are rarely obtained by the used-parts dealers. So, anything that is broken or missing will likely have to be made.

The only actual breakage I have seen is an occasional cracked extractor. These guns have, in miniature, a duplicate of the system used on the Model 98. The extractor is tempered to be its own spring and is retained on the outside of the bolt body by being keyed into a rotating ring. I think that many cases of breakage can be traced to improper disassembly, the extractor being flexed beyond its limits. Unless it's absolutely necessary, the extractor should not be removed. A broken extractor can often be repaired, but the weld must be of steel, as the part will have to be retempered after recutting to shape.

These guns were made with the two-stage trigger pull of the military rifle. It's as smooth as silk, and I like it, but most shooters prefer a trigger with a crisper action. It is possible to alter this trigger system to achieve this type of release, but this is something that should not be attempted by the amateur. The parts are glass-hard, cannot be filed, and I have seen a few .22 Mausers with ruined trigger systems from inept use of rotary grindstones.

Aside from their other good points, these rifles are outstandingly accurate, almost without exception. While the V-notch and inverted-V sights might be a handicap on the target range, they are fine in the squirrel woods. Just remember that those elevation markings on the rear sights are in *meters,* not feet.

This front-end view of the bolt shows the extractor beak and the recess for the cartridge case head. Note the ejector slot at the right.

Mossberg Model 151-M Rifle

An entire book could be filled with the myriad models of the Mossberg rifles, so I've selected the familiar Model 151-M as representative of their .22 automatics. Its Mannlicher-style stock is instantly recognizable, and its firing mechanism is practically identical with the other semiautos made by Mossberg in this time period. The Model 151-M was made between 1946 and 1958, and was quite popular as an economical .22 autoloader.

The firing system of these guns is well-designed and uses heavy parts which are not inclined to break. The mechanical advantage of the sear and trigger bar/disconnector is good and contributes to a trigger pull that is, for a semiauto, smooth and easy. The system is powered by a flat spring which supplies tension to both the sear and the disconnector, and most of these I've seen broken have shown signs of amateur tampering. The spring is not normally flexed severely in operation. If one of these breaks, the replacement may be a problem. Mossberg has *some* parts for these

obsolete guns, but not all of them. If this spring can't be found, it is possible to make a replacement from doubled piano wire, but this is, of course, a job for a gunsmith.

In the receiver of the 151-M, there is a heavy, round hammer that is the same diameter as the bolt, and the flat firing pin in the bolt is not difficult to make if the point should break. As most gunshops have kept Mossberg parts in stock for many years, it is quite possible that a replacement firing pin can be found. The extractors are shaped for ample strength, and these rarely break. Here again, this is a simple part to reproduce.

Entering from the buttplate, the

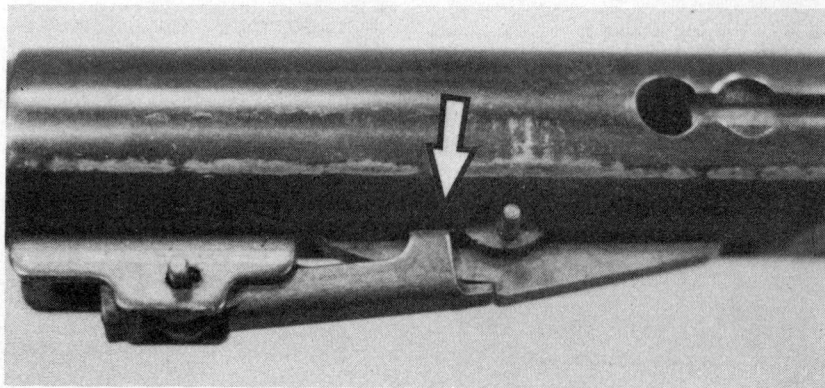

In this photo, the arrow points to the combination trigger bar and disconnector at the point where the disconnector lobes enter the receiver. Note the engagement with the sear, just below and to the right.

Arrow points to one of the two upper projections of the cartridge stop. These are depressed by the bolt as it cycles, and if they become worn, they can cause misfeeding.

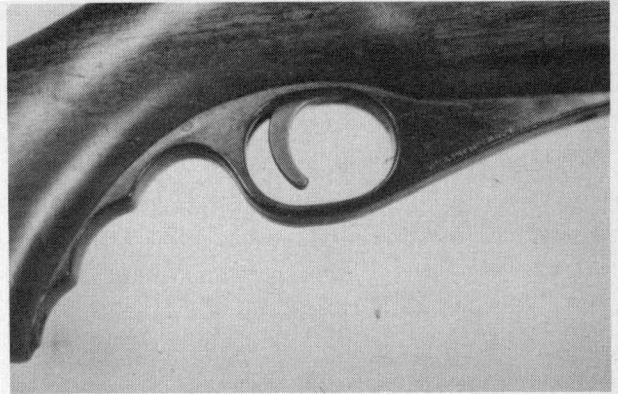

One thing that's characteristic of many Mossberg guns is the extended trigger guard—it's both handsome and comfortable. Unfortunately, the plastic becomes brittle with age.

magazine is a tube type, and at its forward end the tube is saddled from below by a U-shaped spring-powered part which is alternately depressed and released by the bolt as it cycles. This is the cartridge stop, which controls delivery of the next round in the magazine to the chamber. If the twin upper projections of the stop become worn, or the spring weakens or breaks, there will be feeding problems. Correcting this is not difficult, but I have seen many good old Mossberg guns traded off or given away when they began to "jam." When the cartridge stop can be found, it costs no more than a dollar or two, and making one is not terribly difficult. Fitting, however, should be done by a gunsmith, as the proper reach of the bolt contact projections is critical to the feeding. In some cases, it is possible to add a little steel weld to the top of

the contact arms and recut them to shape, saving the original part.

The characteristic extended trigger guard of the Mossberg, with its finger grooves, is both nice looking and comfortable. It is, however, made of plastic and may become brittle with age. If one is broken, it would be well to note that not all of these guards are interchangeable between the various Mossberg rifles, so be sure the one you get is for your particular model.

On the underside of the stock, near the muzzle, there is a large-headed screw with a small shank which holds the separate forward section of the stock to the barrel. This screw is rebated between the head and threads to prevent loss; however through frequent disassembly and overtightening, this screw will frequently break at the rebated section. If this happens, it is easy to make a simple replace-

ment, especially if you clear the threads from the stock escutcheon and just make a straight, unrebated screw. Then, of course, you'll have to be careful not to lose it when taking the gun apart, as it will no longer stay in the stockpiece.

The safety of this gun is quite efficient but may be confusing to those not familiar with it, because it's a little odd in its operation. To place the gun on safe, you draw the bolt handle back until it lines up with a recess in the handle track marked "safe," then push it in toward the receiver, into the recess. The bolt will be held partially open, the disconnector will be depressed, and the gun, if it is in good working order, will not fire. Pulling outward on the handle and allowing the bolt to close puts it back in firing order.

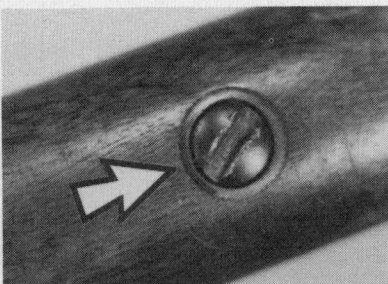

Arrow indicates the screw which retains the separate forward section of the stock near the muzzle. This screw frequently cracks at the rebated section, usually from overtightening.

The only safety provided on the Mossberg 151-M is this intermediate position of the bolt, locked in position by the bolt handle.

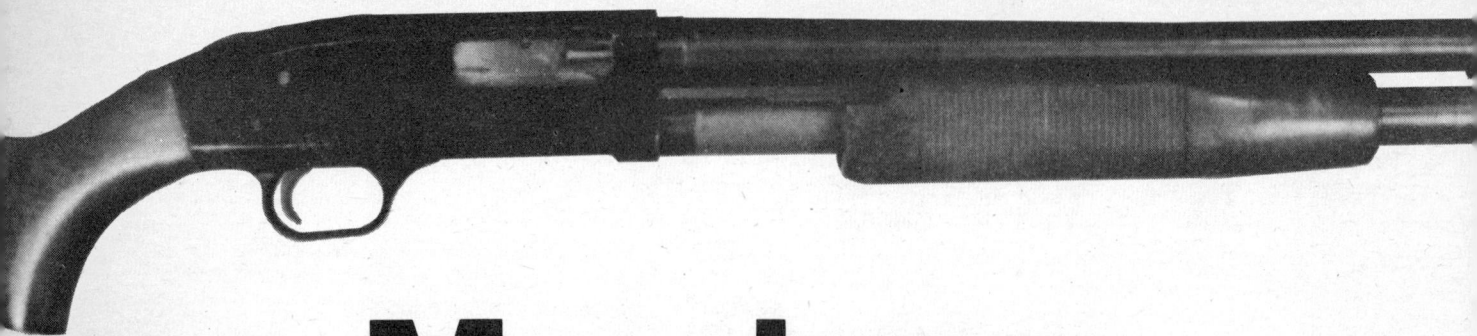

Mossberg Model 500 Shotgun

The 500 series of Mossberg slide-action shotguns began with the standard field grade gun in 1961, and several other models have since been added, designated by letters after the model number. The one shown in our photos, for example, is a Model 500-AT. Most of the Model 500 guns are still in production; nearly all parts are interchangeable; and replacements are readily available.

The Mossberg 500 is a good, solid, low-priced slide-action gun, and unlike previous guns in its price range, it offers interchangeable barrels. The early guns in the production had one chronic ailment—the forend tube tended to break loose from the action slide piece. As originally made, the two parts were joined by three light electric spot welds, and this often proved to be inadequate in taking the shock of the slide operation. The Mossberg company took note of the problem, and later guns have the parts joined with well-run silver solder.

On the early guns, when the action slide parts separate, the amateur re-pairman will often attempt to rejoin them with a torch weld, using steel or bronze rod. This is rarely successful because of the unequal heating properties of the heavy slide base and the thin tube. The tube will usually burn through or wrinkle, causing lumps on the inside which will drag on the magazine tube. When these are ground off, the tube walls will be too thin to anchor the weld. Rejoining the parts with silver solder will work, but care must be taken to get a good flow. When I rejoin these, I usually drill three holes in the prealigned base and tube and install three 6-48 screws, countersinking them into the base and facing off the tips inside. So far, I've not had one of these returned, so it is apparently adequate. You can, of course, simply replace the entire action slide.

On late guns the trigger housing is made of plastic and is retained at the

On the early guns, a chronic ailment was the separation of the forend tube and the action slide. On this one, a crude welding job was attempted—it didn't hold.

On later Mossberg 500s, the trigger housing is made of plastic—the forward retaining lugs (arrow) occasionally shear off.

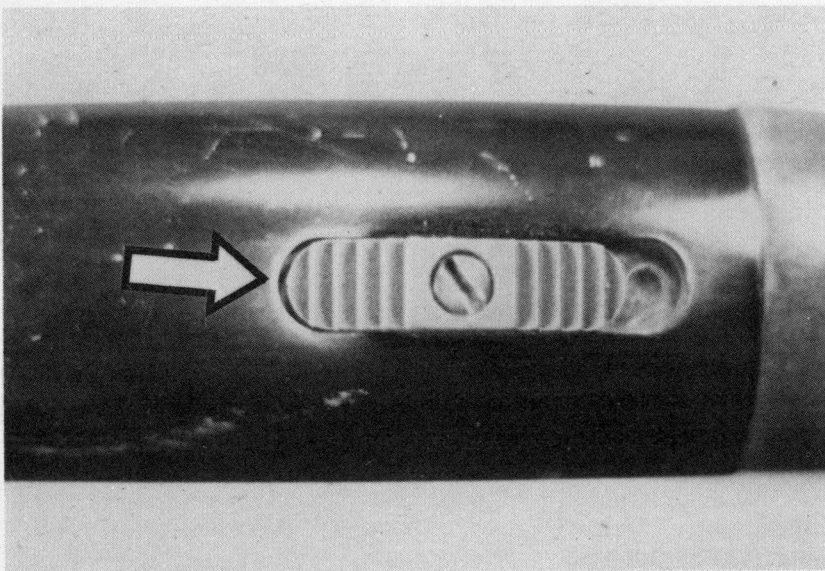

Arrow points to the top-mounted safety catch. The screw that joins it to the internal parts should be checked frequently for tightness.

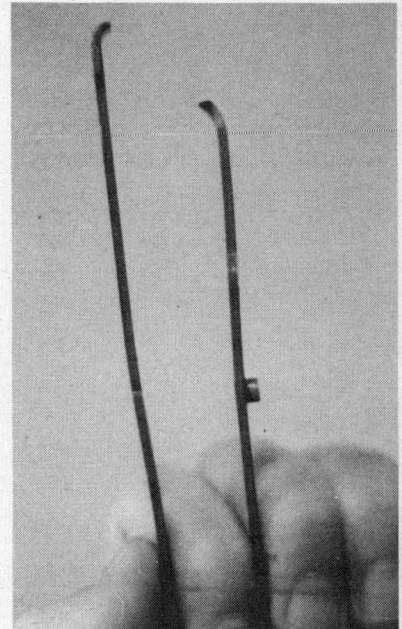

In this "edge-view" of the right and left shell stops, you can see that they are not flat, but slightly angled. The degree of angle is critical to feeding.

rear by a large cross-pin. At the front, a small lug on each side mates with a recess inside the receiver. After long use, these have been known to shear off. To avoid replacing the entire housing, it is possible to drill an angled hole at each forward corner and install steel pins to replace the broken retaining lugs. In time, though, the pins may loosen in the plastic. When this occurs, they can be fixed in place with epoxy glue. In the mechanism of the housing, there are seldom any problems. All of the parts are well-designed, and there are no inherent weak points that might cause trouble.

Conveniently located on the top rear of the receiver, the safety catch is joined to its internal block by a single outside screw. This screw tends to loosen with long use and should be checked frequently for tightness. If a loose safety screw is ignored, and it comes completely out, you will likely lose the screw, the safety and the positioning ball and spring. Also, the internal block will be freed to drop into the action inside, causing further difficulties. If the screw is kept tight, there will be no problem.

The right and left shell stops, lying inside each wall of the receiver near its lower edge, are an occasional problem. When these are removed from the gun, you will note that they are not flat, but are slightly angled. The precise degree of angle is critical to the feeding, and any amateur attempt at reshaping them is likely to cause trouble. When one or both of the stops becomes worn, it is possible to restore them to the proper reach, but this is a job for a gunsmith. Here again, new ones are readily obtainable, and inexpensive, so a defective stop could simply be replaced. It's possible, though, that a new replacement could require slight adjustment to function properly.

The Model 500 has no other quirks and is basically a good design.

Noble Model 235 Rifle

The mechanism of this .22 slide-action rifle has some relation to the old Stevens Visible Loader, but it was made by the Noble company of Haydenville, Massachusetts, between 1949 and 1972. The earliest guns, made from 1949 to 1953, were designated Model 33, and the same gun was offered by Harrington & Rich-ardson from 1952 to 1958 as the Model 422. Considering the bad points of its design, it's amazing that it lasted so long.

The formed sheet steel trigger housing is attached to the receiver by two cross-screws, and the thickness of the sides of the housing is inadequate for proper thread bite. These screws are frequently stripped out. There is a screw through the forward underside of the stock into the housing, and the knurled receiver endpiece has a wood screw which threads vertically into the stock just behind the action. The latter screw is frequently overtightened, stripping out the wood. The entire mounting arrange-

Upper arrow indicates the clip-type double extractor unit. The lower arrow points to the engagement of the slide latch with the slide bar.

In this close-up view of the breech block, you can see the arrow pointing out the slide latch spring—a frequent source of trouble. (The part protruding below is the cartridge lifter.)

ment is a weak one, and the only remedy is the installation of screws of the next larger size. In the case of the cross-screws, this involves some extra work.

The twin extractor unit is a formed sheet steel type that clips over the top of the breech block, and breakage is not unusual. Since the Noble company has been out of business for several years, no new parts are available, and the only possible source would be the used-parts dealers. Any competent gunsmith can make this extractor unit, but it's not an easy job, and the cost may exceed the value of the gun.

The most serious fault of the gun is the slide lock release system. This consists of a round-wire, torsion-type spring mounted on the right side of the breech block, with no other attendant parts. The spring itself is the release. An upper extension of the spring is struck by the striker (hammer) as it falls, tensioning the spring so that its lower arm exerts pressure on the slide latch, forcing it downward and out of engagement with the action slide bar. The slightest deformation or difference in tension of this spring will prevent it from releasing the latch automatically, and when this hap-

pens, the only way to open the action is by manual operation of the slide latch. This spring can often be reshaped to function properly, but it will frequently break when this is tried. Making a replacement is not too difficult, especially if the broken original is available for a pattern. If not, it may require experimentation, as the length of the opposing ends of the spring will be of critical importance.

The cartridge lifter is operated by a lower projection which contacts a stop-surface in the bottom of the housing as the breech block reaches full rearward movement, and the lower arm will occasionally break or bend. The lifter is made of plain flat steel, and making a replacement is not extremely difficult. The exact shape is critical, though, especially the relationship of the rear surface and length of the lower arm to the upper surface of the forward part. Here, again, having the original part for a pattern is helpful, even if it's broken.

With this gun, as with most of the rifles and shotguns produced by Noble, the cost of any repairs must be weighed against the relatively low value of the piece, even when in good working order.

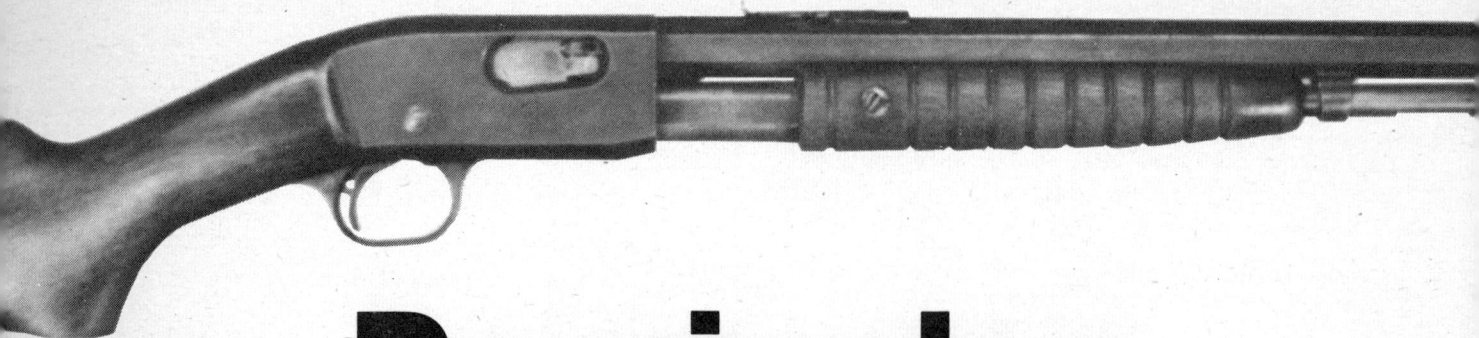

Remington Model 12 Rifle

Like its big brother, the centerfire Model 14, the Remington Model 12 rifle was designed by John D. Pedersen, and its good points kept the basic gun in production for 27 years—from 1909 to 1936. In the latter year it was redesigned slightly to become the Model 121, and continued until 1954. The original Model 12 was available in several sub-models, 12A, 12B, and so on, including special sight arrangements and gallery guns chambered for the .22 Short only. The basic Model 12 rifle fired all three regular .22 rounds interchangeably.

In the transition from the Model 12 to the Model 121, the breech block (bolt) was changed extensively, and some of the late Model 12 guns may have been experimentally altered to Model 121 components. I recently examined a late-numbered gun that was plainly marked as a Model 12, but it had the later style of bolt and firing pin, and there was no sign of alteration. The firing pin on the original was in a recess on left side of the bolt, and the pin had an open track at its center

to accommodate the return spring and plunger, and for passage of the retaining pin. These firing pins are prone to breakage because of the weakened center. They can be repaired, but commercially-made replacements are available. These are a little rough, and usually require some fitting. There

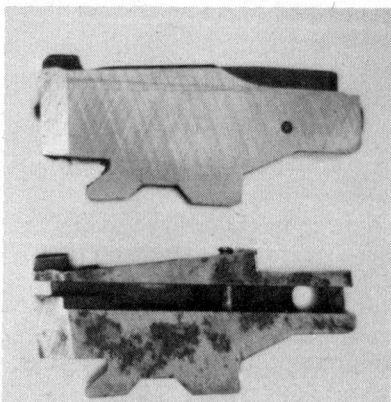

In the transition from the Model 12 to the Model 121, the bolt was redesigned, and the firing pin changed to a central round type. The later version is shown at the top. The firing pin is missing from the older bolt.

are, of course, no original parts available, except from the used-parts dealers. The redesigned bolt of the late Model 12 and Model 121 guns has a centrally-mounted cylindrical firing pin which is less prone to breakage, and easily reproduced.

The single most troublesome part in the Model 12 is the cartridge retainer. This small and narrow piece of stepped steel lies in a groove between the barrel and the action bar, and when a cartridge is fed from the magazine, a beak at its rear tip catches the next round, preventing double-feeding. In actual function, it is the same as a cartridge stop, or cartridge cutoff. The part has a spring-tempered tail, but it is not severely flexed, and rarely breaks. The main problem is that most amateurs taking the Model 12 apart don't realize it's there, and when they remove the action bar and magazine unit from the gun, this small, thin part falls free, never to be seen again. At first glance, the cartridge retainer doesn't appear to be complicated, but it has a number of cuts, steps, and

A comparison between the bolts of early and late rifles. The later bolt is at the right. The firing pin has been removed from the older bolt at the left.

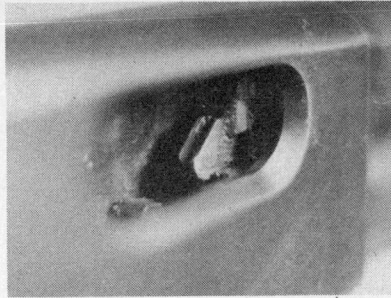

In this view through the ejection port, the head of the cartridge retainer can be seen, forming a ramp below the chamber.

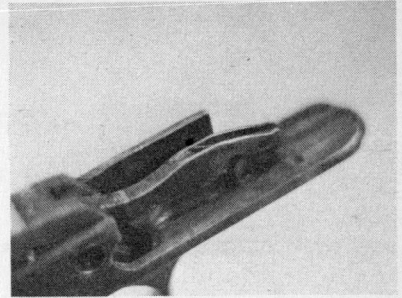

In this oblique view of the cartridge lifter, or carrier, the hammer, at left, is cocked.

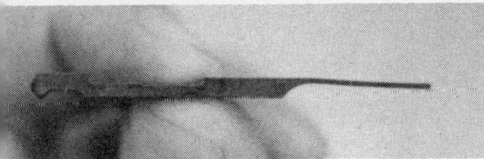

This is the cartridge retainer, a part essential to the proper operation of the feeding mechanism.

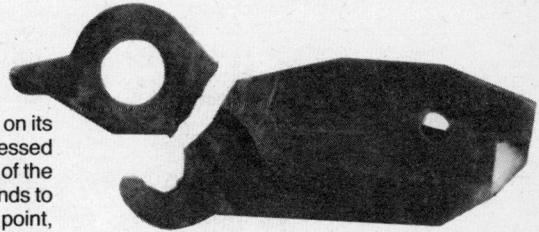

The carrier is thinned on its right side by a recessed track for the lug of the carrier dog and tends to break at its narrowest point, as on the one shown here.

angles that make reproduction by hand a tedious and time-consuming matter. These were, for a time, commercially reproduced, but I'm not sure whether they are still available, as the original supplier is no longer in business. In addition to its function as a cartridge stop, this part has a slanted area at top rear that forms a ramp into the chamber, and without it the Model 12 will simply not work as a repeater.

The motion of the cartridge lifter, or carrier, is controlled by a stud on the carrier dog, which is mounted at the rear of the action bar assembly. The recessed track for this stud, on the right side of the carrier, makes the carrier rather thin at its narrowest point, the neck just forward of its pivot. Breakage at this area is not uncommon. Unless a used replacement can be located, the only alternative is to rejoin it by welding, then recut the track to shape. This will require the services of a gunsmith, of course.

In the Model 12 the firing pin also serves as the ejector, and at the upper rear of the trigger housing there is a small V-blade spring, screw-mounted, which cushions the impact of the firing pin/ejector head as the bolt reaches full rear travel. As with any V-type spring subjected to this sort of impact, breakage is not unusual. If a used replacement can't be found, this spring can be duplicated in doubled round wire. The other springs in the gun are helical coil; and if age-weakened, they can easily be replaced with modern coil springs of proper tension and diameter.

The cartridge retainer (arrow) is located between the barrel and the action bar.

In this right-side view of the trigger housing, the hammer is at the left, shown in the uncocked position. At the right is the cartridge lifter. Both parts pivot on the hollow sleeve that forms a tunnel for the takedown screw.

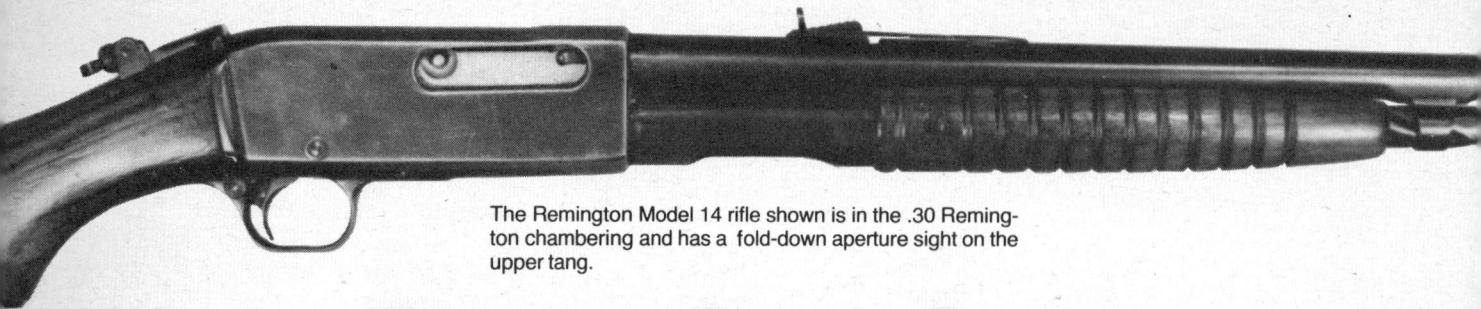

The Remington Model 14 rifle shown is in the .30 Remington chambering and has a fold-down aperture sight on the upper tang.

Remington Model 14 Rifle

This neat little slide-action centerfire rifle was made between 1912 and 1935, and was chambered for the .25, .30, and .32 Remington rounds, the latter two being in the same power class as the .30-30 Winchester cartridge. The bolt locked by tipping into lug recesses in the inside top of the receiver, and the bolt itself was intricately machined from a solid block of steel—it's a strong system. The rifle is easily recognized by the "twisted" appearance of its tubular magazine, which has deep spiral indentations at intervals along its length. These had the effect of tilting the cartridges inside the magazine, keeping the bullet noses away from the primers of the next rounds in line. With this system, pointed bullets could be used—a practice that is unwise in a normal tubular magazine. Another interesting touch is the gas port on the left side of the receiver, surrounded by the head of the cartridge case, and showing at a glance the round for which the gun is chambered.

The action slide unlocks auto-matically, of course, when the gun is fired. The breech block can also be unlocked manually, and the release button is in an unusual location. It is on the bolt itself, accessible at the upper rear of the ejection port on the right side of the receiver. The bolt, or breech block, contains the entire firing mechanism, and it is sufficiently complicated that takedown by the amateur is definitely not recommended. In fact, it's best not to remove the breech block from the receiver, since taking it out will release the ejector rod and plate on its left side, and replacing these parts in the proper order can be tricky, even for a gunsmith, if he's not thoroughly familiar with the Model 14 rifle.

The action of this gun was derived from the earlier Model 12 in .22 caliber, and, as in that gun, the magazine tube moves with the action slide. The safety is a cross-bolt type, located be-

On the Model 14 the breech block is an intricately machined block of solid steel. Breakage is unlikely, and disassembly is not recommended.

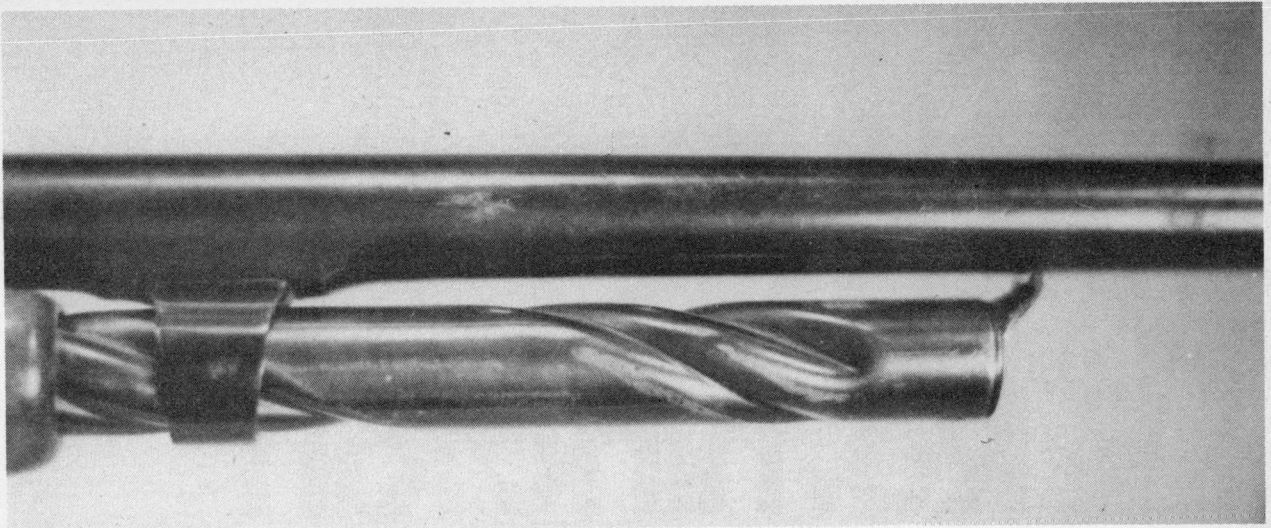

Unique spiral indentations on the magazine of the Model 14 were designed to tip the cartridges, keeping the points of the bullets from resting against the primers of the next rounds in line.

hind the trigger. Loading is through a gate on the underside of the magazine tube, just forward of the receiver, and can be done only with the action closed. (Magazine capacity is five rounds.)

The Model 14 was made in an era of solid, hand-fitted parts, and such things as the extractor, firing pin, and carrier are heavily made and not prone to breakage. In the event something does eventually let go, parts can be a problem, as the gun is long obsolete. If the used-parts dealers don't have what is needed, any replacements will have to be made by a gunsmith. Fortunately, this gun has no chronic ailments. I have worked on only one in the past 30 years, and that job was the installation of a set of sling swivels!

Popularity of these guns seems to have been somewhat regional. They are seldom seen here in the Midwest, but my Editor, Bob Anderson, says that many of them are still in use in the woods of New England. Those who want them for practical purposes must now compete in the market with the Remington collectors, as these guns were not produced in the large quantities of other Remington models. The .30 and .32 Remington rounds are still commercially loaded, but the .25 Remington was discontinued around 1950.

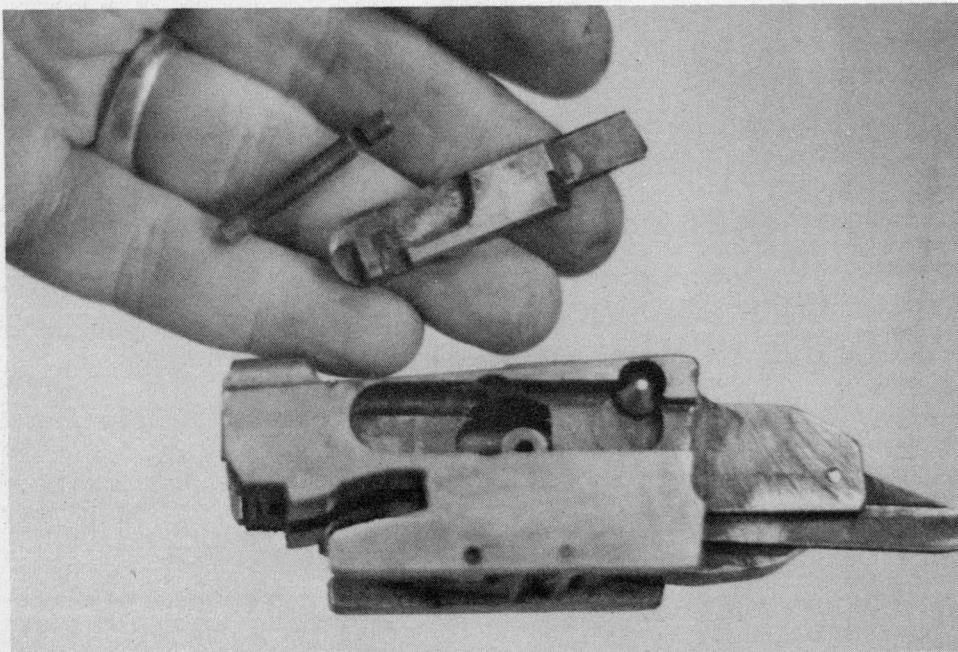

When the breech block is taken out of the receiver, the ejector rod and a long plate on the left side are free to fall off, and replacing them in the proper order can be tricky.

Remington Nylon 66 Rifle

If an old-time gunsmith could look inside the Du Pont Zytel "receiver" of the Nylon 66 rifle, he might come to the conclusion that it was some sort of elaborate toy—but he'd be wrong. What appears to be a Chinese-puzzle arrangement of formed sheet steel parts and expansion-type springs is actually a fine demonstration of modern engineering, performed by Wayne Leek and the design team at Remington. When you consider that it first appeared 18 years ago, it's even more remarkable. The gun doesn't have the good "feel" of the traditional wood stock, but for many shooters, this is outweighed by its other good points. The Zytel stock is impervious to extremes of heat, cold, and moisture, resists accumulation of powder residue, and is very difficult to break. The internal surfaces, in contact with the steel parts, require no lubrication. You can mistreat the gun, fail to clean it, and it will just keep on working.

I can think of only one part that I have replaced with any frequency —the disconnector. The Nylon 66 has a "prop"-type sear system with a wide step on the disconnector supporting the sear, the sear having an angled striker contact surface rather than the usual sharp-edged detent.

When the trigger is pulled, the disconnector moves forward, releasing the sear to be cammed downward by the striker. The disconnector usually breaks in one of two places—either the bolt-contact lobe, or the long arm

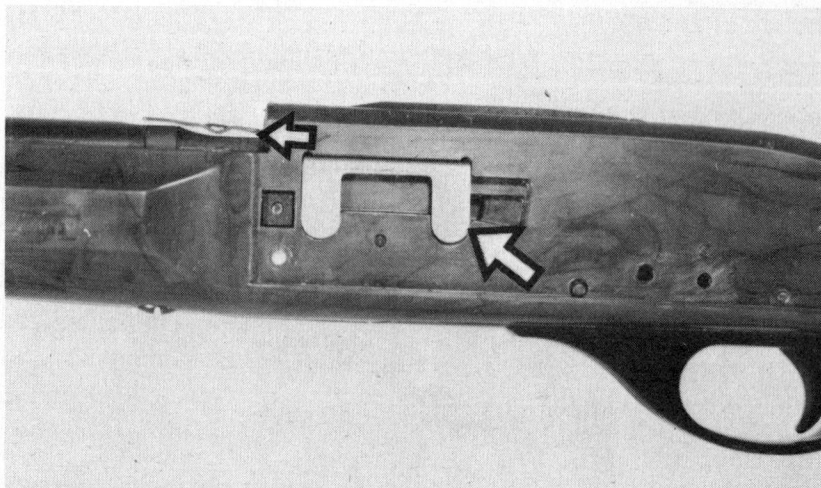

When reassembling, the cartridge guide (small arrow, upper left) must be in the position shown. The semi-horseshoe shaped ejector (large arrow) is retained only by the receiver cover—it can easily fall out when that cover is removed.

94

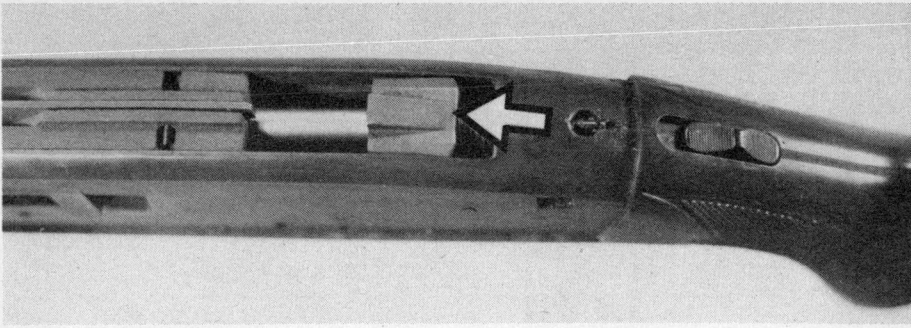

When the Nylon 66 is taken down for cleaning, be careful not to release the hammer (arrow), as repositioning it can be quite tricky.

which goes to the rear and meets the safety lever. In either case, everything will stop working. The part is available at most gunshops, and also from Remington, and it is very inexpensive. Installing it, though, is definitely not a pleasant way to spend your weekend. This operation is best left to your gunsmith.

Most difficulties with the Nylon 66 arise when the amateur decides to give it a thorough cleaning, which this gun normally needs only about once a year. A partial takedown is not beyond the skills of the average shooter, as long as he knows where to stop. Making sure that the rifle is empty, cycle the bolt to cock the striker (hammer), and move the safety back to the on-safe position. Then, pull the cocking handle straight out to the right. Remove the two cross-screws to free the receiver cover, and lift this straight up and off the gun. The ejector lies in a shallow recess on the left side of the receiver, and only the cover keeps it in place, so be sure it doesn't fall off and become lost. Do *not* remove any of the other screws or cross-pins that are exposed by removal of the cover. There is a large, coin-slotted screw on the underside of the stock, just forward of the receiver area. Loosening this will allow the barrel retaining yoke to be moved upward, and the barrel slid forward out of the stock. Now, grasp the bolt by the pivoted cartridge guide at its top front, and run the bolt forward until it is clear of the receiver. The recoil spring can also be removed at this time. *Don't* release the striker, as it is rather tricky to re-install. For routine cleaning, this is far enough.

When you're putting it back together, be sure that the ejector is back in its recess on the left side and that the cartridge guide is flipped over forward to lie on top of the barrel. I have only one real criticism of the Nylon 66, and this has nothing to do with the firing mechanism. It seems incongruous that a gun as rugged and dependable as this one has a rear sight that is so fragile and easily deformed.

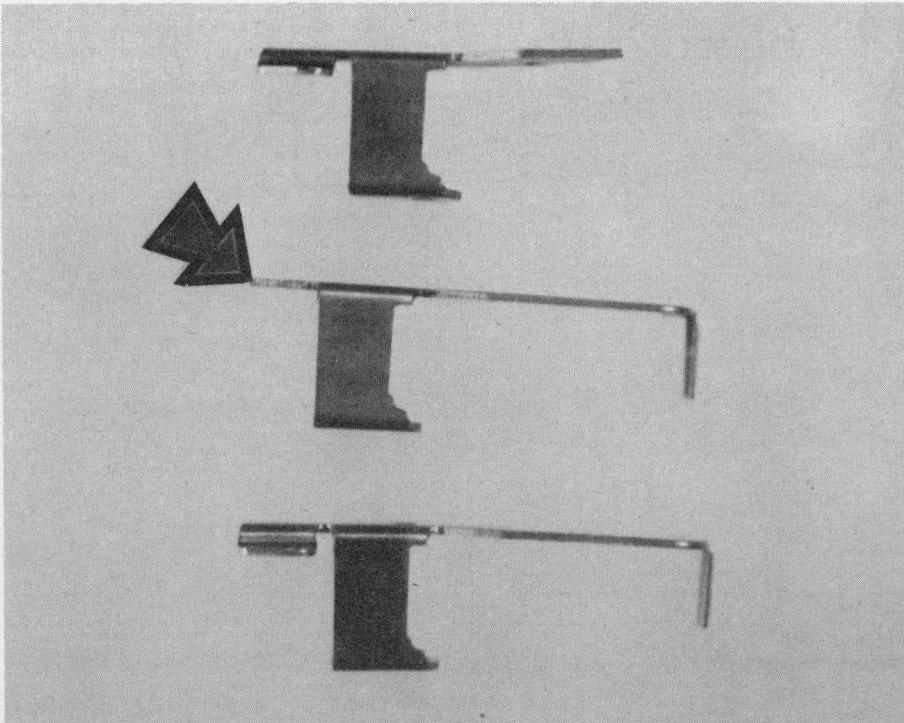

If there is one part on the Nylon 66 that's subject to breakage, it's the disconnector. The one at the top has a broken safety contact extension, while the one in the center has lost its bolt contact lobe (arrow). The disconnector on the bottom is intact.

Remington Model 341 Rifle

This tube-magazine .22 bolt-action and its ancestor, the Model 34, were both made for relatively short periods. The Model 34 was in production from 1932 to 1936; and, the Model 341, the gun covered here, also covered a 4-year span, from 1936 to 1940, when it was replaced by the Model 512. The Model 341 was made in three styles—one with standard open sights (341-A), one with a Remington peep sight (341-P), and another designed to function with .22 shot cartridges, a smooth-bore (341-SB).

The Model 341 has several outstanding features, one of the most notable being the bolt locking system. With the relatively low power of the .22 rimfire cartridges, most .22 bolt-action rifles simply lock the bolt by bearing the bolt handle base against a shoulder in the receiver. The Model 341 has this, but it also has a large additional lug on the opposite side, locking firmly into an opening in the side of the receiver. If this gun had still been around for the introduction of the .22 Magnum round, it could

have simply had the barrel and feed system altered to the dimensions of the longer cartridge. The bolt locking system would have been quite adequate, with no change.

Most .22 bolt-action rifles simply lock on the base of the bolt handle. The Model 341 has an additional lug (arrow) which bears against the receiver on the opposite side.

The combination firing pin and striker of this gun is long and heavy, and lock time is very fast, a feature that aids accuracy. There are no regularly available commercial parts for

The Model 341 has a Mauser-type safety at the rear of the bolt. It is shown in the on-safe position.

The heavy carrier is designed to fully enclose the cartridge, and there is little chance of misfeeding.

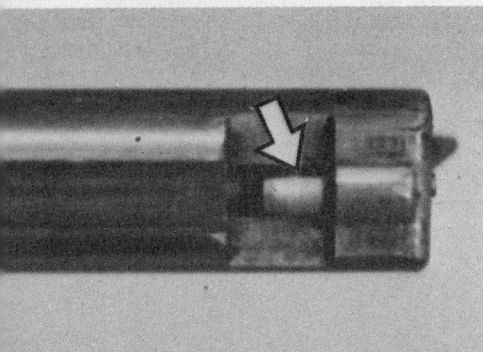

As the bolt reaches full rear travel, the ejector emerges from the bolt face. It is actuated by a lug (arrow) on the underside of the bolt which contacts a frontal beak on the sear. This also acts as the bolt stop.

In this view of the bolt face, the ejector is the small pin protruding just below the extractor. The larger opening at the right is the firing pin aperture.

this gun, so any breakage of the firing pin tip will have to be repaired by a gunsmith. The point is offset, and re-pointing is difficult, but not impossible. The manual safety, a Mauser-style flip-up lever, is cross-pinned directly to the striker at the rear of the bolt. It is very efficient, and is not inclined to break. Over to the left is firing position, and straight up is on-safe. In the latter position it obscures the sights, a most effective reminder.

The heavy carrier fully encloses the cartridge, and there is little chance of misfeeding. The round is precisely controlled from the time it leaves the magazine until it enters the chamber, an excellent system. The extractor is a vertically pinned pivoting type, powered by a coil spring and plunger, and is not the source of any trouble. The ejector is mounted in the lower front portion of the bolt, its cartridge contact pin emerging from the bolt face in the lower part of the cartridge head recess. On the underside of the bolt, it has a beaked lug which meets a like surface on the front of the sear, sliding the ejector forward to kick out the fired case. Its underlug also serves as the bolt stop. These do not break often, but when one does let go, it is not too difficult to make.

Holding the trigger back while opening the bolt allows the bolt to be taken out, but on the guns equipped with the peep sight it is also necessary to loosen the adjustment screw and swing the sight up out of the way. Takedown of the bolt itself should be left to a professional, as there are some points in the reassembly where a mistake could cause damage.

This advice also applies to the receiver. If extensive cleaning is required, it would be best to leave this to a gunsmith.

Remington Model 512 Rifle

Thirty years ago, when a boy got his first repeating bolt-action .22 rifle, it was probably this one. It was one of the very popular Remington "500 Series" guns which had model numbers running from 510 to 514, with various letters added to the number denoting target and hunting types, and the sights that were supplied. The Model 512, fairly typical of the group, was a good little gun. Even though many thousands of them were made, I have seen very few that required repair. I have, on the other hand, seen several that were simply worn out from years of faithful service, and these were still shooting, more or less, at their demise.

Other than routine replacement of extractors and firing pins, the sort of thing expected with any gun, the only cases of breakage I have seen involved the cartridge lifter, or carrier. This is a stamped steel part, hardened after shaping, and is actually an assembly of two shaped plates of thin stock, with an integrally mounted coil

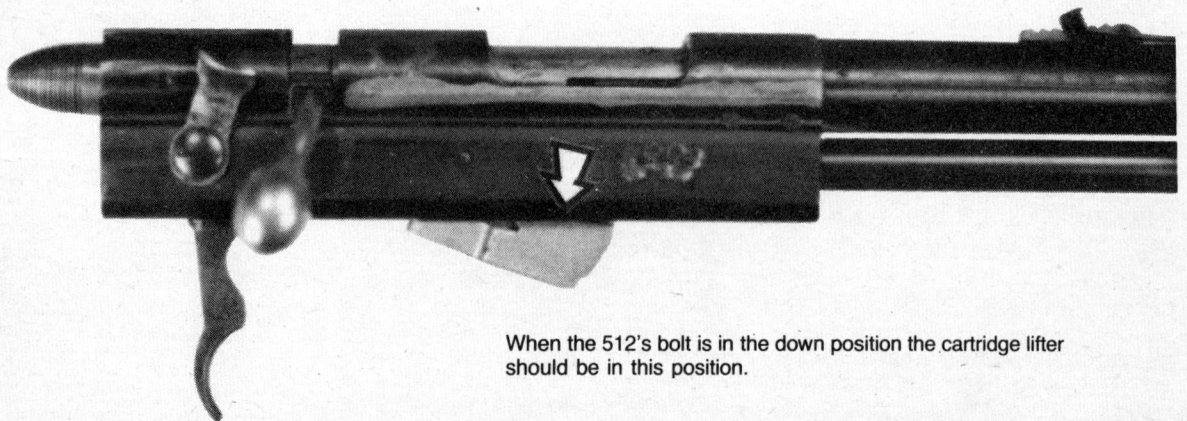

When the 512's bolt is in the down position the cartridge lifter should be in this position.

In this view you can see (arrow) the broken upper lobe of the two-piece cartridge lifter—new lifter is seen on the right.

spring. As the bolt is pulled to the rear, a shelf on its underside strikes an upper rear extension on the carrier, tipping the forward part of the lifter upward to raise the cartridge into the feed lips of the guide. I have seen several cases in which the rear arm of the carrier was broken off, presumably from repeated impact of the bolt. Repair of this thin steel part is not feasible, and the broken ones were simply replaced with new parts.

It should be noted that Remington still has *some* parts for these rifles, so it would be worthwhile to inquire for any that you might need. Keep in mind, though, that certain individual parts are exhausted, and no more are being made. It may be that you can obtain several parts for this gun at your local gunshop, as these rifles were popular and sold in large quantities, and most shops kept such things as extractors, firing pins, and lifters in stock.

The Model 512 has a couple of points regarding maintenance and disassembly that should be mentioned. When the lifter is in the raised position, a small spring-powered plunger engages a detent notch on its lower front surface. This keeps the lifter up, and the cartridge it has raised in line for pickup by the closing bolt. As the bolt chambers the round, the carrier is pushed back down to pick up the next cartridge from the magazine. Occasionally, the little plunger-detent will become gummed with dirt and will stick in its hole in the sub-frame block. If this occurs, and it fails to make proper contact with the notch on the carrier, the gun will misfeed. In many cases, a squirt of good penetrant will cure this. If not, consult your

gunsmith, as getting to that tiny part requires extensive disassembly.

I have seen one case of breakage involving the domed endpiece at the rear of the bolt (Remington calls it the "bolt sleeve"), but this was no fault of the gun. The owner had attempted to dismantle the bolt and had used an oversized drift punch to start the retaining cross-pin out. One entire side of the endpiece just broke away. This part is tempered as hard as glass and is not very tolerant of impact, especially

when delivered by a carpenter's hammer and a 3/16-inch punch. Actually, the bolt of this gun should be disassembled only when absolutely necessary, and then preferably by a gunsmith. This advice also applies to the internal parts of the receiver, as there is an interdependence of several things that can prove confusing for the nongunsmith. When the action is removed from the stock, several pins and screws become visible, and they are best left alone.

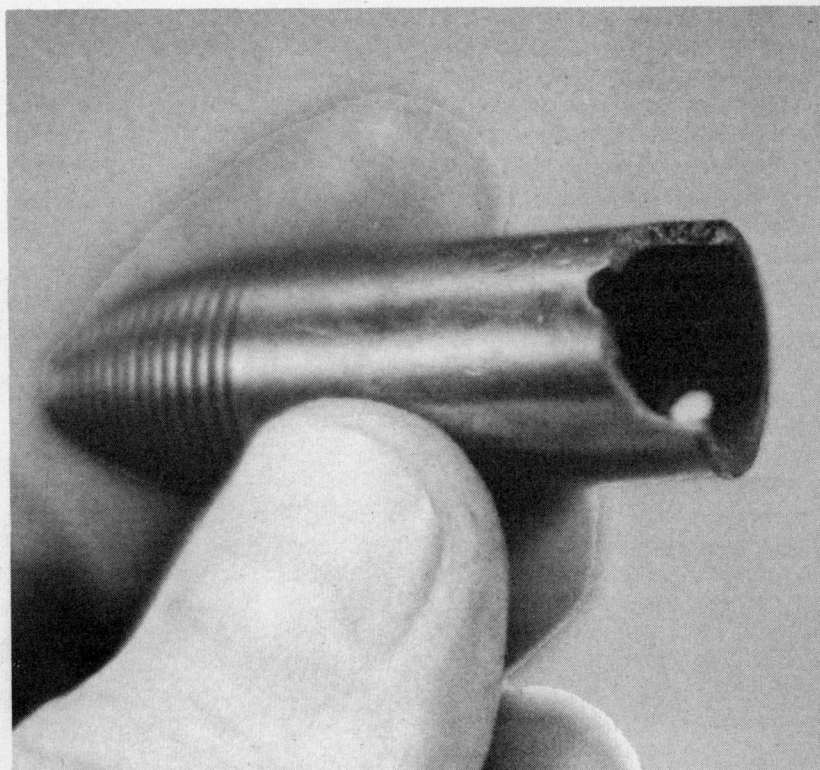

The bolt endpiece of the Remington 512 is hard—so hard that it's brittle. This bolt endpiece was not broken in normal use—it shattered when someone attempted to drive out the cross-pin with a tapered drift.

Remington Model 552 Rifle

In 1958, Remington replaced their Model 550 rifle with a new .22 semi-auto that was designed to have handling qualities similar to their larger centerfire self-loader, the Model 740. The new .22 auto was the Model 552, also called the "Speedmaster," a name that had been previously used on their old semiauto, the Browning-designed Model 241.

Still in production, the Model 552 has a receiver and trigger group of alloy. In an unusual arrangement, the bolt cocking handle is on the left side, forward of the receiver, and the recoil spring surrounds the rear portion of the magazine tube. On some of the guns, the rear sight is also of alloy, in the same shape as the original steel sight. These alloy sights are less resistant to breakage than the ones of steel.

The mechanism of the trigger group is of good design, and breakage is quite rare. On the left side of the housing the long rear arm of the disconnector meets the left arm of the sear connector, and in careless reassembly it is possible to reverse the engagement.

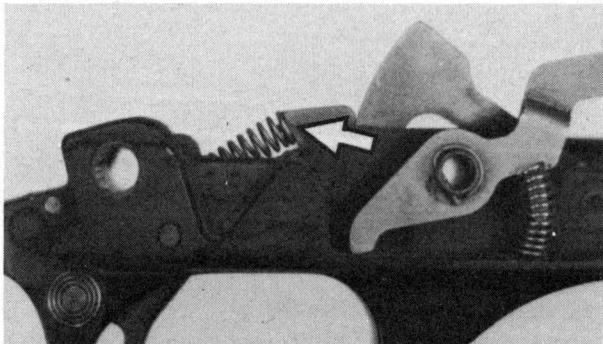

In the Model 552, one coil spring powers both the sear and the trigger (arrow). The spring to the right powers the cartridge lifter—the degree of tension of both of these springs is critical to proper functioning.

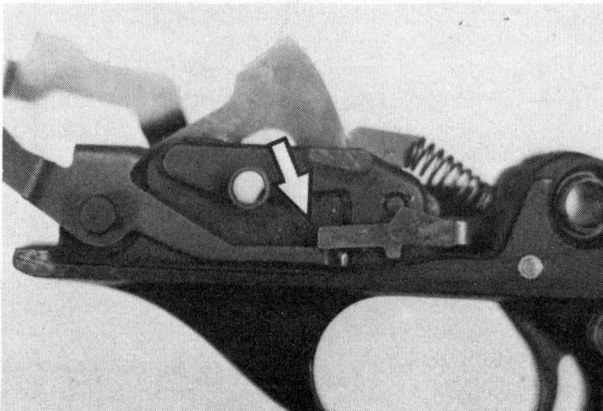

Arrow indicates the proper engagement of the rear arm of the disconnector with the left arm of the sear connector. *CAUTION:* If careless reassembly takes place, reversal of the engagement is possible.

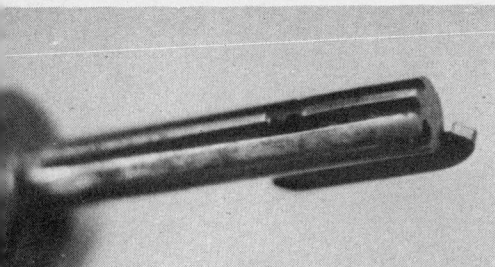

One of the interesting features of the 552 is the forward section of the bolt—it's barely larger than the rim of a .22 round and is extensively cut away to accommodate the extractor, ejector and firing pin.

Tightness of the retaining screw for the outer magazine tube (arrow) should be checked often. If it's loose, you might end up losing the tube!

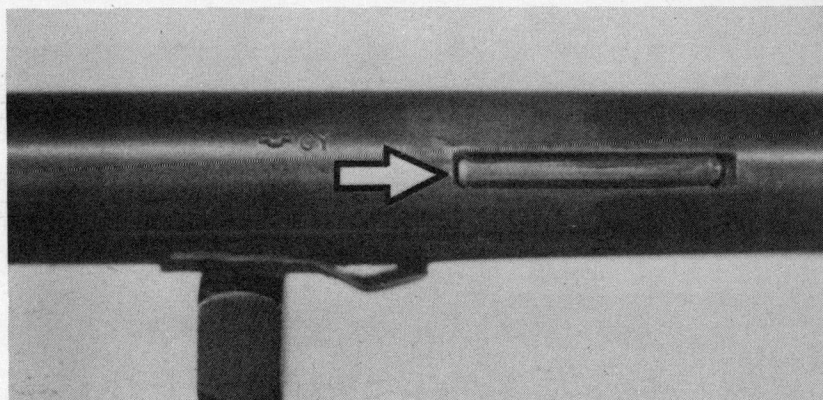

The 552's ejector is keyed in place by its twin rear projections. For removal (bolt must be out), the ejector is pulled outward by its forward end (arrow).

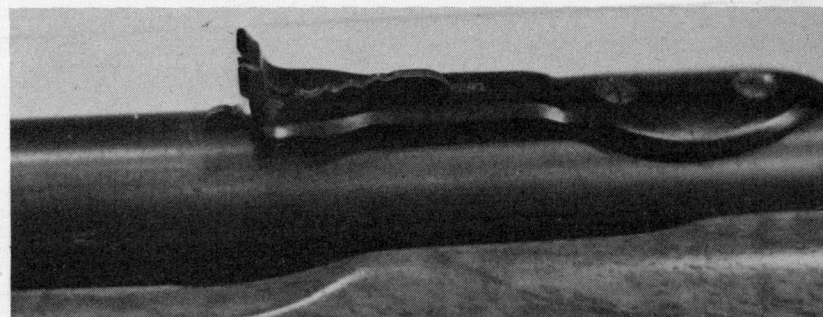

On some 552s, the rear sight is made of alloy—these are somewhat less durable than the steel type.

As the photo shows, the proper position is for the disconnector arm to lie below the sear connector.

A single coil spring, a fairly heavy one, powers both the sear and the trigger and is mounted between studs on the two parts with no other retention. It is easily detached when the trigger group is out of the receiver, and if it should be lost, keep in mind that the tension strength of this spring is critical, both for proper operation and to keep it in place. If a non-original replacement is installed, it must have the same weight as the original. Replacements are, of course, readily available, and this applies to all of the parts. In regard to tension, the cartridge lifter spring is in this same category for the same reasons.

The bolt of this gun is of unusual design, having a large rear portion and a forward section that is not much larger than the rim of a .22 cartridge. The small front portion is slotted rather extensively, to allow for mounting of the extractor and firing pin and for passage of the twin projections of the ejector. In spite of this, I have seen only one or two cases of breakage. The ejector lies in a long slot on the left side of the barrel extension and is keyed in place by twin projections toward the rear. To take it out, the bolt must be removed, and the ejector pivoted outward by its forward end.

Extending toward the rear to beyond the rear edge of the chamber, the barrel surrounds the small forward part of the bolt. With this arrangement, the feed lips of the magazine system are actually cut into the under-side of the barrel extension. This works fine, as long as the surfaces are sharp. In a few cases I have seen, long use had worn the feed lips, and there was only one way to correct this—by replacing the entire barrel! It should be noted, though, that it takes many thousands of rounds before this sort of extreme wear is apparent.

The outer magazine tube is retained in the gun by a single screw in the underside of the hanger loop below the barrel, and this screw threads directly into the loop. Since the loop wall is relatively thin, the screw has a grip of only three or four threads, and its inner tip is curved to conform to the inside of the tube. This screw should be checked frequently for tightness, but keep in mind the very small thread bite, in order to avoid over-tightening. If this screw is lost, not only will the magazine tube slip out, but it will release the recoil spring inside the fore-end. When replacing a lost magazine tube screw, be sure that an original part is used, as any makeshift substitution will likely cause trouble.

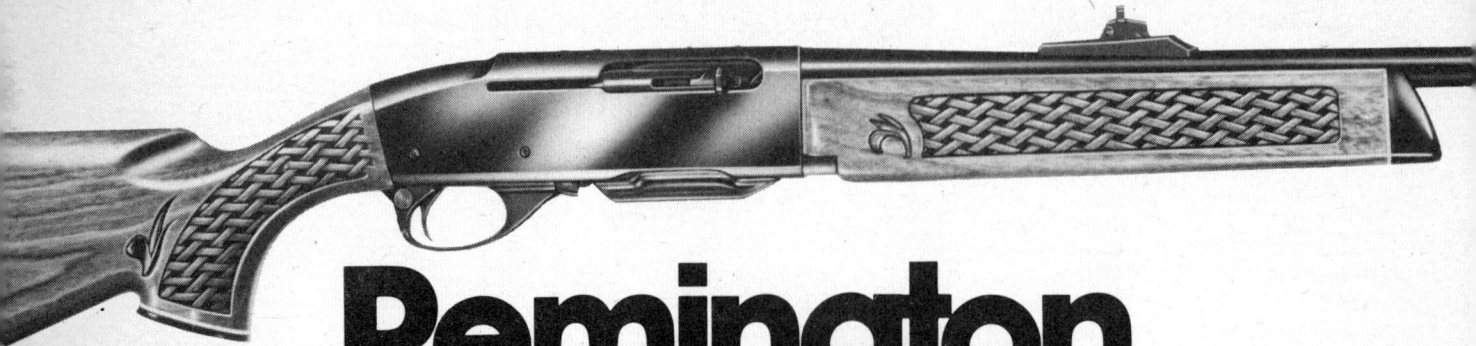

Remington Model 742 Rifle

In basic design, the Model 742 is simply a slide-action Model 760 converted to a gas-operated semi-automatic rifle. Several of the parts not directly related to the operation of the

Remington solved the problem of unequal tension on the forend by designing this retaining bolt with separated threads.

different actions will, in fact, interchange without alteration. Three years after the introduction of the Model 760 pump, Remington brought out the original version of this gun, the Model 740. Several quirks developed in that gun after extensive field use, and it was redesigned in 1960 to become the Model 742. One of the problems of the Model 740 was a sensitivity to the degree of tightness of the forend retaining screw, and this required the use of a special spacer block in the forend assembly. In the 742, this was solved by making the

retaining screw with two separate sets of threads, equalizing the forend tension without the block. The breech ring nut of the 740 was a capstan type, requiring a special wrench for barrel removal. On the 742, this was changed to a hexagonal nut that can be turned with an ordinary wrench. This nut, by the way, should be checked occasionally for tightness, since it retains the barrel in the receiver. If the barrel has not been removed since the gun left the factory, the nut is not likely to loosen in normal use.

The gas system of this gun does not

The smaller projection between the barrel and action guide is the gas tube. It should be kept clean, never lubricated, and guarded against any blow that might deform it.

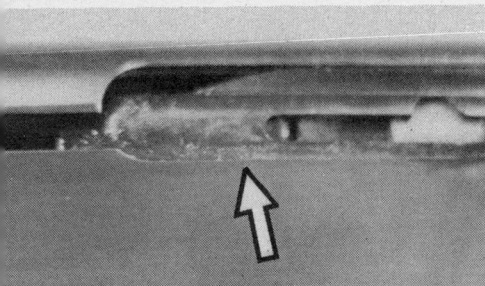

On late production guns, the ejection port cover (arrow) is made of plastic—these break with some frequency.

use a moving piston. Instead, it has a short hollow tube protruding from the barrel lug which contains the gas port, and this tube directs the ported gas against the action bar assembly. This tube is susceptible to damage, especially during amateur disassembly and reassembly, and any deformation or burring which restricts its gas transfer will cause malfunction of the system. As long as it is undamaged and kept clean and free of any lubricants, it will continue to work indefinitely and is self-adjusting to any normal commercial load. There are limits, though. This rifle will usually not function properly with very light or very heavy handloads, as the system is balanced for cartridges within a certain level of power.

There is only one part on the current Model 742 that causes any chronic difficulty. On the Model 740, and possibly on early Model 742 guns, the ejection port cover was made of formed sheet steel and caused no trouble. On the current Model 742, this part is of plastic, and it is extensively skeletonized to accommodate the cocking handle. From examples observed, it is safe to say that the plastic will eventually crack at its thin lower edge. If this is the only crack, it will continue to function, and there will be no problem. If another crack develops, and it comes apart in two or more pieces, the portion that is freed can drop into the action, causing a jam. The ejection port cover costs less than a dollar, but installation requires removal of the barrel, and for most people this means a trip to the gunsmith.

Another part that should be handled with care during takedown and reassembly is the disconnector, the long arm extending forward from the left side of the trigger housing. If it becomes deformed, it will fail to properly contact the rear edge of the action bar and will also bind the magazine. The disconnector can usually be straightened, but it's best left to a gunsmith, as this is a hardened part and will snap off if this is tried cold.

The long forward arms of the disconnector, located on the left side of the trigger housing, can be deformed during careless reassembly.

When the trigger housing is out of the gun, the magazine catch and its spring are easily detached, as they are retained on the pivot stud only by the inner wall of the receiver. When this happens, the catch will usually be found, but the little spring is under tension, and will often depart, never to be seen again. All parts are readily available, of course.

On the left side of the magazine, at its lower edge, there is a button which can be pushed forward to release the locked-open bolt. The button is connected to a lever, and a pin at the top of the lever lowers the rear of the magazine follower to release the bolt. This assembly is riveted together at the factory, and no attempt should be made to take it apart.

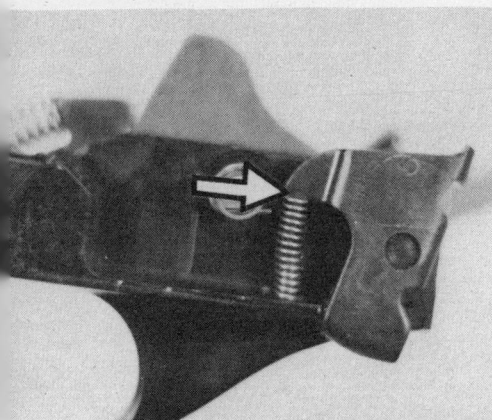

When the trigger housing is out of the gun, the magazine catch and its spring (arrow) are easily detached and lost.

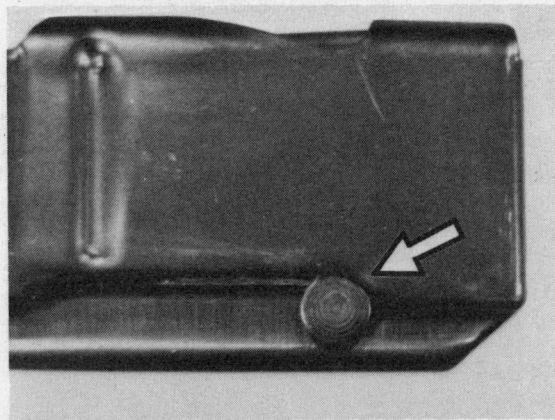

On the left side of the magazine there is a button (arrow) which can be pushed forward to release the locked-open bolt.

Remington Model 760 Rifle

Remington's earlier slide-action rifle, the Model 141, was only a redesigned version of the old Model 14 and did not have sufficient action strength for the more powerful modern cartridges. In 1952, Remington replaced it with an entirely new slide-action gun, the Model 760, and this one is still being made. The Model 760 has a two-piece bolt with a rotating head, and the head has four rows of multiple locking lugs which mate with matching recesses in the barrel extension. This arrangement gives adequate strength for even such cartridges as the popular .30-06, and the Model 760 has become the gun of choice for those who prefer a powerful slide-action rifle.

There are several small differences between early and late production Model 760 rifles, and most of these have been improvements. Early guns have a rather flimsy spring-type rear sight, similar to those used on .22 rifles, but later guns have an excellent solid steel ramp with a sliding leaf, adjustable for both windage and elevation. The early guns had an ejection

The rotating head of the two-part bolt has four sets of locking lugs like the ones shown here. Keep them clean and the gun will function perfectly.

On late Model 760 guns, the rear sight is Remington's excellent solid steel ramp type.

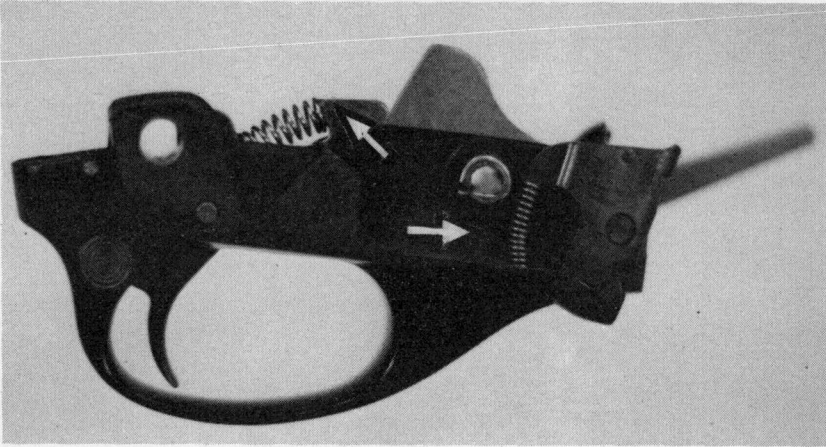

Combination sear and trigger spring (left arrow) can be lost during careless disassembly. The magazine catch and its spring (right arrow) are even more easily detached when the trigger housing is out of the gun.

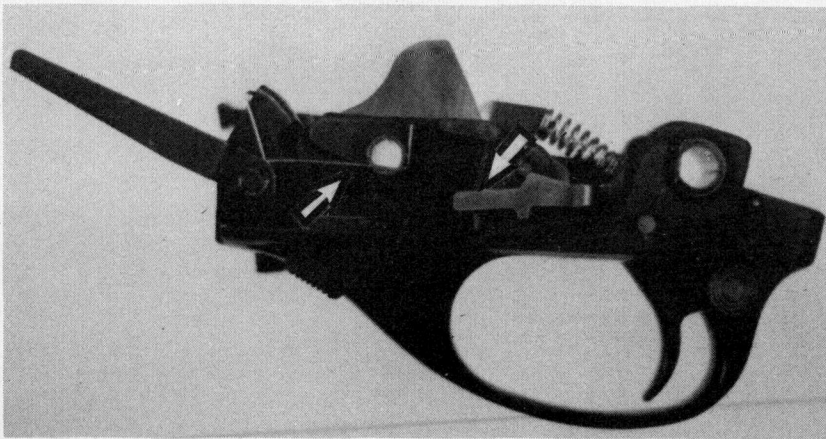

The rear arm of the slide latch spring (left arrow) also serves to retain the front trigger housing pin. The left connector (right arrow) disconnects trigger from sear when the action is opened.

port cover of lightweight steel, while those of current production have this part made of plastic. This causes no operational difficulty, as this part is under no extreme stress, but it cheapens the appearance of the gun.

The multiple locking lugs of the bolt system work perfectly, but care should be taken to avoid any buildup of powder residue in the lug recesses or the action will begin to be very stiff. This is true of any gun, of course, but the Model 760 is particularly sensitive in this area.

The trigger housing is easily removed for cleaning by pushing out the two large cross-pins which retain it. When the housing is out of the gun, take care that the combination sear and trigger spring isn't detached and lost. This same advice applies to the magazine catch and its spring, as they will come off even more easily. Both of these springs are under compression and can travel quite a distance

when freed. On the left side of the housing, at the front, the slide latch spring extends an arm rearward to fit into a slot in the front housing pin sleeve. This arm serves to hold the pin in the receiver. When replacing the housing in the receiver, be sure that this arm of the spring is in the slot. Midway on the left side, be sure that the left connector arm of the trigger is located above the tail of the slide latch, as shown in the photos.

On late guns, there is a large screw at the front of the forend piece, and this screw should be checked occasionally for tightness. The action tube assembly must also be kept tight, but unless it has been removed since installation at the factory, it probably will need no attention. If this is loose, it will be immediately apparent, as it retains the barrel in the receiver!

The extractor used in the Model 760 is of the same pattern as the one in the Model 788 (q.v.), and shares the

same liability—cracking at the rivet hole. In this case, replacement is not simple, as the entire gun must be taken apart to get to the bolt.

For those who prefer a slide-action rifle, the Model 760 is a good, dependable gun, and with normal cleaning and maintenance has no chronic ailments.

Be sure the forend screw is checked occasionally for tightness.

Remington Model 788 Rifle

Five years after the introduction of their very successful Model 700 in 1962, Remington began production of a moderately-priced high-powered rifle called the Model 788. Early in the production, the gun was offered in .30-30 and .44 Magnum chamberings, and these guns had a different bolt head, a separate rotating arrangement. In the current standard model—in chamberings from .222 up to .308—the bolt is of one-piece design. The bolt is unusual in having nine locking lugs located at the rear, just forward of the bolt handle, locking into matching recesses in the receiver. One advantage of this system is its very reliable feeding, as the cartridges don't have to pass over a lug recess in the receiver ring as they are fed from the magazine into the chamber.

The bolt handle is joined to the bolt body with what appears to be a high-tensile-strength silver solder, and I have observed three cases in which the handle separated from the bolt. This may have been caused by an inadequate flow during the joining pro-cess—a freak occurrence. In one of the cases, the shooter was firing "rather warm" hand-loads, and a stuck case made him decide, unwisely, to rap the bolt handle with a mallet in an attempt to force it open. In two of the detached-handle cases, the guns were returned to the factory, and Remington replaced the bolts at no charge. When the bolt handle breaks, the amateur gunsmith may be tempted to rejoin it to the bolt with steel weld, and this should *not* be done. The extreme heat of welding would be likely to affect the hardness of the nearby lock-ing lugs, with possibly disastrous results. If it's tried at all, it should be done with a low-temperature silver solder, with the lugs protected by wet cloth or welder's clay. Personally, I'd prefer to rely on the excellent facilities at the Remington plant in Ilion, New York. Bear in mind that there are many thousands of Model 788 rifles in constant use to which this has never happened. It's not a common ailment.

The only thing that falls into the category of a common ailment is breakage of the extractor. The plain cylindrical head of the 788 bolt is

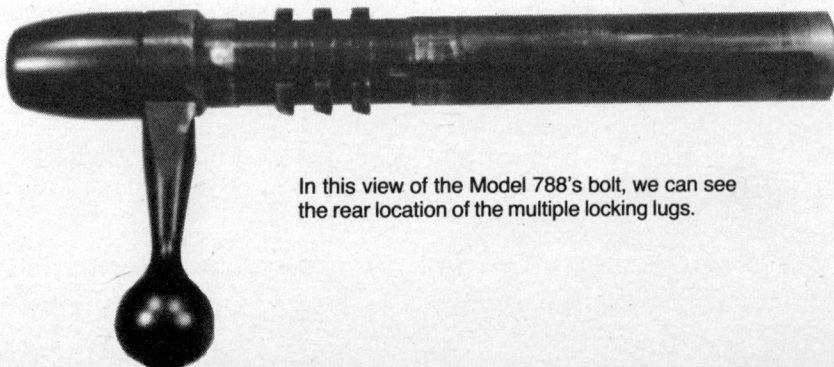

In this view of the Model 788's bolt, we can see the rear location of the multiple locking lugs.

nicely recessed to enclose the entire head of the cartridge; and, the crescent-shaped extractor, which is tempered to be its own spring, is mounted in a groove inside the recess. The extractor is attached by a single tiny rivet which passes through the side wall of the bolt and a hole in the spring-end of the extractor. The extractor will frequently fracture at the rivet-hole. Both the extractor and its rivet are very inexpensive, but installation is an interesting operation, and one that is best left to the professional.

Plastic is used in several locations on the Model 788, a manufacturing expedient that is not unusual in modern firearms. The rear sight rib, actually a sub-base, is plastic, and in this usage it causes no difficulty. The operating knob of the safety-lever and the release button for the magazine are also plastic, molded around the ends of these parts. The safety is not likely to be damaged, but the magazine release is mounted on the magazine itself and could be broken if the magazine is dropped on a hard surface.

At the point indicated by the arrow, the bolt handle will occasionally separate from the bolt body.

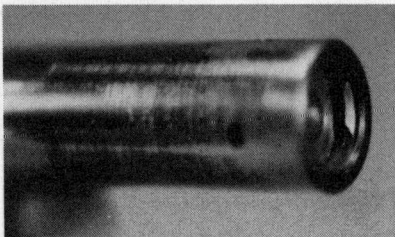

The breech face of the bolt completely encloses the cartridge head, and the crescent-shaped extractor can be seen, mounted within this recess.

As can be seen here, the extractor is retained inside the bolt face recess by a small rivet (arrow). Replacement is rather difficult.

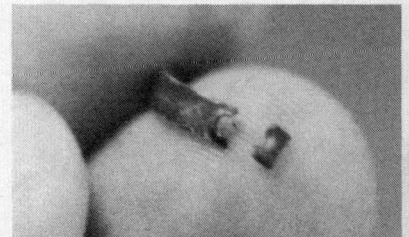

When the extractor breaks—it usually happens at its rivet-hole—replacement is definitely a job for the gunsmith.

While the rear sight itself is made of steel, the sight mounting rib (arrow) is of plastic.

Since the plastic is molded in place, it is not available separately for these two parts, and breakage would require the replacement of the entire parts. It should be noted that this seems to be a very tough plastic, and I have seen only two cases of breakage.

The trigger and sear system of the 788 is of very good design, and every one I have examined has had an *excellent* trigger pull. This system uses the familiar prop-up sear design, and the engagement of the sear trigger, and striker should not be disturbed by the amateur. Besides, it is not usually necessary. Worth noting is the 788's reputation for superb, and in some cases, phenomenal accuracy.

Another plastic part is the operating knob of the manual safety. When this is broken, the entire safety-lever must be replaced.

The magazine release (arrow) is mounted on the magazine itself, and its operating button is also made of plastic.

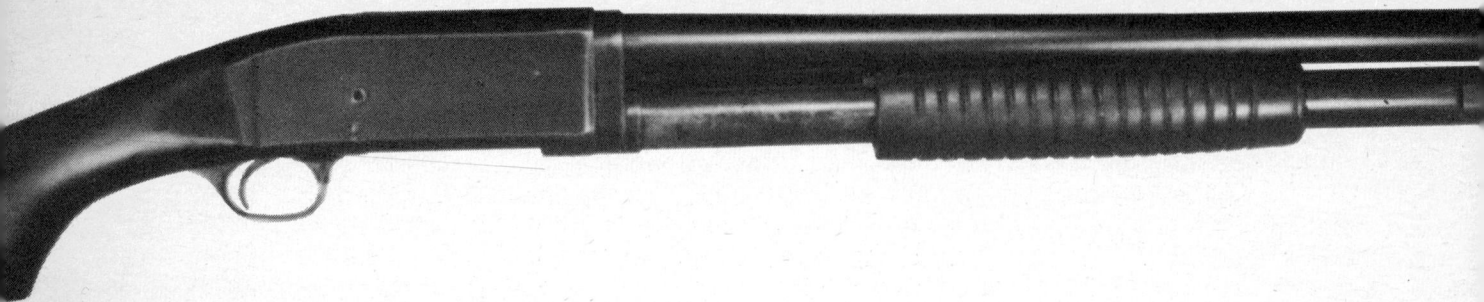

Remington Model 10 Shotgun

Designed in 1901 and patented in 1903 by John Douglas Pedersen, the Remington Model 10 was the first successful hammerless repeating slide-action made in the U.S., and it pioneered the "streamlined" receiver shape that is used on most currently-made shotguns of this type. The gun was put into production by Remington in 1907, and very early catalogs referred to it as the "Model 1908," but this was soon dropped in favor of the "Model 10" designation. There were several minor mechanical alterations along the way, but the basic gun was made for 22 years, until being replaced by the Model 29 (1929). The Model 10 had several noteworthy features, the main one being that it both loaded and ejected from the bottom of the receiver, and the solid top and sides kept rain and dirt out of the internal mechanism. Because of its bottom ejection and centrally-mounted safety it also could be readily used by either right- or left-handed shooters.

For the time it was designed, the Model 10 was a remarkable achievement. There were, however, several weak points which showed up after long years of use. The ingeniously designed carrier is controlled by a headpiece at its rear pivot point which has intricately-machined curves that mate with like surfaces on the right side of the breech block. The mating of the curved surfaces is critical to proper operation, and either accumulated dirt or extreme wear can make the system malfunction. Also, the headpiece has a tendency to break off, and replacement carriers are very scarce, being available only occasionally among the used-parts dealers. If the broken-off head is not lost, it is often possible to rejoin it to the shaft of the carrier. It should be noted though, that the headpiece must be oriented on the shaft in exactly the same position as when it was part of the carrier, or the carrier arc will not be timed correctly in relation to the bolt movement, and everything will stop. I have seen one example of this in which the head was rejoined nearly 180 degrees off, and the action was

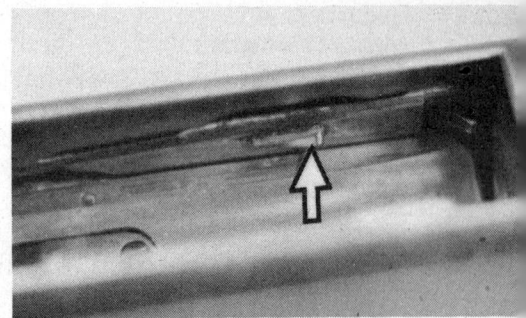

When the bolt is closed, the carrier (arrow) is swung upward to lie beside the bolt, against the right inner wall of the receiver.

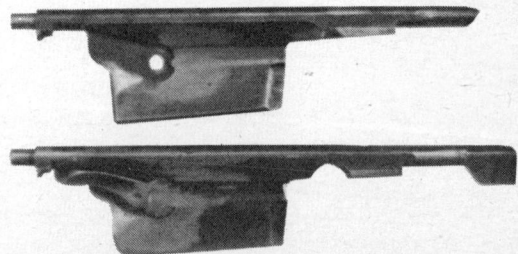

The carrier is the weakest point in the design of the Model 10. The lower one is intact, while the one at the top has lost both its camming head and its shell stop.

Arrow indicates the curved recess on the right side of the breech block which controls the movement of the carrier. This area must be kept clean and lightly oiled.

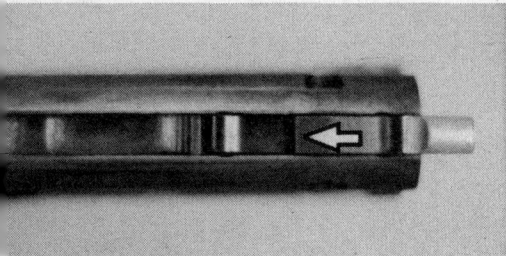

Located on top of the breech block, the extractor is powered by a folded blade spring. These break with some frequency.

solidly jammed. (The one thing I could never determine was how the owner managed to get it back together in that condition!)

Slot-mounted in the inside top of the receiver, there is a medium-weight blade spring which curves downward when the bolt is opened, and serves to kick the empty shell case down to be struck by the carrier and ejected. This spring is flexed upward to lie in a groove when the bolt closes, and breakage is not unusual. The spring is a simple piece of curved flat stock and is not difficult to make if a replacement can't be found.

The action slide is released automatically when the gun is fired, of

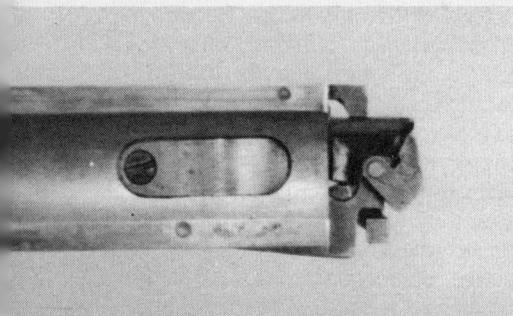

The lower rear portion of the breech block houses the sear, striker head, and bolt locking mechanism in an arrangement that defies logical description. If anything goes wrong, consult a gunsmith. The sear spring screw, visible here on the underside of the bolt, must be kept tight.

course. When it's necessary to open the action without firing, there is a button on the right side of the receiver which is pushed inward to unlock the action. The button is retained in the wall of the receiver and powered by a small flat spring, and this spring will break occasionally. Here, again, making a replacement is not difficult, but the installation is interesting, to say the least, as it requires complete removal of the parts in the receiver. There is one other unfortunate note about trouble in this area—if the spring breaks in such a manner that the button is freed, it can fall out of the receiver and disappear into the tall grass. Making one of these little buttons from rod stock is another interesting project, if the used-parts dealers happen to be out of it.

In the Model 10 the barrel, magazine and forend assembly can be easily separated from the receiver and buttstock unit, and the initial key to this takedown is a small button at the forward end of the magazine endpiece. When pushed downward to clear an edge of the endpiece, it allows a large milled block to be turned across through the end of the magazine, beginning the takedown sequence. This small button has a tendency to break, either at its head or at the pivot point inside the locking piece. If exact duplication is not necessary, a workable latch button with an L-shaped head can be made fairly easily.

The breech block of the Model 10 contains the complete firing mechanism except for the trigger, and takedown of this unit is definitely *not* recommended for the amateur. This particularly applies to the lower rear portion of the bolt where the sear, striker head, and bolt locking mechanism is arranged in a manner that defies logical description. If anything goes wrong in this area, just consult a gun-

smith, preferably one who is familiar with the Model 10. On the bottom of the breech block, the sear spring and its retaining screw are visible in an oblong recess, and the screw should be checked occasionally for tightness. The extractor, mounted at the top front of the bolt, is powered by a folded blade spring, and this spring breaks with some frequency. It is, however, possible to make a workable replacement from doubled round-wire spring.

The shell stop, or cutoff, is mounted in a recess in the forward portion of the carrier and is riveted in place. The stop is tempered to be its own spring, and this results in considerable stress on the rivet, which will often loosen. If this is discovered in time, before the shell stop is lost, the rivet can be reclinched or replaced. When the shell stop breaks, it is a real problem, as they are difficult to make.

At the lower edge of the receiver on the right side near the trigger, there is a small T-shaped block which can be slid out of the receiver only after the trigger housing is removed. This little block is the rear pivot point of the carrier shaft and retains the carrier and the bolt in the receiver. When the gun is completely taken down, this part is easily lost, and its multiple cuts, planes, and studs make it difficult to reproduce.

On the right side the trigger has a hook-like extension which reaches forward to contact the sear arm on the bolt. I have seen a few of these broken, mostly as a result of using force during amateur reassembly. If both parts are saved, they can be rejoined by welding, then refitted to the sear. This is a job for a gunsmith, of course.

The sliding safety is mounted in the front of the trigger guard and directly blocks the movement of the trigger. The safety travel is very short, and its positioning is not positive. Because of the limitations imposed by the area in which it is mounted, it's difficult to improve on its action. All things considered, it might be best to give the Model 10 an honored place in your collection as a milestone in the design of the slide-action shotgun and get a more modern gun for practical use.

Remington Model 870 Shotgun

This is one of those guns which really needs no introductory comments. Since its introduction in 1950, it has become one of the most-used slide-action shotguns in the world, and with good reason. It is reliable, has a relatively simple mechanism, and is reasonably priced. The Model 870 has been available in as many as 14 distinct sub-models, but a few of these were dropped from the line in 1963. Even so, there is still a fairly wide choice today in stock styles, barrels, sight arrangements, and so on. The gun has quite a few advantages, one of which is an easy takedown procedure for cleaning.

By simply driving out two spring-detained cross-pins in the receiver, the entire trigger group can be removed, and the group and the inside of the receiver sprayed clean with solvent. The gun can usually be sufficiently cleaned this way, and no attempt should be made to dismantle the contents of the trigger housing. The non-gunsmiths who do this often manage to replace the disconnector arm of the trigger and the rear arm of the slide latch in reversed position of engagement, and this is only one of several opportunities for misassembly. While on the subject of amateur tinkering, it might be wise to mention that I have never seen a worn-out hammer and sear in an 870, but I have seen several in which someone had attempted to "adjust" the trigger pull by grinding on the sear and/or the sear step on the hammer, with disastrous results. Be-

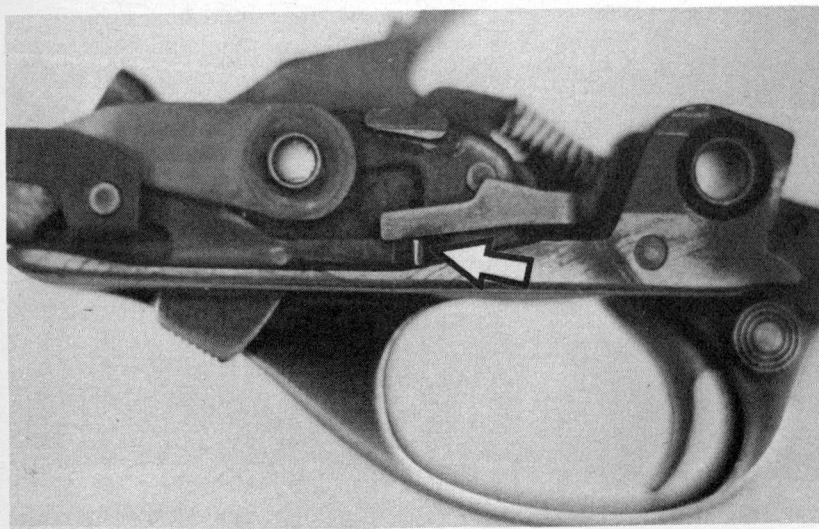

Arrow indicates the engagement of the rear arm of the slide latch with the disconnector arm of the trigger, shown in the proper position.

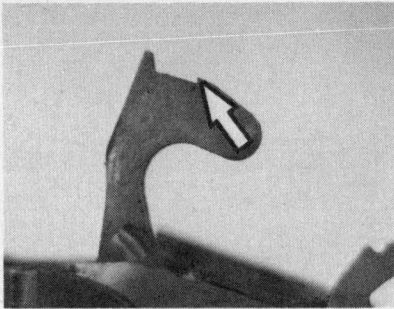

Here the arrow indicates the sear step on the rear lobe of the hammer. This is not a problem area in normal operation, but amateur attempts to adjust the trigger pull will usually ruin the hammer.

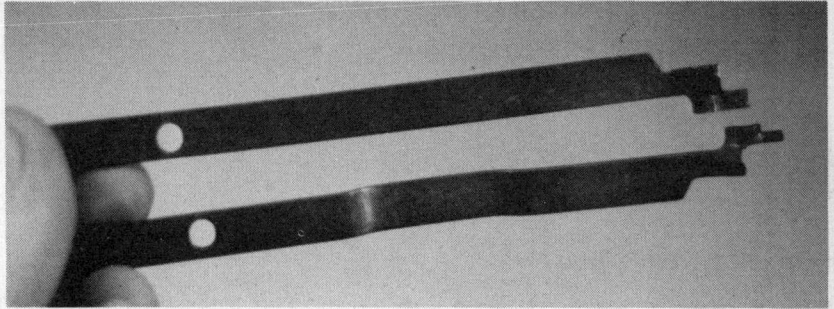

Right and left shell stops are shaped irregularly and are not supposed to be "straight." They occasionally require adjustment, but this is a job for the professional.

cause of the design of the sear and hammer engagement in this gun, it's best to leave it as fitted by the factory. A professional can smooth up the pull, if necessary, but the angle should not be changed.

The shell stops, which control the release of the shells from the magazine during feeding, lie in shallow wells on each side of the receiver near the lower edge. These two parts are formed of flat steel stock, and tempered after shaping. They extend almost the full length of the receiver, being retained at the rear by having the edges of their receiver recesses peened over into twin notches in each part. The forward ends of the stops have a rather complicated shape, with curved fingers to contact the shells, and side tabs which are acted upon by beveled surfaces on the slide bars. These parts rarely break but, after many years of hard use, one or the other of them may lose some spring tension and begin releasing shells at the wrong time. It is possible to re-shape the shell stops to restore the proper tension, but since parts are readily available at almost every gun shop in the country, replacement might make as much sense. New replacements will often require some fitting, so it's best to leave this job to a gunsmith.

I have seen one or two cases of major parts breakage in the 870, and one of these was a cracked breech block (bolt). In this case, however, there was good cause: The firing of a 3-inch Magnum shell in a standard (2¾-inch) chamber. It should be

noted that even though the bolt cracked, the gun stayed together, and there was no harm to the shooter. About the only thing that could approach being called a chronic ailment is breakage of the ejector spring. The ejector is a long piece of formed steel with a square-U cross-section, riveted inside the left wall of the receiver. Riveted in its center is a narrow piece of spring steel which is shaped to protrude outward and assist in the expulsion of the fired case. With only a few days of hunting use each year, this little spring will seemingly last forever. With once or twice a week on the Skeet or trap range, though, it's only a matter of time before it breaks. The part is inexpensive and can be replaced without removing the main body of the ejector, but the reriveting process may mar the outside of the receiver slightly, as the rivet goes all the way through—the services of a *competent* gunsmith may be in order here.

All of the other springs in the gun are of round wire, either helical coil or torsion type, and these never cause any trouble. All in all, the Model 870 is relatively trouble-free. It is this factor, plus its good handling qualities, that have made the 870 such a long-time favorite.

A close view of the shell stops shows the complicated form of their shell contact tips.

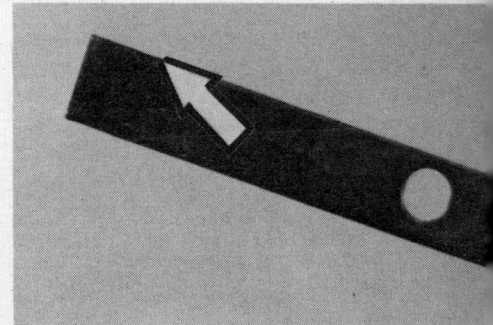

The arrow points to one of two recesses at the rear end of the shell stops, where the edge of the stop channels in the receiver is peened over to retain them.

Seen through the ejection port, the ejector and its center spring are riveted inside the left wall of the receiver.

111

Remington Model 1100 Shotgun

Since its introduction in 1963, the Model 1100 has become the preferred choice of many shotgunners, and with good reason. One of the first of the "new generation" gas-operated guns, its well-balanced system allows the use of several different loads without adjustment; and, like most guns with this type of action, the "felt recoil" is markedly reduced. The Model 1100 is still in production, and Wayne Leek and the design engineers at Remington can be justifiably proud of it. The gun has very few points for criticism. It should, however, be kept clean and properly maintained.

On the early production guns, the only actual complaint I have noted is occasional loss of the operating handle, otherwise known as the bolt handle or cocking handle. In the older guns, the handle was retained by a spring-powered plunger which entered a well in the underside of the handle; and, with frequent takedown or age weakening of the spring, the handle would occasionally fly out to disappear into the tall grass. I have altered a

few of these by deepening the well and extending the plunger for a more positive lock. Remington was also aware of the problem, and guns of more recent production have the retaining plunger mounted at the rear, entering a deep notch in the rear edge of the handle for more certain retention. Later production handles will work in both early and late guns, but early handles must have the rear notch cut if used in recent guns.

The heart of the gas system is the flexible barrel seal, a small ring of special rubber that fits into a groove on the magazine tube, just forward of the piston and the piston seal ring. The composition of the barrel seal is resistant to gas erosion, but over a period of time and many shots the little rubber ring can lose some of its sealing qualities. This can adversely affect the proper operation of the gas system. For a gun that will see a lot of use

This is the proper arrangement of the gas system components. The barrel seal is in its groove at the right. Next is the piston, and on the left is the piston seal ring.

The interceptor latch (arrow) has a narrow rear projection which is struck by the disconnector in its downward arc. The rear arm will occasionally break.

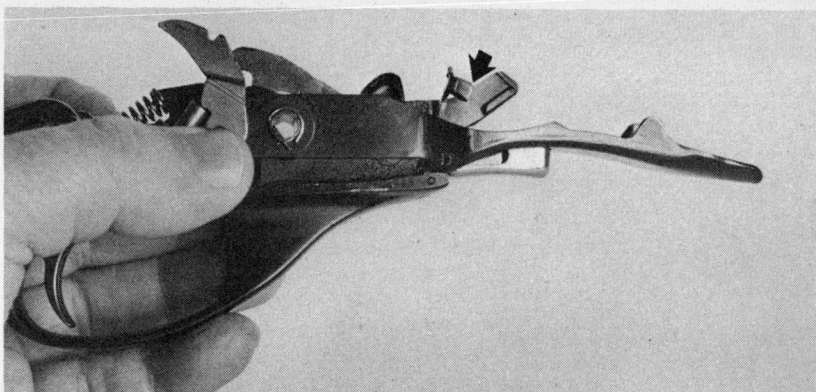

The carrier latch (arrow) is activated by the head of the shell as it travels from the magazine onto the carrier. A weak magazine spring may cause failure to disengage.

Here, the arrow points to the disconnector which is subject to wear at its contact point with the action bar.

the year around, in hunting, trap, and Skeet, it's a good idea to keep a couple of spare seals on hand. The part is quite inexpensive, and changing a barrel seal is an extremely simple operation. Aside from this, the only maintenance of the gas system is to keep the operating parts clean and free of powder scale, and keep all oil or other lubricants away from it. Any type of lubricant in this area will soon bake to a very hard residue that is difficult to remove, and this stuff can retard the proper movement of the parts. When you are cleaning the gas system, take note of the arrangement of the three parts, and replace them in order. The grooved piston seal ring goes on first, nearest the receiver, the beveled piston next, and the barrel seal last, toward the muzzle, resting in its shallow groove.

There is one internal part which gives occasional trouble. The interceptor latch—one of the two shell stops—is located inside the left wall of the receiver at the front lower edge. It has a narrow extension to the rear, the underside of which is grooved for a torsion-type spring. During the firing cycle, this rear arm is struck by the disconnector in its downward movement, and I have seen a few cases of breakage in this area. The part is not expensive, but replacement is rather difficult without a special tool to release its retaining clip-ring, and this job should be left to your gunsmith. Fortunately, this doesn't happen often.

During the firing and feeding cycle, the carrier latch is activated by being struck by the head of the next shell fed from the magazine onto the carrier. If the magazine spring has become weak, the fed shell may have inade-

quate energy when propelled back against the catch, and may fail to disengage it. The simplest way to correct this is to replace the magazine spring with a new one having full strength. If a replacement magazine spring is not immediately available, the same effect may be obtained by an adjustment of the carrier latch spring, but view this as a temporary repair.

The disconnector, located on the left side of the trigger housing at its forward edge, is subject to wear at its contact point with the action bar, but it takes a good many rounds over the years before wear will be of any significance. More often, in amateur reassembly, the forward arm of the disconnector can be bent out of alignment to the point that it no longer makes proper contact with the action bar and the interceptor latch. Unless the deformity is very severe, it can usually be repaired.

The ejector is a simple, solid stud that is rivet-mounted in the left wall of the barrel extension. I do not know of any incidence of breakage, but if one of these should chip off, it would not be difficult to repair. All parts are, of course, available at most gun shops, and from the factory.

Breakage of the ejector (arrow) is rare. It's rivet-mounted in the left wall of the barrel extension.

113

Remington Model 550 Rifle

Semi-automatic .22 rifles have been around since the first decade of this century, but each of them was made for a particular .22 cartridge—usually, either the Short or Long Rifle. The half-way round, the .22 Long, would *usually* function in those made for the Long Rifle, but otherwise the shooter had to use the specified cartridge. Then, just before WWII, Remington introduced their Model 550, and true interchangeability had arrived. The gun had a separate movable chamber that was slightly shorter than the case of the .22 Short cartridge. When the gun was used with Long or Long Rifle rounds, the longer case sealed the chamber, retarding the motion of the floating piece. When Short rounds were used, the separate chamber was driven back sharply to start the rearward movement of the bolt, compensating for the lower power of the Short cartridge.

This system works perfectly, its only drawback being a tendency to influence the shooter to use the economical Short cartridge exclusively.

With any gun which will chamber both the Long and Short-cased rounds, this can become a liability. Perpetual use of the Short in a gun not specifically chambered for it can produce a very slight "burn ring" in the chamber at the point where the short case ends. If this heat erosion becomes severe enough, subsequent use of Long or Long Rifle cartridges can give extraction problems, as the longer case will swell into the eroded area, retarding movement of the case from the chamber after firing. Bear in mind

This is the "floating chamber" which allows the Model 550 to fire the .22 Short and Long Rifle interchangeably.

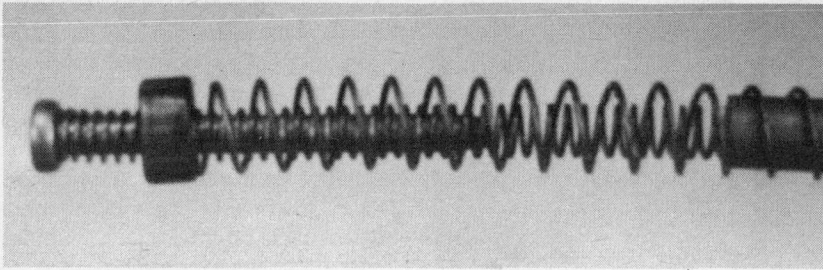

The striker spring is the smaller one at the center, and the larger one is the bolt or recoil spring. During disassembly, take care not to lose the recoil spring collar, shown on the spring at left.

that it takes *thousands* of rounds to produce this effect, so there's no need to worry about *occasional* use of the .22 Short.

The Model 550 was a well-designed gun and has no inherent weaknesses. It does not, however, tolerate any degree of amateur tinkering. The once-a-year complete takedown for cleaning should be left to your gunsmith. There are several points where the person who is unfamiliar with the internal mechanism can get into real trouble. The recoil spring and striker are concentrically mounted, the recoil spring has a thin collar at its forward end which can easily be lost or deformed, and the springs are easily kinked when screwing the receiver endcap back into place.

On the bottom of the receiver, between the trigger and the cartridge lifter, there is what appears to be the head of a large screw. Actually, this is the sear spring housing, a large hollow screw which not only contains the spring, but also has an internal collar which holds the sear at the proper level in relation to the striker and disconnector. This ''screw'' is often found staked in place to prevent rotation, with good reason. Once the unwary tinkerer has backed it out, it is impossible to replace it correctly without first driving out the sear pin, an action which leads to another assembly problem. Except for an occasional check of the various screws for tightness, it's best to leave the pins and screws of the Model 550 alone and take any problems to a gunsmith.

The gun has a fairly low incidence of parts breakage. The combined striker and firing pin has a long, narrow nose which looks delicate, but seldom breaks. When one does let go, any good gunsmith can rejoin the point to the striker base, or, if necessary, make a new point.

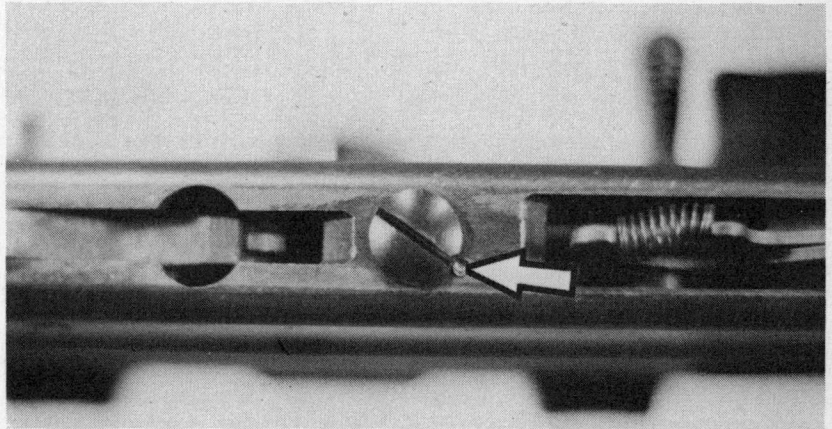

The sear spring case not only holds the sear spring, but also has an internal collar which holds the sear at the proper level. Its screw-head is staked in place (arrow) for good reason. Removal and replacement is not a job for the amateur.

From left to right, the arrows indicate the sear and lifter pin, the trigger stop pin, and the trigger pin. These should *never* be disturbed by the amateur.

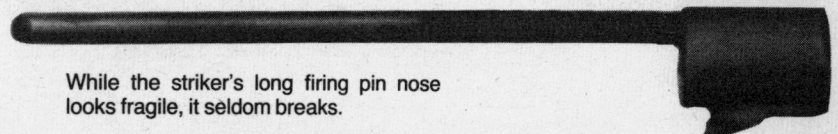

While the striker's long firing pin nose looks fragile, it seldom breaks.

The cartridge lifter, or carrier, assembly, which raises the rounds from magazine level to the feed lips, consists of two flat, irregularly-shaped leaves, a pivot sleeve, and a coil spring. An upper arm contacts a recess in the side of the bolt, and the movement of the bolt controls the arc of the carrier. The upper arm is under a good deal of repeated stress, and the

With the stock removed, the cartridge lifter (carrier) assembly can be seen at the bottom of the receiver. When replacement is necessary, it should be done by a professional.

carrier leaf from which it extends will occasionally fracture at the base of the arm. If both parts are saved, they can be rejoined. If not, a new leaf can be made, but the dimensions must be exact for proper operation. Replacement parts are usually available from the used-parts dealers, and some, but not all parts, are still available from Remington.

The receiver endpiece is threaded into the rear of the receiver, and there is an L-shaped spring detent plate below it that has a projection which locks into the endcap's serrated inner edge. The detent plate is screw-mounted to the bottom of the receiver, and these will occasionally break at the screw hole. This part is not absolutely essential, as the end piece can often be tightened sufficiently to prevent loosening. If not, and if a new detent plate is not available, a lower edge of the receiver can be staked into the cap serrations to hold it in place.

The Model 550 has been made in several slight variations during its period of manufacture, these being designated Model 550-A, Model 550-1, and so on. Many thousands were made between 1941 and 1971, and most of these are still in use. I recently discovered that its unique floating chamber allows it to function with the new CCI .22 Short CB cartridge, a very light load that is almost silent in the long barrel of the Model 550. Some of the starlings in my area are doubtless still wondering what happened to the next bird on the limb.

Threaded into the rear of the receiver is the receiver end piece—a projection on a spring detent plate below it locks into serrations on the edge of the cap to prevent loosening.

The detent plate for the receiver end piece is screw-mounted in the bottom of the receiver, and occasionally breaks at the screw hole.

Rossi "Overland" Double Hammer Shotgun

The Rossi company of Brazil has been recreating the well-liked guns of yesteryear for quite a while. About 15 years ago, they manufactured a nice little copy of the diminutive .22 "Ladies Model" Smith & Wesson revolver. Another of their well-received pieces has been a close copy of the Winchester Model 62 rifle. In the smoothbore department, a quick favorite was the double hammer shotgun. First offered only in 12 and 20 gauge, with a .410 recently added, the gun was named the "Overland," in remembrance of the man who once sat beside the stage driver, "riding shotgun."

With its twin hammers, their spurs angled slightly outward, the Rossi closely follows the pattern of the early double hammer guns. It is a true sidelock, having removable plates that hold the hammers, tumblers, sears, and their attendant springs. Inside the old-fashioned lockplates, though, the antique approach ends. The hammer spring is a heavy helical coil, and its guide head is a rebound cam that returns the hammer to safe position after its strike. The sear spring is equally modern, a round-wire torsion type. The bridle is a straight oblong bar secured by two screws, and if many years of hard use wear out its tumbler-pivot hole, it is easily replaced by a piece of strap steel cut to the right dimensions. Any parts eventually needed are, of course, available from the importer, Interarms.

The barrel latch system of this gun is particularly good, a sliding plate bearing on double lugs below the barrels. If years of shooting should slightly loosen the action, it can be tightened by careful peening of the rear face of the lugs, just below the step, to raise the locking surfaces. Since the Rossi guns I have examined close with a vault-like click, I doubt that this operation will be needed in the near future.

The forend latch is a push-button type, the button located at the forward

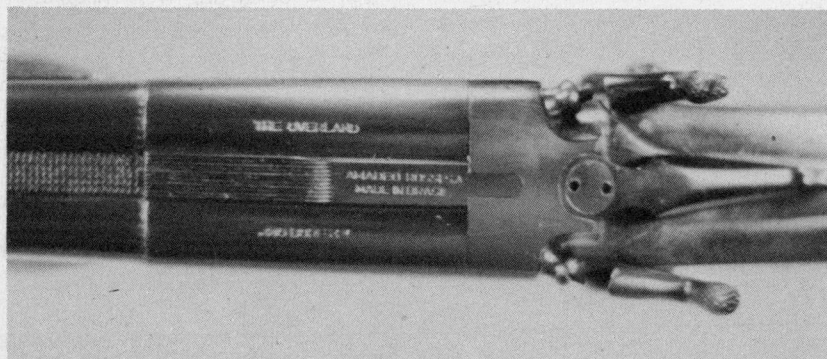

A top view of the breech area shows that Rossi closely followed the pattern of the early hammer doubles. Note the slightly canted hammers, and the good fitting at the breech.

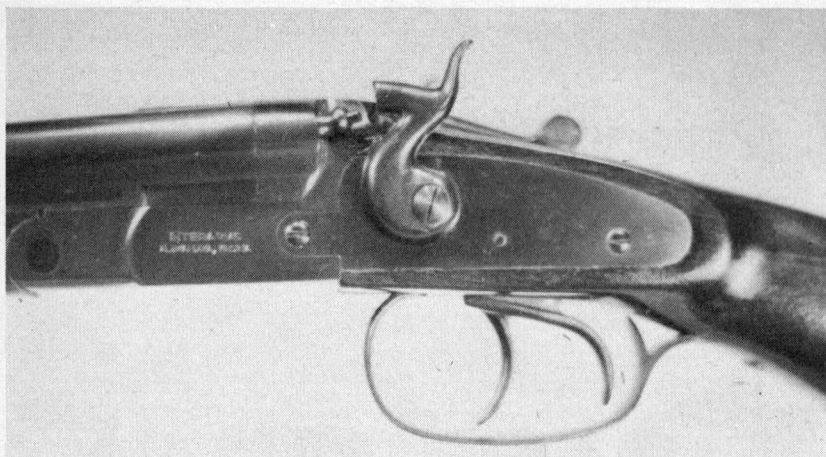

The Rossi is a true sidelock gun, complete with double triggers. Many guns of this variety have "false" side plates—not the Rossi.

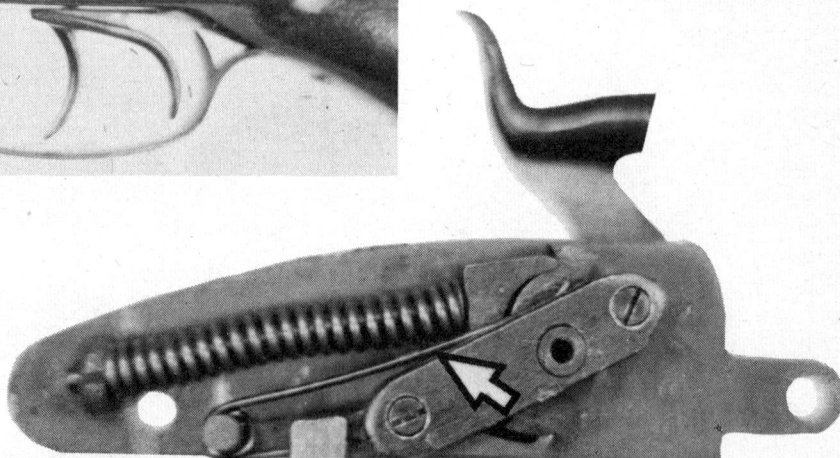

An inside view of the Rossi lock, showing the coil hammer spring and rebound cam. A round-wire torsion spring (arrow) powers the sear.

tip of the forend, and the latch lug below the barrels has an angled beak which should automatically tighten the latch as it wears. The firing pins are of simple cylindrical configuration, and would be easy to reproduce if a replacement were needed and original parts were not immediately available. The firing pins are retained by old-fashioned screw-in bushings, and these should be checked occasionally for tightness. This advice also applies to the large screws that retain the hammers on the tumbler

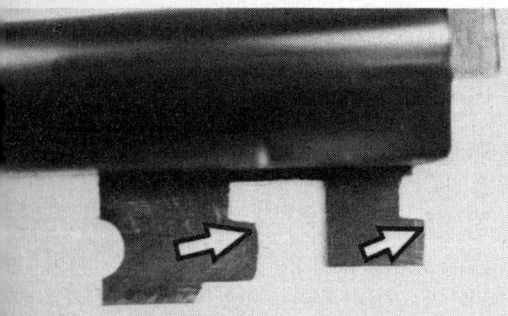

The Rossi has a very strong barrel latching system, with double lugs. After years of shooting the action may become loose; it can be tightened by peening at the points indicated by the arrows.

shafts. If these should need tightening, be sure to use a screwdriver that has a very wide, very thin blade. If one can't be found, a few seconds on a grindstone can convert an ordinary one into a perfect fit, and it's worth the trouble. These screws are prominently seen, and a screw slot deformed by use of the wrong tool is an abomination. If the aesthetics of these don't bother you, the loss of value will.

All of the springs in this gun are of round-wire type, in helical coil or torsion applications, and there is an ample allowance for age weakening. The ejector is a simple non-automatic type, cammed by a lever in the forend

base, and there is very little that can go wrong with it. Because of the inletting necessary to fit the side locks, any gun of this pattern has a little less strength in the wrist area of the stock than the box-lock with a stock-mounting through-bolt from the rear. In normal use, the strength of the Rossi stock is quite adequate.

The Rossi line of guns was formerly imported by the Garcia Corporation, a firm now entirely out of the gun business. Some of the very early Rossi guns were a little rough in fit and finish, but the more recent Interarms imports, including the Overland double, are very well made.

The forend latch (left) is a push-button type, and its latch lug on the barrels (right) has an angled beak that automatically tightens as it wears.

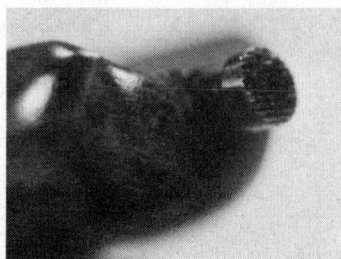

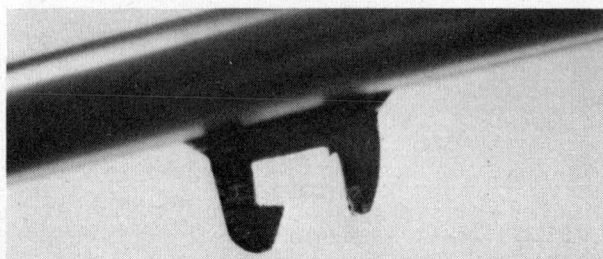

Ruger Model 77 Rifle

In 1968 Ruger introduced a centerfire rifle that had all of the best elements of the classic Mauser action, along with a number of original Ruger features. It was designated the Model 77, and it's perhaps not the best subject for the troubleshooting concept, because hardly anything ever goes wrong with it. Like most of the guns bearing the Ruger name, it was designed with ample

Of classic Mauser design, the extractor is tempered to be its own spring. Breakage is quite rare.

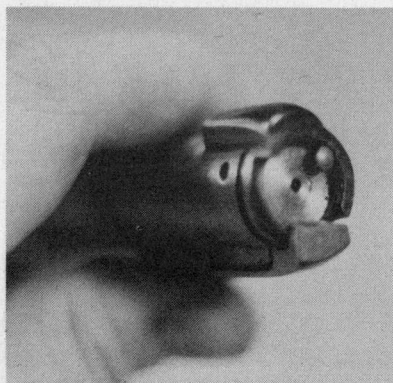

The bolt face has a half-shroud, and the ejector is a spring-and-plunger type. Note the large, well-shaped extractor beak.

allowances for wear and basic parts strength, and there are no weak spots at all.

Of Mauser pattern, the extractor is mounted outside the bolt body, and retained by the usual T-slot and ring arrangement. It is tempered to be its own spring; and, I suppose with a long passage of time one of these might weaken and require replacement or retempering, but this is looking far into the future. Both the extractor and its retaining ring seem to be slightly heavier than the original Mauser type, and I doubt that breakage will ever be

a problem. If it does happen, it will probably occur during amateur takedown or reassembly of the bolt. The bolt can be taken apart without much difficulty, but the extractor should not be removed except in cases of repair.

The bolt face has a half-shroud, and the ejector is a spring-and-plunger type that should be entirely trouble-free. If the ejection should become sleepy after many years of use, it will be a simple matter to install a stronger ejector spring. The ejector spring is made of helical coil, and the plunger is retained by a simple cross-pin. The

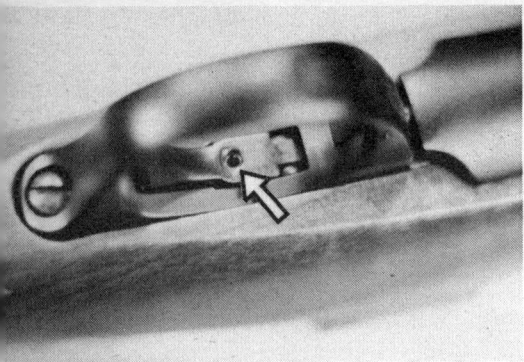

Weight of the trigger pull is adjustable by means of this Allen screw (arrow) without removal of the action from the stock.

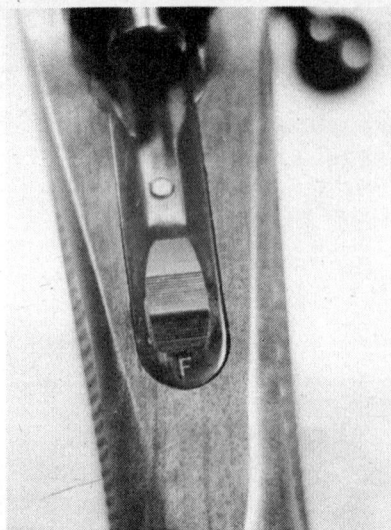

On the Ruger 77, the sliding safety is in the best possible location, on top of the upper tang. Here is it shown in the off-safe position.

Not only is the magazine floorplate latch conveniently located at the front of the trigger guard, it's easy to use due to its reasonable size.

pin should be checked for tightness and staked if necessary, because if it should loosen and creep out, it can catch on the edge of the bolt lug recess and jam the action.

Trigger pull weight can be adjusted without taking the action out of the stock, by means of an Allen screw in the top underside of the trigger. For adjustment of the trigger and sear engagement, and over-travel, the action must be removed. The pull adjustment is done by simply turning the Allen screw, but the other adjustments should be done by a gunsmith. The engagement screw, in particular, should not be disturbed by the amateur.

The Model 77 has a sliding safety in the best possible location, on the upper rear tang of the receiver. The off-safe motion is forward, and the internal engagement is very efficient. The magazine floorplate latch is conveniently located in the front of the trigger guard and is a modern version of the excellent latch that was first seen on the Japanese Arisaka (q.v.). While its design makes it easy to operate, it's unlikely the latch could be released accidentally.

With the ejector mounted in the bolt face, the bolt stop at the left rear of the receiver performs only that function, and the one on the Model 77 is perhaps the ultimate refinement of the original Mauser type. Instead of the complex blade spring of the German

original, the Ruger is powered by a coil spring and plunger, and its internal stop lug is well-shaped and strong.

Several variations of the Model 77 are available, including some which feature a round-topped receiver that is drilled and tapped for standard scope mounts. The basic Model 77, though, has integral bases cut into the top of the receiver, and special matching scope mount rings are supplied with each gun. This system is well-designed, having both vertical and horizontal locking recesses, and giving an extremely firm mount.

In case of eventual routine breakage, such as a firing pin point, all parts are readily available from gunsmiths and from the factory. The Model 77 is one of the *very* good ones.

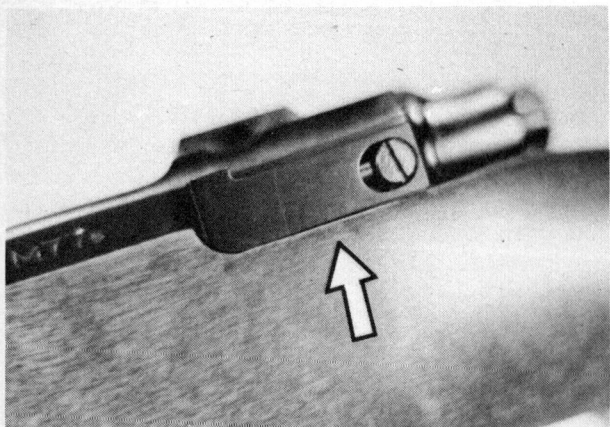

The bolt stop (arrow) is perhaps the ultimate refinement of the original Mauser type and is powered by a coil spring and plunger.

On the standard version of the Model 77 the scope mount bases are integral with the receiver and a set of rings comes with each gun. This close view of the rear mount base shows the vertical and horizontal locking recesses.

Ruger Mini-14 Rifle

In 1973, Bill Ruger came up with another of his excellent ideas. He took the basic pattern of the old military M-14 rifle, the ultimate refinement of the Garand, and scaled it down to carbine size and .223 chambering. In the process, he strengthened and simplified the action, adding several Ruger design features. The result was the Mini-14 rifle and, judging from the number that have been sold, its acceptance by the public has been enthusiastic. The gun has applications in the areas of varminting (with a scope added), general sport shooting, and also in police and guard use. Recently, the receiver was redesigned to include a push-button manual hold-open device, but so far this has been the only change in the basic configuration. The change in the receiver will mean that certain scope mounts will no longer fit, so when buying a mount, be sure which version of the Mini-14 you have.

The gun is gas-operated, and uses a fixed piston, the ported gas acting directly on a slide which rotates the bolt for unlocking. As with any gas system, the piston must be kept clean and dry, and no oil or other lubricant should ever be used in that area of the action. The bolt is very similar to the one used in the military rifle, but un-

like that gun, and its ancestor the Garand, the right rail of the receiver is not fragile. On the Mini-14 this area is heavier, and any problem from wear is unlikely.

Engagement of the sear and the sear

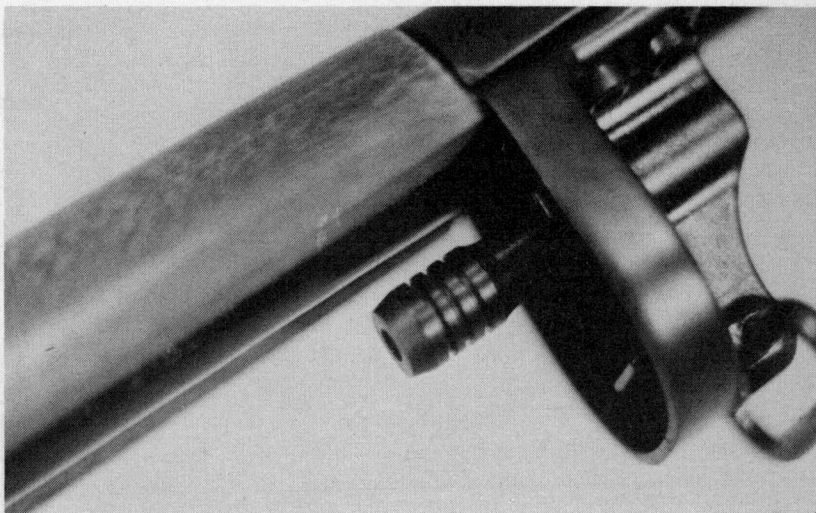

This is the fixed gas piston of the Mini-14. It should be kept clean and dry, and *never* lubricated.

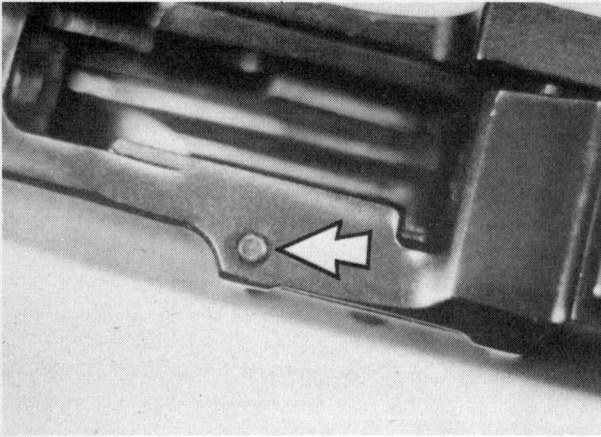

The receiver of the Mini-14 was recently redesigned to include a manual hold-open button (arrow).

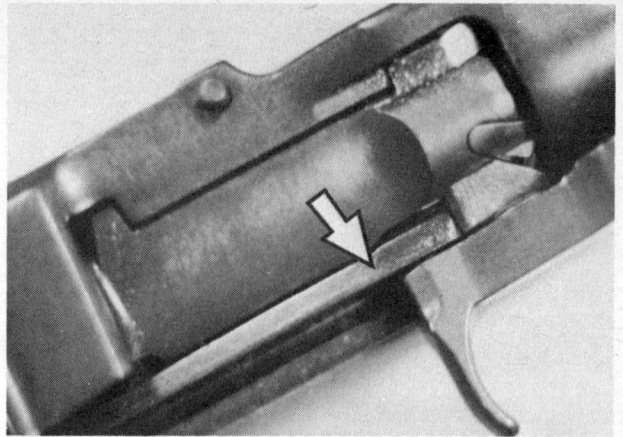

On the original military rifle the right rail of the receiver was a weak point—it's stronger on the Ruger.

step on the rear extension of the hammer is precisely engineered, and no alteration should be attempted by the amateur. If the trigger pull happens to be a bit stiff on a particular gun, this can be corrected, but it should be done by a professional. The cost will likely be less than the price of new replacements for a ruined sear and hammer.

Located at the left forward base of the trigger guard the safety catch is pushed toward the rear for the on-safe position. It is designed so that it must be in the on-safe mode to allow take-down—a good feature. The floor plate of the sturdy magazine is made of a very tough plastic, and breakage is very unlikely. This is probably the

Engagement of the sear and the sear step on the hammer (arrow) is precisely arranged and should not be altered by the amateur.

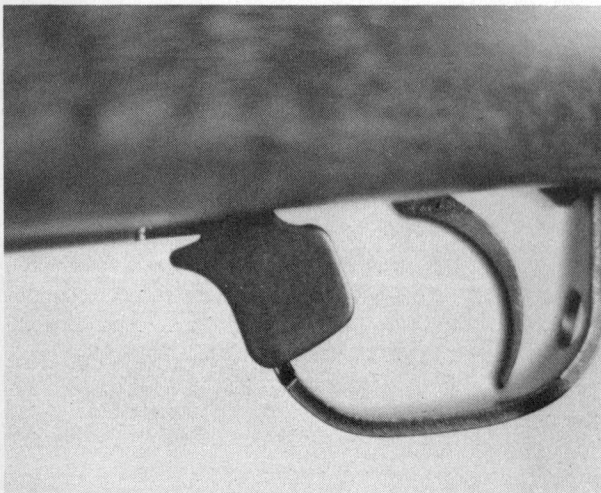

The safety catch is located at the forward base of the trigger guard and is pushed to the rear, as shown, to lock the firing mechanism.

When the Mini-14 is to be disassembled, the safety catch (arrow) is designed so that it must be in the on-safe position (shown) to allow takedown of the action.

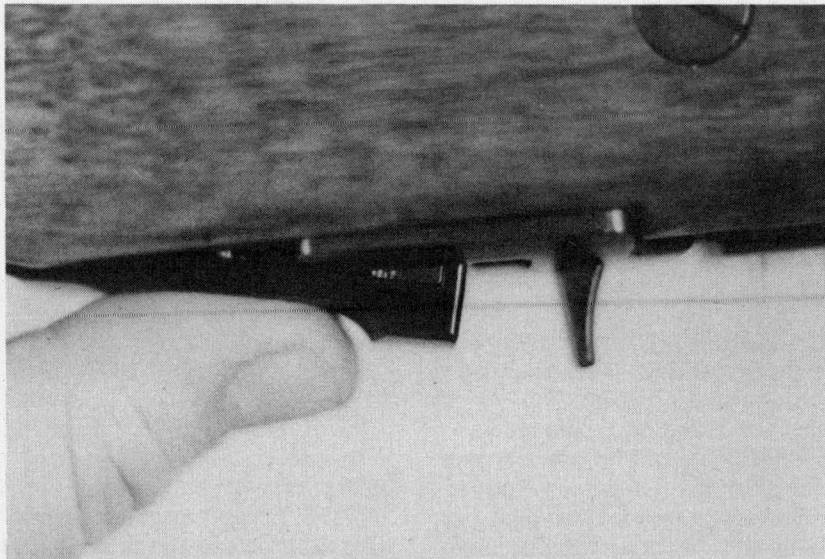

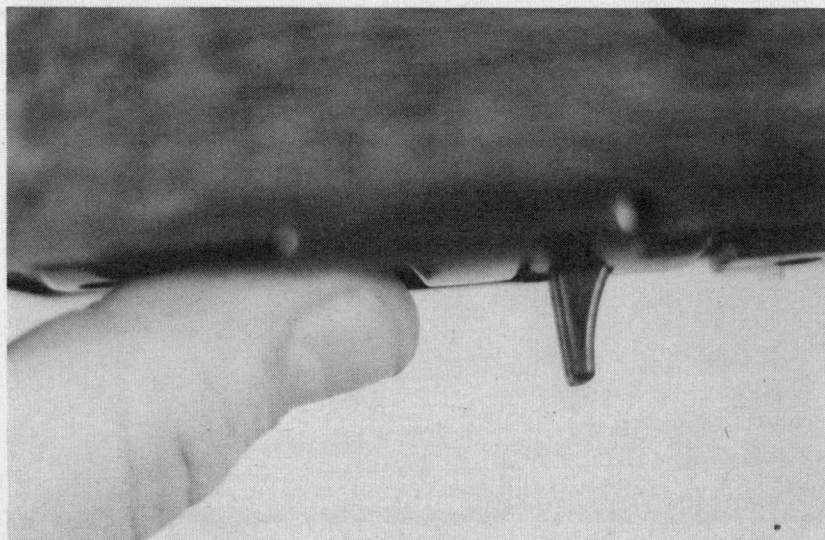

The floor plate of the magazine is made of a very tough plastic. Breakage is very unlikely.

same plastic used for the body of the magazine in the Ruger 10/22 rifle, and those are practically indestructible.

For those who are unfamiliar with the Mini-14, the method of inserting the magazine may seem puzzling at first. The magazine is first started at an angle, tilted toward the rear, its front face against the forward portion of the wide magazine recess. It is then pivoted upward and toward the rear until it locks in place. Although this might seem a bit awkward in description, it becomes a smooth and easy operation when you are used to it.

The Mini-14 seems to be entirely free of any chronic ailments. If there is some routine breakage in the future, such as an extractor or firing pin, parts are readily available from the manufacturer, and at most of the larger gun shops.

For those unfamiliar with the Mini-14, the method of inserting the magazine may seem a puzzling operation. It is started at the angle shown (top), then pivoted back and upward until it locks in place.

Ruger .44 Magnum Carbine

The .44 Magnum cartridge, with its rimmed case and intense obturation, is all wrong for a self-loading action. In spite of this, the expert design engineers at Ruger managed to solve all of the problems, and in 1961 they perfected a compact, reliable carbine in the .44 Magnum chambering. In the 18½-inch barrel of this gun, the cartridge develops around 1700 foot-seconds of velocity, and about 1500 foot-pounds of energy, demonstrating that a good deal of power is lost when this round is used in a handgun of normal barrel length.

The action of the Ruger carbine features a short-stroke gas-operated piston, a turning bolt, and an extra-sturdy extractor, elements which take care of the heavy obturation. The rimmed case is efficiently handled by a four-round tubular magazine, a well-designed cartridge stop, and a carefully-contoured carrier. In earlier writings about this gun, I ventured the opinion that the cartridge lifter latch should have been made of steel instead of alloy. The latch has an upper extension which is struck rather sharply by the cartridge heads as they are fed from the magazine. This pivots the latch, releasing the lifter to transport the round upward. I was worried that this repeated impact on a relatively narrow projection of an alloy part might in time cause deformation or breakage. Well, I should have trusted the Ruger engineers. Several years have passed, and I have not seen a single broken or deformed lifter latch. The only valid complaint I can make is that its black anodized finish tends to scratch in time, but this is strictly a matter of appearance.

In fact, the only mechanical quirk I have noted is one that is familiar to most shooters of .44 Magnum revolvers—a tendency toward loosening of

The arrow points to the lifter latch. This part is made of alloy, but no incidence of breakage has been observed.

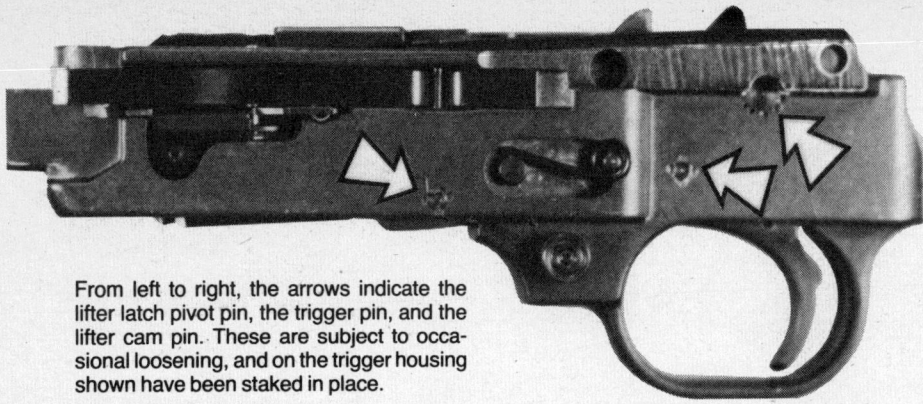

From left to right, the arrows indicate the lifter latch pivot pin, the trigger pin, and the lifter cam pin. These are subject to occasional loosening, and on the trigger housing shown have been staked in place.

certain parts because of the heavy recoil. In revolvers, the screws tend to back out, a condition often cured by a drop of Loctite. Later revolvers have nylon plugs set into the threads to prevent loosening. In the Ruger carbine, this same problem applies to several of the pivot pins. In the trigger housing, the ones usually affected are the lifter latch pivot pin, the trigger pin, and the lifter cam pin. The cure for this is simple and easy—just use a small punch to make stake marks beside each of the pins, on both sides of the housing.

The same condition affects the two pins in the bolt, and these are even more likely to loosen, because of its movement and impact. If the extractor pivot pin and the firing pin retaining pin do loosen, the results can be serious, as their protrusion can jam the action, and there is even the possibility of damage. The cure is the same, staking the pins firmly in place. When

this is done properly, they will not loosen again.

Internally, the carbine shows the beautiful engineering and attention to detail that is characteristic of all Ruger firearms. The receiver is made from a solid block of steel, a welcome change in today's ghastly trend to formed and welded sheet steel. The bolt, when locked in place for firing, has four surfaces bearing against strong shoulders inside the receiver—one at the front, three at the rear.

Takedown for extensive cleaning is a job best left to a competent gunsmith, preferably one who knows this gun. The Ruger carbine is not unnecessarily complicated, but there is an interdependence of certain parts which can make takedown and reassembly quite difficult for those who are not familiar with this mechanism.

One word of caution, regarding the rounds used in this tubular-magazine gun. Most shooters are aware that

cartridges with pointed (Spitzer-type) bullets should not be used in any tubular magazine, since the points of the bullets will rest against the primers of the other rounds, and there is the danger of recoil ignition. With the growing popularity of metallic silhouette shooting, full-metal-jacket bullets have been developed for the .44 Magnum cartridge for use in handguns. While these bullets are not exactly pointed, their noses are less flat and more solid than the standard .44 Magnum slug. The Hornady Company tested some of these new bullets in a Ruger carbine, and on the first shot, all of the cartridges in the magazine tube detonated, demolishing the carbine. No fault of the gun, of course, but be warned: *Never* use any cartridges having pointed, or semi-pointed FMJ bullets in a rifle with a tubular magazine, this one or any other.

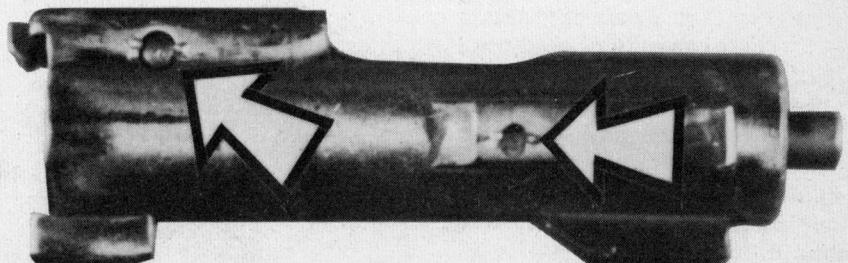

In this view of the bolt, the left arrow indicates the extractor pin, the right arrow the firing pin retaining pin. These are especially susceptible to recoil loosening unless staked in place as shown.

The Ruger 10/22 Carbine shown here has the "International" style stock—one of a limited number in this pattern.

Ruger Model 10/22 Carbine

In 1964, Ruger introduced a small-caliber companion to their .44 Magnum carbine, and in reference to its caliber and magazine capacity it was named the Model 10/22. As a subject for "troubleshooting," this one is going to be very difficult, since hardly anything ever goes wrong with it. The cartridge feed system is particularly outstanding, and a 10/22 that jams is almost unheard of. In fact, in the past 14 years, I've not encountered a single one. I can even recall one case in which the gun had a ruined sear as a result of amateur tampering, and this one was firing full auto. It would empty the magazine in a single burst before the finger could be removed from the trigger, but it didn't jam! Now that, friends, is an efficient feed system.

The key to this reliability is, of course, the design of the magazine. The 10/22 magazine is really sort of strange looking to those accustomed to the usual type. It is a squarish, box-like affair of plastic, containing a nylon rotor which brings the car-

tridges around in a circle, clockwise, to deliver them to the steel feed lips at the top. For the rimmed, lead-bulleted .22 Long Rifle round, I don't think a better system could be devised. In regard to the material used for the body of the magazine, I remember years ago seeing a Ruger representative demonstrate its strength by putting one on the floor and standing on it,

balancing on one foot. Can you imagine what would happen if you tried this with a magazine made of sheet steel? Apparently, that special Cekon plastic is really tough. Also, as previously noted, the part that takes the friction wear, the feed throat, is of hardened steel. *One note of caution:* At the front of the magazine there is a large screw. Check occasionally to

On the International model, the stock endpiece often fits the muzzle rather tightly. If this part is exceptionally tight you'll have to remove it in order to get the action free of the stock. *CAUTION:* While parts for the basic Ruger 10/22 Carbine are readily available (and will serve to repair the International style Carbine), external parts such as the International style stock and all its accompanying furniture are *competely* exhausted. Exercise care in disassembling the International—if something gives or breaks you're in for a trip to an *experienced* gunsmith.

see that it stays tight, but otherwise, don't fool with it. If you back it out, it will release the hexagon-headed end of the rotor shaft from its recess at the rear and let the tension off the rotor spring. Regulating this is a job for a gunsmith unless you are thoroughly familiar with the construction of the magazine.

The firing mechanism of the 10/22 is so beautifully engineered that I have repaired exactly *one* since the gun was introduced—the ruined sear mentioned earlier. I have, on occasion, reworked the sear and the sear step on the hammer to give these guns a lighter trigger pull, and this is a job that should not be attempted by the amateur. The parts have surfaces that are glass-hard, and the angle of contact is quite critical.

At the end of a day of shooting, when the gun is to be put away, many of us like to let down the hammer, rather than leaving the spring under tension. With most "hammerless" .22 rifles, it is necessary to put an empty cartridge case in the chamber when doing this, to protect the firing pin point and chamber edge. In the 10/22, you can just pull the bolt back slightly, about ½-inch, hold the trigger back, and ease the bolt forward. This will let the hammer down gently. Needless to say, this should never be done with a live round in the chamber, as the firing pin point would then be resting firmly against the rim of the cartridge, and any sharp jar could set it off.

During its time of production, the 10/22 has been made in four models, and two of these are no longer available. The International model, which had a full Mannlicher-style stock, was made in limited quantity only between 1965 and 1969. The early Sporter model has a screw-mounted stock, without barrel band and sling swivels, and the forend portion of the stock was deeply fluted on each side. The currently made version of the Sporter has a screw-mounted stock, without barrel band, and the pistol grip and forend area are checkered, the buttplate is straight and sling swivels are provided. The Standard model, which has been available during the entire production, has a barrel

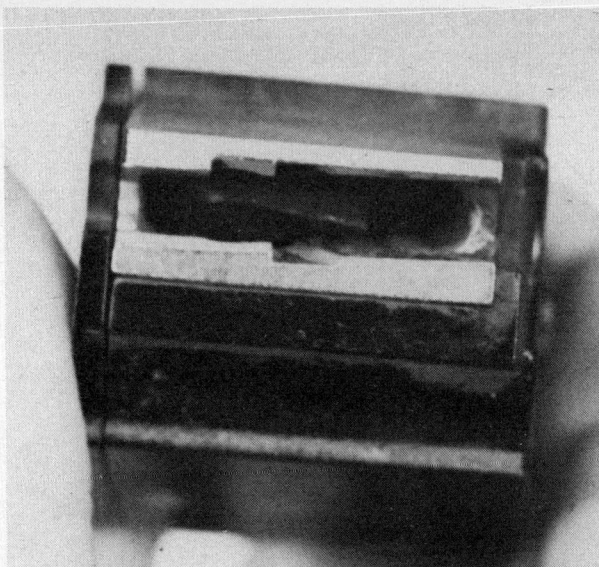

"Reliability" is one word which aptly describes the 10/22 series of Ruger autoloaders. The key to that reliability is the 10/22's rotary magazine. While the body is made of plastic the feed lips are of steel. The magazine works.

At the front of the magazine is a coin-slotted screw (arrow). It should be checked occasionally for tightness, but the amateur should resist any temptation to remove it.

band retaining the action in the stock, a carbine-style curved buttplate, and no sling swivels or stock checkering. All of these models are mechanically identical.

Sako Forester Rifle

These fine rifles were made by Oy Sako, A.B., of Riihimaki, Finland, and the original L-57 Forester model was first offered in 1958, chambered for the then-new Remington .244 and Winchester .243 cartridges. Two years later, in 1960, Sako redesigned and improved the L-57 action, the main change being a different bolt sleeve to function with a trigger mechanism that featured a built-in sliding safety. Another change was in the design of the extractor, from the old self-spring type to a separate coil spring and plunger, a good alteration. The revised gun was designated the Model L-579, but was still called the Forester. The Sako rifles were originally imported by Firearms International, and are currently offered by Stoeger. Their quality of materials and workmanship is excellent. The later L-579 is the gun covered here.

One of the reasons for the ultra-smoothness of the Sako action is a full-length guide rib on the bolt, pivot-ring mounted in the manner of the old-style Mauser extractor. As men-tioned above, the extractor is powered by a coil spring and plunger, and is mounted just above the right bolt lug. The bolt face recess fully encloses the head of the cartridge case, and the only cut in the lugs is a narrow slot in the left one for the receiver-mounted ejector. The latter part is located in the bolt stop, Mauser-style, and one piece serves both functions. No incidence of breakage has been seen.

At the rear center of the cocking piece is what appears to be a screw, but this is definitely not the case. This is actually the rear tip of the firing pin, which is threaded into the cocking piece, and the screw slot simply allows adjustment of the protrusion of the firing pin point from the breech face. This adjustment is not the sort of thing that should be attempted by the amateur, as a miscalculation can

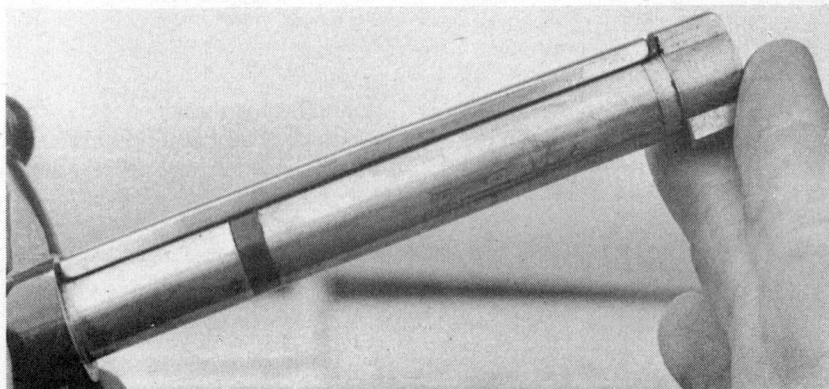

One of the reasons for the smoothness of the Sako action is a full-length pivoting guide rib on the bolt.

The extractor is powered by a coil spring and plunger. Note the guide rib behind the right bolt lug.

The bolt face is fully recessed for the cartridge head, and the left lug is slotted for the receiver-mounted ejector.

What appears to be a screw is actually the rear tip of the firing pin shaft. This should not be disturbed by the amateur.

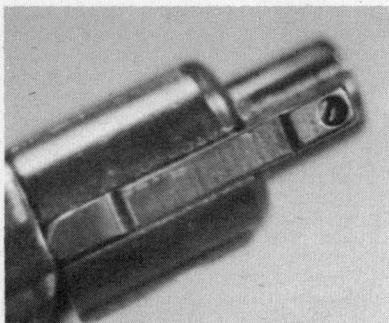

In this underside-view of the bolt endpiece, the small screw visible at far right locks the firing pin, which is threaded into the cocking piece. This screw must be kept tight.

Arrow at left indicates the lock nut and screw which tighten the trigger housing in place. The right arrow points to the screw and lock nut for adjusting the weight of the trigger pull. Just below this (not visible in the photo) is a screw for over-travel adjustment.

On the right side of the trigger housing, the safety mounting screws should be checked occasionally for tightness.

cause either misfiring or pierced primers. For the benefit of any gunsmiths who might be reading this, the proper protrusion is .055-inch, and you'll need one of those neat little gauges that Brownells, Inc. sells for around $10. On the underside of the cocking piece there is a small setscrew which locks the firing pin adjustment, and this one should be kept tight.

The trigger mechanism of this gun is fully adjustable for both weight of pull and over-travel, but the action must be removed from the stock for this. On examining the trigger housing, you will note a screw and lock nut at the extreme front, the nose of the screw bearing on the underside of the receiver. This one simply snugs the trigger housing in place, and has nothing to do with trigger adjustment. Above the trigger, on the front face of the housing, is a screw and lock nut that will adjust the weight of pull. Just below this, with no lock nut, is the screw which limits the over-travel. On the weight adjustment screw, the lock nut must be loosened before the screw can be turned, and the screw must be held in the desired position while tightening the lock nut. Unless you are very familiar with this sort of operation, it might be best to leave adjustment to a professional.

The safety is mounted on the right side of the housing by two screws having neutral shanks on which the safety slides, and these should be checked occasionally for tightness. If they should loosen, the inside of the stock will prevent their loss, but extreme looseness can affect the safety operation. Other screws that may occasionally loosen are the two which retain the housing for the bolt-stop/ejector, and the same advice applies. The Sako rifles are among the very good ones, and seldom require repair.

Available in a number of different models, this is the Savage Model 24 "Field Grade."

Savage Model 24 Combination Rifle/Shotgun

If I were asked to choose one gun for use in a survival situation, it would be the Savage Model 24. To be more specific, the Model 24-C, with the upper barrel in regular .22 rimfire, and the lower barrel in 20 gauge. An added feature of the 24-C is a storage compartment in the buttplate that holds one shotshell and 10, .22 cartridges. Even without this embellishment, the standard Model 24 is a versatile gun. The original version, introduced in 1950, had a regular .22 barrel over a .410 shotgun bore, and it has since been offered in a variety of combinations, including a top barrel chambered for the .22 Magnum round. These guns, in different chamberings and varying degrees of finish, are designated by various letters following the model number, 24-D, 24-E, and so on. The gun covered in the close-up photos here is the Model 24H-DL, chambered for .22 Long Rifle and 20 gauge.

The early models of these guns had an internal selector system, operated by a sliding button on the right side of the receiver. Over a period of years, several different selector designs were tried. The first had a plate which moved vertically between the hammer and the firing pin heads, a long arm extending downward from the right side of the plate to contact a screw-mounted button. These selectors were prone to breakage, usually occurring in the arm of the plate, and installation was not a simple matter. It is possible

Before the selector was located in the hammer, several different button-controlled internal selectors were used. They are *not* interchangeable.

to install replacement selectors in these older Model 24 guns without entirely stripping out the receiver, but it's a very tricky operation which would take a few pages of description—more space than we have here.

After several selectors of similar design were tried, the Savage designers arrived at the current pattern, a rocking lever mounted in a slot in the top of the hammer. With the lever tipped back, the hammer will fire the upper barrel. Tipped forward, the lower barrel will fire. The sides of the hammer are stamped with small guide arrows to show the position for each barrel. The lever is held in each of its positions by a spring-and-plunger detent inside the hammer. The selector lever and its pivot pin sustain quite a bit of impact when the hammer falls, but there seems to be an ample strength allowance for this; and, I haven't seen one of these broken as yet.

The ejector for the lower barrel is of sturdy design, and is retained by a large cross-pin in the underlug of the barrel. The .22 ejector is rather small,

While the retaining screw for the .22 ejector (arrow) should be kept tight, it shouldn't be over-tightened—you can easily break it.

The barrel selector is shown in position to fire the top barrel (upper photo) and the lower barrel (lower photo). Note the small guide arrows stamped into the hammer side.

its shaft offset into the upper left quadrant of the lower barrel, and it is retained by a small headless screw which crosses a recess in the ejector shaft. This screw should be kept snug, of course, but beware of over-tightening, as the slotted top of the screw is easily split if too much force is used.

On some of these guns, especially the early ones, the rear sight is mounted with a double dovetail fitting. This can be a problem when one

of these is broken or lost, as no other commercially-available sight will fit that double-dovetail arrangement, and you have to get an original Savage replacement. While on the subject of sights, it would be well to note that the upper barrel of later guns is grooved for a standard .22 scope mount, but shooters are cautioned to remove the scope before firing the shotgun barrel. Not only do the scopes tend to shift toward the rear during the increased recoil of the shotgun, but .22 scopes are not built to take this sort of jolt without the possibility of some internal damage. The front sight on early production guns is a small ramp-type, mounted with a single tiny screw, and these should be checked frequently for tightness. Here, again, be careful not to over-tighten, as the bite of this screw is rather shallow.

The trigger guard is retained by two screws, the rear one entering the lower tang from the outside, where it can easily be checked for looseness. When the front screw loosens, it's a real problem, since it enters the front base of the guard from *inside* the re-

ceiver, its head hidden below the hammer and barrel latch assembly. To avoid taking the gun completely apart, it's possible to tighten this screw if you can find a screwdriver that has a slim shaft and a wide blade. By cocking the hammer and inserting the screwdriver in front of it, you can look into the receiver from the front (with forend and barrels removed) and position the blade of the screwdriver in the slot of the screw.

Because of the heavy, snake-like spring that forms the forend latch, forend retention on these guns is very firm, and that's good. For some, who take these guns apart frequently for stowage in a camping pack, the forend latch may seem too stiff, and I have seen some cases in which the latch lug on the lower barrel had been filed to lighten the compression of the spring. I don't approve of softening this latch at all, but if it must be done, *don't* do it that way, as the thinning of the lug will eventually cause breakage. Instead, remove a very small amount of steel from the tip of the wavy blade spring of the latch.

Usually, the forend latch of the Model 24 is very tight. In an effort to make it work more easily, the owner of this gun has altered the lug on the barrel, making it dangerously weak.

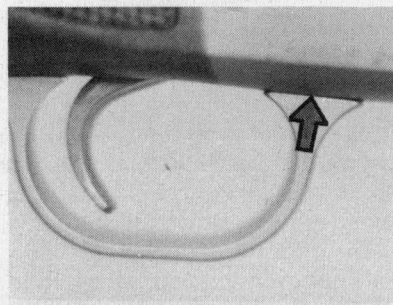

The front trigger guard screw enters the guard from inside the receiver, at the point indicated by the arrow. Tightening without complete disassembly is not easy.

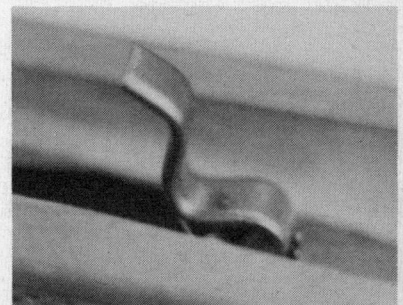

Normally, the snake-like forend latch spring is very stiff. Its action can be eased by removing a tiny amount of steel from its tip.

Savage Model 340 Rifle

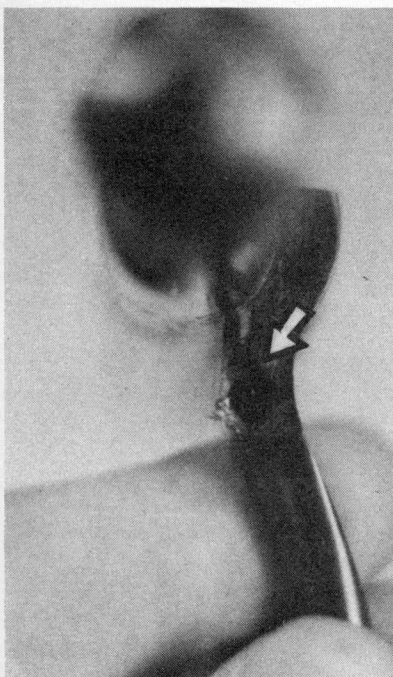

When the safety lever is in the on-safe position, a forward projection enters a hole (arrow) in the bolt handle, locking the bolt against opening. This feature is often removed.

For the hunter who wants a good varmint or deer gun at a moderate price, the Savage 340 is often the choice. Introduced in 1950, the gun is currently available in four chamberings: .22 Hornet, .222, .223 and .30-30. Its open-topped receiver is unusual in a modern bolt-action gun and requires the use of a side mount when installing a scope sight. Its detachable box magazine is a good feature, allowing the carrying of a spare magazine, the extra possibly containing a different load for altered ranges or conditions.

The barrel mounting system is also of unusual design, having a serrated lock nut just forward of the receiver to secure the barrel in place. I have known the nut to work loose on occasion, and anyone who shoots one of these rifles extensively should check this nut every so often for tightness. With the action removed from the stock, a brass or aluminum drift can be set into the grooves on the nut and tapped with a hammer to tighten it. This can be done on the underside grooves, normally hidden by the stock, to hide any marks that might be made on the nut.

The bolt is quite complicated, and if disassembly is required this should definitely be done by a gunsmith. The forward section of the bolt has a single lug, and the bolt handle base on the rear section acts as the second lug, locking into a deep cut in the side of the receiver. On top of the bolt is a long, flat part called the "gas shield" which also acts as a bolt guide, and this part is retained at each end by rings which surround the body of the bolt and by small cross-pins which hold the part to the rings. The forward cross-pin also retains a part called the gas shield key, and this pin tends to loosen after long use, its protruding end preventing full travel of the bolt. This pin should be checked occasionally and staked in place if necessary.

The very small extractor is both retained and powered by a flat spring—the spring held in place by a cross-pin. The system appears fragile, but the design is apparently better than it looks, as breakage is not frequent. In

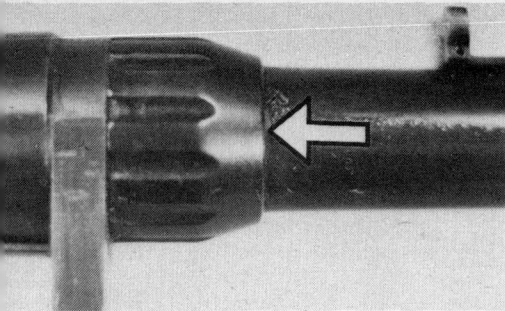

Tightness of the barrel lock nut (arrow) is very important.

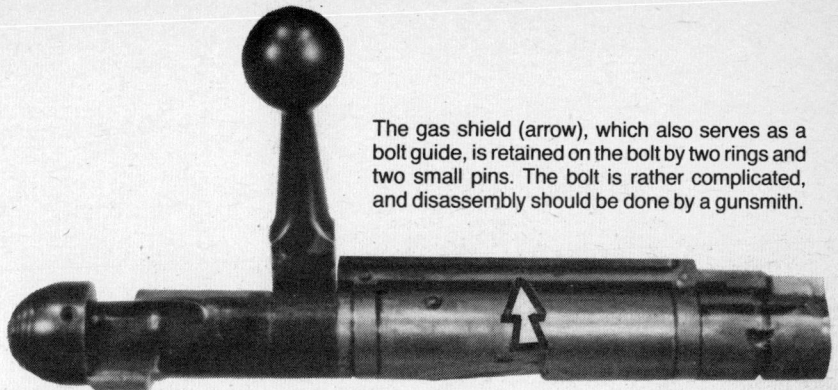

The gas shield (arrow), which also serves as a bolt guide, is retained on the bolt by two rings and two small pins. The bolt is rather complicated, and disassembly should be done by a gunsmith.

Arrow at upper left indicates the safety lever screw, which should be checked for tightness. Arrow at center points to the magazine catch, which is tempered to be its own spring. The arrow at far right indicates the magazine guide.

the case of temporary parts unavailability, the spring could easily be made, but parts are usually on hand at most gun shops.

The safety-lever is screw-mounted on the right side of the receiver. This screw also serves as the pivot for the lever, and it should be checked occasionally for tightness. Although it is insured against loss by being inside the stock when the gun is assembled, there is sufficient clearance for looseness to affect the operation of the safety.

The magazine catch is a formed piece of sheet steel, tempered to be its own spring, and occasional weakness is more common than breakage. It can usually be reformed to restore lost tension. Replacements are very inexpensive, but installation requires removal of the trigger housing. Forward of the magazine there is a heavier piece of formed steel which acts as a magazine guide, and this part is occasionally deformed by careless takedown and reassembly. It can usually be reshaped and is easily replaced if this is unsuccessful.

When the safety lever is in the on-safe position, there is a small forward

Arrow points to the small extractor which is both retained and powered by a flat spring. The system appears fragile, but breakage is not frequent.

projection which enters a hole in the base of the bolt handle, locking the bolt against opening. Many shooters prefer being able to operate the bolt with the rifle on-safe, and I have often removed the safety lever projection for this purpose—a simple operation.

With routine maintenance, the Model 340 can be a good, dependable rifle. Its only real disadvantage is that its firing system is relatively complicated, and any adjustments or extensive cleaning/takedown should be handled by a professional. A number of variations on the basic "340" theme are around as the gun has been produced for many, many years. Fortunately, the folks at Savage can handle your parts needs.

The bolt head has a single locking lug, the bolt handle base serving as a second lug. Note the fully recessed breech face, and the spring-plunger type ejector.

The Swiss Schmidt-Rubin rifle shown is the 1911 model.

Swiss Schmidt-Rubin Rifle

A roster of the world's military rifles having a straight-pull bolt-action would make for a very short list. The only ones made in any appreciable quantity, and actually used by the military in action, were the U.S. Navy Lee, the Canadian Ross, the Austrian Steyr, and the Swiss Schmidt-Rubin. The other three named disappeared rather quickly, but the Schmidt-Rubin lasted in the Swiss service for 68 years, being officially replaced by a modern assault-rifle in recent years—the Model 57 (SG510). Between 1889 and 1931 there were several model variations of the Schmidt-Rubin, but the one most familiar to the average gun person is the Model 1911, the one shown in the photos. The basic idea of the small-caliber high-velocity military rifle for the Swiss service was that of Colonel Edward Rubin, also the designer of the 7.5mm Swiss cartridge. The man who actually designed the rifle was Colonel Rudolf Schmidt.

In 1911 the Swiss service cartridge was increased in power, and the de-

Here we have the straight-pull bolt system of the Schmidt-Rubin, removed from the receiver. Taking this assembly apart is *not* recommended for the amateur.

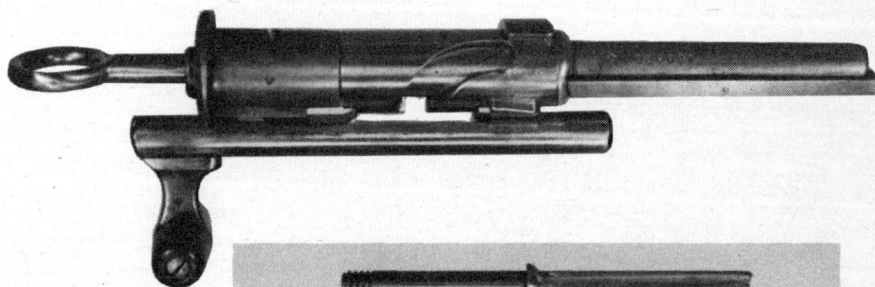

When the Schmidt-Rubin bolt assembly is stripped, you can see the care of manufacture that went into this rifle. Note the spiral track in the bolt sleeve and the locking lugs at its forward edge.

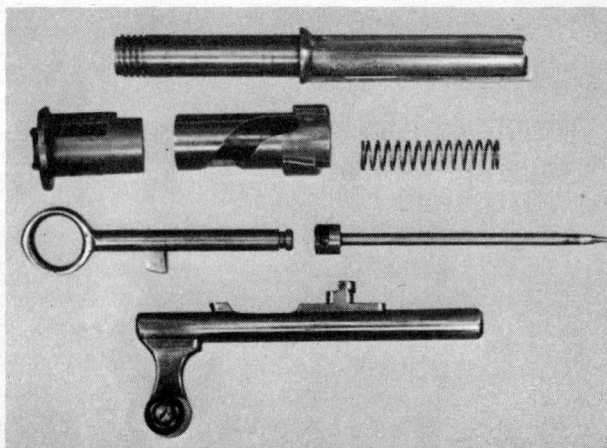

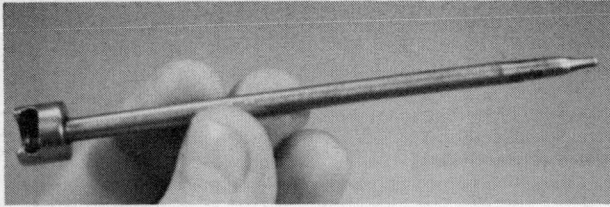
The Schmidt-Rubin's long, slim firing pin is not prone to breakage, and this is fortunate, as making a replacement would be difficult.

Tempered to be its own spring, the extractor is a heavy part, and it seldom breaks.

sign of the rifle's action was changed to give more strength for the hotter round. The bolt was shortened, and the locking lugs moved from the rear to the front of the bolt sleeve, giving a greater section of receiver behind the lug recesses for an added safety margin. The modern 7.5mm Swiss cartridge should not be fired in the older rifles and carbines. (Norma is the only company that presently loads this round commercially.) I know of several cases in which Schmidt-Rubin rifles and carbines have been altered to the .308 Winchester (7.62mm NATO) round, but I have had no actual experience with these guns, so can't comment on their safety and performance. The two cartridges are in the same power range, but their length is different, so the magazine would have to be altered for proper feeding.

The Schmidt-Rubin rifles are made with characteristic Swiss quality and precision, and many of the internal parts appear to have been electro-polished. The bolt system, when removed from the rifle, is a work of art, having the fine finish of surgical equipment. Bolt removal is easy, as there is a large latch lever on the right side of the action which is pushed downward for release. The amateur may safely remove the bolt assembly for cleaning, but be cautioned against taking the bolt system apart. For the non-professional, reassembly is likely to have some of the elements of a Chinese puzzle. For those who are unfamiliar with the gun, but have wondered about the large ring at the rear of the bolt, this serves two purposes: It allows manual cocking of the striker in case of a defective primer; and it also is the handle for the manual safety.

Parts breakage in the Schmidt-Rubin is practically zero. Most of the parts are of rather heavy construction, and the heat treatment was done by perfectionists. The firing pin is long and slim, and its striker attachment is of unusual design, so it's fortunate that they don't often break. The extractor is tempered to be its own spring, but here, again, the part is heavy and well designed. Parts for these guns are usually available from the various surplus dealers, if any should ever be needed.

The magazine catch is unusual, being mounted on the right side of the magazine. It's an effective system, and causes no problems. The Schmidt-Rubin is an extremely accurate rifle, and within the pressure limits of its original cartridge its straight-pull action is quite safe. Aside from practical use, I like to keep one around just to admire the quality and precision of its unique mechanism.

The magazine catch (arrow) is mounted on the magazine, and this system causes no problems.

Located on the right side of the receiver is the release lever for bolt removal (arrow). It's pushed downward to free the bolt.

This is the Sears Model 31 rifle, easily identified by the wood forend panels that extend back along each side of the receiver.

Sears Model 31 Rifle

This .22 semiautomatic rifle, made for Sears by High Standard, has one instantly recognizable feature—the narrow panels of wood that extend from the forend back along each side of the receiver. Several models in this series were made with different numerical designations, and some of these also had an ingenious retractable nylon sling with a spring-powered reel inside the buttstock.

The design of the Model 31 has several weak points, and each of these is the source of some difficulty at one time or another. For some unknown reason, the extractor cut at the edge of the chamber has a raised rib of steel at its center. To fit this, the extractor has a twin beak. These beaks are quite thin, and the lower one does most of the work. Breakage is not unusual, and neither Sears nor High Standard can supply any parts for this obsolete model. If you are unable to locate one among the used-parts dealers, it will be necessary to have your gunsmith add steel weld to the extractor beak, and recut it to shape, then reharden it.

When I do this, I make a solid, undivided beak and remove the dividing rib from the extractor recess, correcting the weakness.

The lifter, the part that brings the cartridges from magazine level up to feeding position, is a good, solid unit, but it is powered by a strangely-shaped little round-wire torsion-type spring that is mounted on a cross-pin in the bottom of the trigger housing. In operation, this spring is severely flexed, and its design is not suited to this. At this point, I will propose what might be called, "Wood's Law of Gun Parts," as follows: The more weird the design, the more likely it is to cause trouble. When this little monstrosity breaks—and it will, eventually—the installation of a new replace-

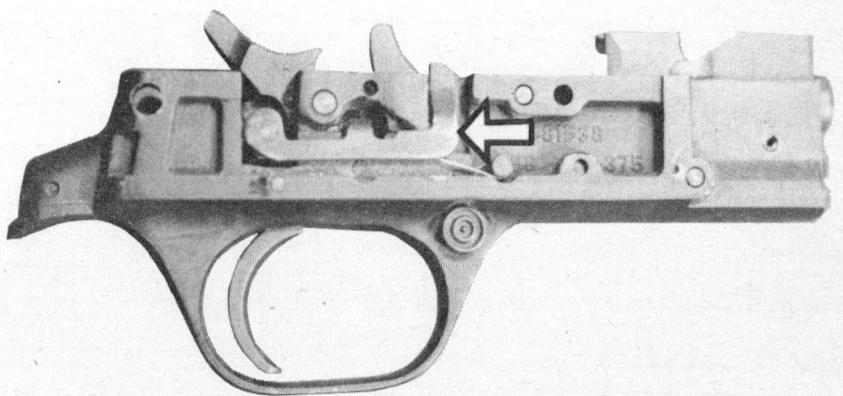

In this view of the right side of the trigger group, the arrow points to the trigger bar/disconnector, a frequent source of trouble.

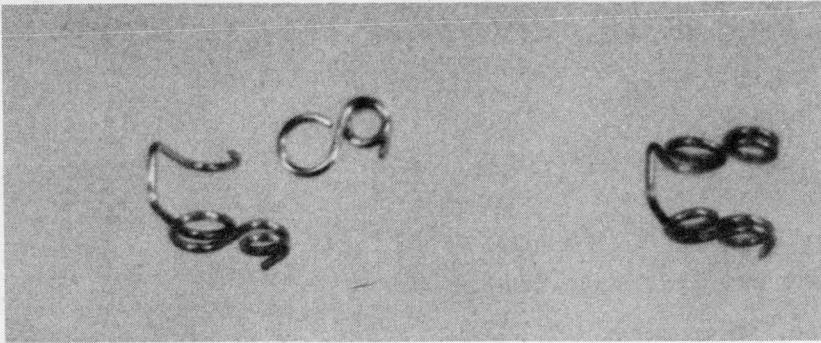

A broken cartridge lifter (carrier) spring is to the left while an intact one is to the right. Both of these springs are of original pattern—breakage is not uncommon.

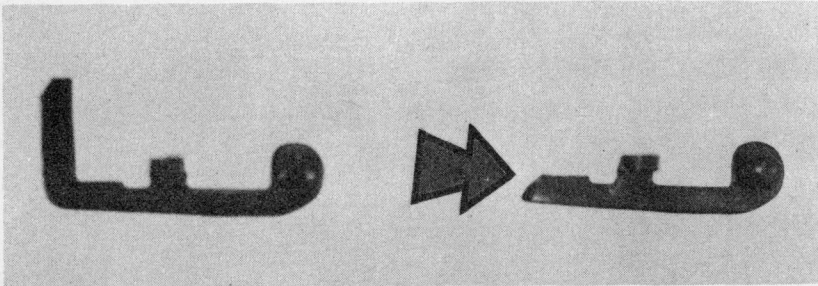

The trigger bar/disconnector at left is intact, while the one on the right is broken (arrow) at the usual place.

An intact extractor is on the left—the arrow indicates the portion of the extractor beak that usually breaks (the lower one when the part is installed in the gun).

oted on the trigger at lower rear. Although the upper end of the arm is beveled, the system has poor mechanical advantage, and the arm breaks with some frequency. When replacements were available from Sears, installing a new disconnector took all of 5 minutes and the part was not expensive. Now, you have a real problem, as this part is not of simple shape and is not easily made. I usually square off the broken arm and make a separate vertically-sliding part that will duplicate its function, utilizing the remainder of the original disconnector.

The cocking handle for the bolt is of excellent design. Unfortunately, it was made of alloy and usually breaks at the point where the handle enters the receiver. Making a replacement out of steel, by using the broken handle as a pattern, is not too difficult for the knowledgeable amateur, and this would be a permanent repair. Aside from the things mentioned above, the Model 31 is not a bad design.

The Sears Model 31 has a cocking handle that's constructed of alloy—they break. The one on the right is broken (arrow) in the usual place while the one to the left is a new replacement.

ment, if you can find one, is best left to your gunsmith. I don't even try to find the original type—I replace it with a shop-made spring that has more loop and less severe flexing.

The disconnector lies in a recess on the right side of the trigger housing and extends forward from the top of the trigger, mounted there by a short integral cross-pin. At its center, there is a side projection that contacts the sear, and there is a vertical arm at its forward end that is pushed down by the recoiling bolt to disengage the unit from the sear. The arm is struck a horizontal blow by the bolt and is piv-

Sears Model 20 Shotgun

This is another of the guns made for Sears by the High Standard company, and it's basically a good slide-action shotgun. The trigger group mechanism is particularly well-engineered, and the bolt locking system shows the same good elements in design. There are some slight differences between the early Model 20 guns and those of later manufacture, and each of the two variations has a particular trouble spot.

As in most modern slide-action shotguns, the locking of the bolt is activated by a sliding plate below the breech block that is connected to the slide bar. In most guns, this connection is direct, the action slide bar engaging a recess on the plate. On the early Model 20, the L-shaped end of the bar engages a separate block set into the plate. This block is held in place by a small plunger powered by a coil spring, the end of the plunger contacting a depression in the block. For a part which is under considerable stress and subject to countless jolts as the action is cycled, this arrangement

Arrow indicates one of the two opposing retaining lugs found on the forward portion of the trigger group. On the later alloy units, these tend to break off.

(Top) Shop-made replacement parts are not unfamiliar to the experienced gunsmith. The arrow points to one of these shop-made gems—in this case, the slide connector which fits into the bolt locking plate. In the photo above you can see this part and its relationship to both the bolt and the bolt locking plate when fully assembled in the gun—as viewed through the loading port.

is far from adequate. Eventually, the block will simply fall out the bottom opening of the receiver, to disappear into the tall grass. Neither Sears nor High Standard has this part, and making a replacement from heavy steel stock is a complicated and expensive endeavor. Since removal of the connector block is not necessary during takedown for cleaning or other repair, I can't see any reason for its existence, and I wonder why it was in the original design. In later Model 20 guns, it was eliminated, the bar making direct contact with the plate.

When I make a replacement for the connector block, I drill a deep hole in its rear face and reduce the end of the plunger to enter the hole. With this arrangement, the replacement won't fall out. In fact, it can be removed only with difficulty.

The trigger group is held in the receiver by a large cross-pin at the rear, and by a small projection on each side at the front, these front lugs fitting into recesses inside the lower edge of the receiver. On the early guns, which had trigger groups of steel, this was a good mounting system and caused no trouble. Later, however, the trigger housing material was changed to alloy with no increase in the size of the frontal retaining lugs. As might be expected, the alloy lugs break with some frequency and would require replacement of the entire trigger housing, except for one fact: There aren't any available.

I repair this situation by drilling slightly angled holes in the front corners of the housing and installing steel pins that protrude forward and slightly outward, facing them off to match the recesses in the receiver. This will solve the problem for a good long while, but the pins may eventually loosen in the alloy, so they should be checked during future disassembly.

The Model 20 seems to have no other chronic ailments, and once these two are corrected, the gun will give long and dependable service.

Sears Model 66 Shotgun

This gun was made for Sears, Roebuck & Company a few years ago by the High Standard factory and was the lowest-priced of the gas-operated shotguns of that time. It also had two advantages over the rest of them. The gas piston is hollow, surrounding the magazine tube, and the tube will accommodate five rounds. Added to this is the gas system, which automatically adjusts to various loadings. Sears called it the "Autojuster," and it accomplished its automatic adjustment by a group of eight flat, circular springs and three spacer rings, their tension controlled by a slotted circular nut on the forward end of the magazine tube. As originally installed, the system requires no adjustment. Often, though, the amateur will fool around with it, and the nut will be either backed off too far or cinched down too tightly. Since this has a direct effect on the amount of gas impelling the piston, malfunctions will be likely. Restoring this system to proper balance is a job for your gunsmith, but with a large number of assorted loads and some patience, you can do it yourself.

The gas piston and the parts near it should never be oiled, as this will soon cause a buildup of scale and residue that will retard movement of the piston. The piston and its attendant parts should be cleaned often and kept dry. In any gas-operated gun, a good rule to follow is to avoid using any oil from the front of the receiver to the end of the forend.

The Model 66 has one chronic ailment—breakage of the cocking handle. The handle is a rather small part, projecting from the right side of the receiver. It is an integral part of a long, narrow connecting bar which links the gas piston to the bolt. The bar, and the handle, are drawn to a

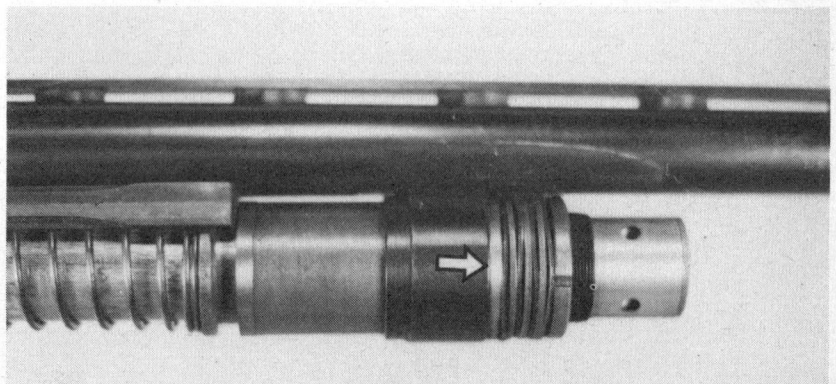

The Sears Model 66 allows the shooter to adjust his gun for high or low base shotshells. The arrow points to the "Autojuster" gas system. From the left: the gas ring, springs and spacers, and adjustment nut.

Arrow indicates the location of the bolt cocking handle, broken off on the gun shown. The handle is an integral part of the bar which connects the piston to the locking plate.

The cocking handle on this Model 66 is unbroken. Be assured it's a rare sight!

hard temper, and it may be that the breakage is due to repeated impact against the forend base as the action is cycled. The original instructions supplied with the gun warn against allowing the bolt to slam shut on an empty chamber. When the bolt is loading a round, the impact is slightly lessened by the feeding process. So, when closing on an empty chamber, it is probably best to ease the bolt closed by hand, rather than letting it slam by just pushing the release button.

When the cocking handle on this gun breaks, you have a real problem. The gun has been discontinued for some time, and neither Sears nor High Standard can supply the bar with its attached handle. It may be possible to find one among the used-parts dealers, but if not, it will be necessary to improvise. I have repaired these by drilling and screw-mounting a serviceable knob in that location. It is also possible to weld on a replacement, but this will affect the heat treatment of the bar, and may lead to future troubles.

Aside from the two problems mentioned, the Model 66 was a good gun, and the bolt locking system and the trigger group are excellent examples of good engineering. If the cocking handle quirk can be solved, this gun will go on working indefinitely.

Smith & Wesson Model 1000 Shotgun

A large number of Smith & Wesson Model 1000 shotguns have been sold in my area since 1973, and so far, I have not repaired a single one. Although the company is most noted for fine handguns, this gas-operated shotgun is one of the best of its type on the market. The gas system is particularly outstanding, and its design is unlike any of the others, with a connector ring riding outside the tube, and a cross-pin mating it to an internal piston. At the end of the tube is a heavy valve which compensates for the varying pressures of different loads, and the main parts of this system are plated with hard chrome. This,

coupled with other features of the design, results in a gas system that is truly self-cleaning. I personally know of one Model 1000 that has been fired more than 1,800 times and shows no extensive buildup of residue in the gas system. It has, by the way, never jammed, even though a number of the rounds were handloads.

The trigger housing and its components are well-designed, and no chronic ailments have developed thus far. When the trigger group is out of the gun, take care not to pull the trigger without gently lowering the hammer, as the hammer has no stop other than the breech block when the unit is

in the gun. Outside the gun it can pivot forward to such an extent that the hammer spring and its sleeve are released. If this occurs, they will not travel far, but if it happens outdoors, a short distance might be enough to cause loss of the parts.

In the entire design the only point that might possibly cause a future problem would be the carrier stop, a projection at the front of the trigger housing. The housing is alloy, and the carrier gives the projection a tap each time the action cycles, so there is a slight chance of breakage in this area after many years of use. On the other hand, the stop is quite heavy, and there seems to be an ample allowance for strength. On this question, time will tell. The ones that I have examined show no signs of strain at this point.

Although made of formed steel, the shell stop has ample strength and wear allowance and is activated by a beveled surface on the right action bar. The bevel is also well-proportioned, to allow for eventual wear. The oper-

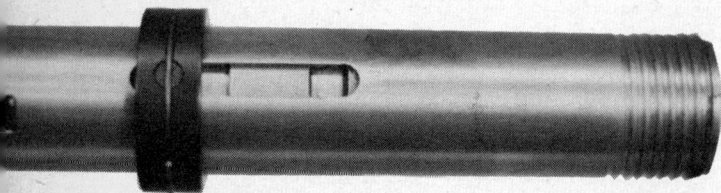

Plated with hard chrome, the gas system of the Model 1000 rarely needs cleaning.

This Model 1000 has been fired extensively without cleaning the gas system. Note the small amount of residue in the grooves of this component, the gas valve.

The carrier stop (arrow) is an integral part of the alloy trigger housing. There seems to be an ample allowance for strength.

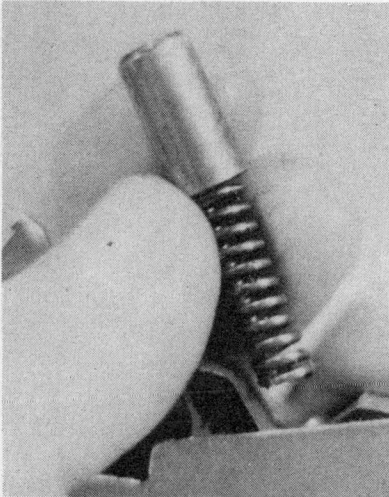

When the trigger group is out of the gun, take care not to pull the trigger without gently lowering the hammer or the hammer spring and sleeve can fly out and become lost.

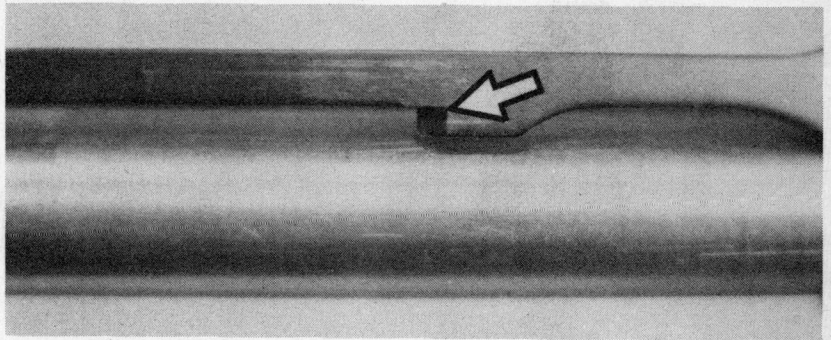

A bevelled surface on the right action bar activates the shell stop. There is good allowance for eventual wear.

ating handle is retained by a spring-powered plunger which contacts a depression in the rear edge of the handle, and in the guns I have seen, the retention is tight, requiring a determined pull to remove it. It is not likely to fly out in normal operation.

The ejector is a solid bar of steel, slot-mounted inside the left wall of the receiver. Its design appears to be very strong, and breakage is unlikely. As you may have gathered by now, the Smith & Wesson Model 1000 is one of the very good ones.

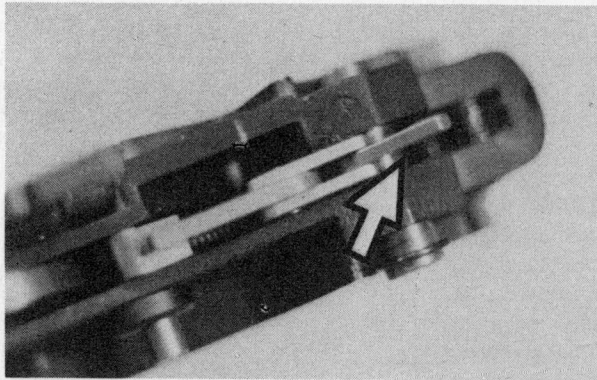

The "auto safety" (arrow) serves the same function as a disconnector. It is not subject to great stress and should not be susceptible to damage.

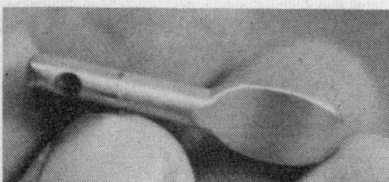

The ejector (arrow) is slot-mounted in the left inner wall of the receiver. Breakage is not likely.

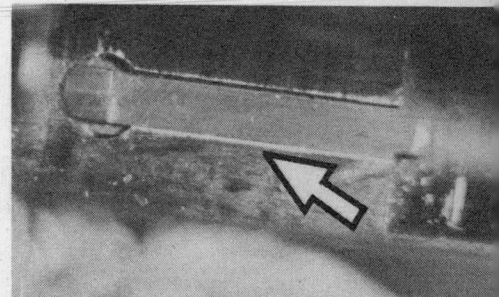

The operating handle is retained by a spring powered plunger which contacts a depression in the rear edge of the handle. In the guns examined, retention has been tight.

"Snake-Charmer" .410 Shotgun

In 1977, H. Koon, Incorporated, of Dallas, Texas, introduced a small .410 shotgun called the "Snake-Charmer," the name indicating one of its intended uses—an anti-snake device for those whose outdoor activities take them into areas where they are likely to encounter poisonous reptiles. With the idea that much of its use will be around water, the working parts of the gun are all of stainless steel, and the forend and small buttstock are of tough plastic. The gun is sort of a cross between a handgun and a shoulder arm, but it has the necessary overall length and barrel length to make it meet the legal specifications. In actual use, it functions as a handgun, the diminutive "buttstock" serving to steady it against the arm. In keeping with its close-range capabilities, there is no front sight, as none is needed.

Although it is intended to be a working gun, not a pretty one, the matte finish is attractive and nonreflective, and the fitting of all parts is very well done. Almost too well

done, in one instance. On my gun, the trigger pull is beautifully crisp, the let-off just under 3 pounds. On a shotgun of this type, I think it should be a bit heavier for safety reasons. This would be easy to correct, though. Also, the manufacturer figured the gun should have an external hammer so it wouldn't be cocked unless immediate

use were intended—it's a smart safety feature.

The springs for the hammer, trigger, ejector and barrel latch are all round-wire types, either torsion or helical coil, and breakage or weakening should be extremely rare. The barrel latch is of particularly good design, allowing for future wear in the lockup

The Snake-Charmer's ejector is a simple, spring-loaded part, without automatic trip. It is large and heavy and not likely to break.

system. The ejector is a massive part, and I can't see any way that it could break in normal usage. It is not a trip-type automatic ejector, it just eases the fired shell out to be removed with the fingers. Like the stock and forend, the trigger guard is of plastic. I am generally opposed to this material for a guard, but this one seems heavy enough to resist cracking. The forend, too, is of sturdy construction and is not likely to break under any normal use.

The buttstock is also well-made, but its margin of strength is not as great as the other plastic parts. It consists of two pieces, held together by three screws, and these thread directly into posts on the opposite inside wall of the stock. Over-tightening should be strictly avoided, and the buttstock should be treated with some care, as repeated impact could break the screw posts. In normal use, with the mild recoil of the .410 shell, there should be no problems. Although the stock material is entirely unaffected by water or dampness, it is not impervious to heat. If the gun were left on the deck of a boat in the blazing sun for several days, the plastic would likely begin to heat-warp. Bear in mind, though, that this sort of treatment would probably have a detrimental effect on a wood stock, as well.

In the butt of the stock is a sliding cover which is moved upward to expose four holes that are just the right size for storage of spare .410 shells. Because of the design of the pistol grip portion of the stock, the top hole will accommodate a 3-inch shell, while the lower three holes will take only the 2½-inch version. Although the stock material is impervious to water, this compartment is not watertight. The sliding lid has a raised nub on its undersurface and is retained in the stock only by friction. Also, there is no stop on the lid—when it is slid upward, it comes completely off, so keeping a couple of extra lids on hand would be a good idea.

The stock was not, of course, intended to be used on the shoulder. It serves as a convenient handle and also helps the gun to attain its legal length. In this regard, it is inevitable that someone will think of lopping it off

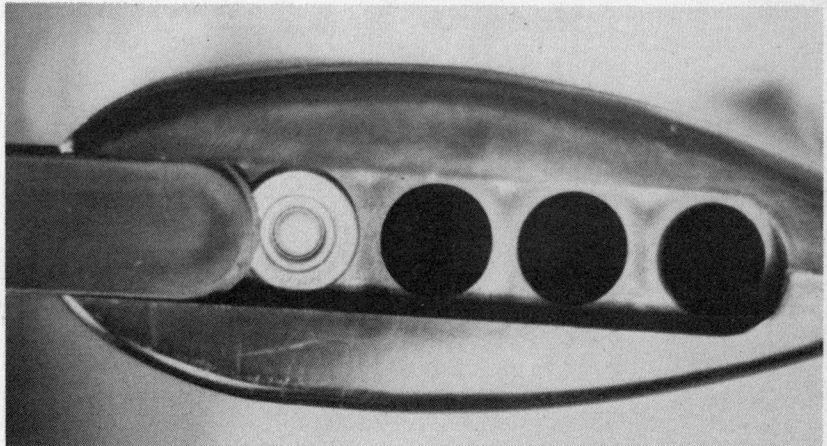

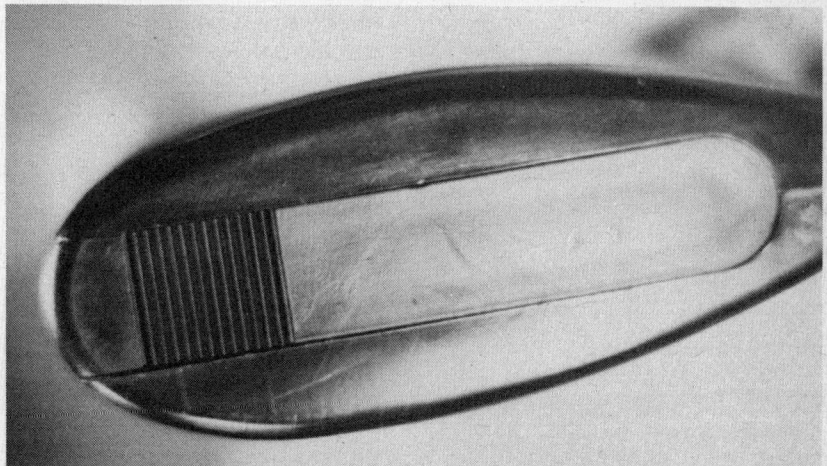

Opening the sliding trap in the buttstock (top) gives access to a storage compartment for four .410 shells. (Center) The hole at far left will accommodate a 3-inch shell, but the following three will hold only the 2½-inch version. (Below) While the sliding trap works nicely, it's locked only by a plastic nub—something a bit more positive is needed to prevent loss.

just behind the pistol grip, to make the gun even handier. *Don't,* or you are likely to become acquainted with an officer of the BATF, and I doubt that it would be a pleasant encounter.

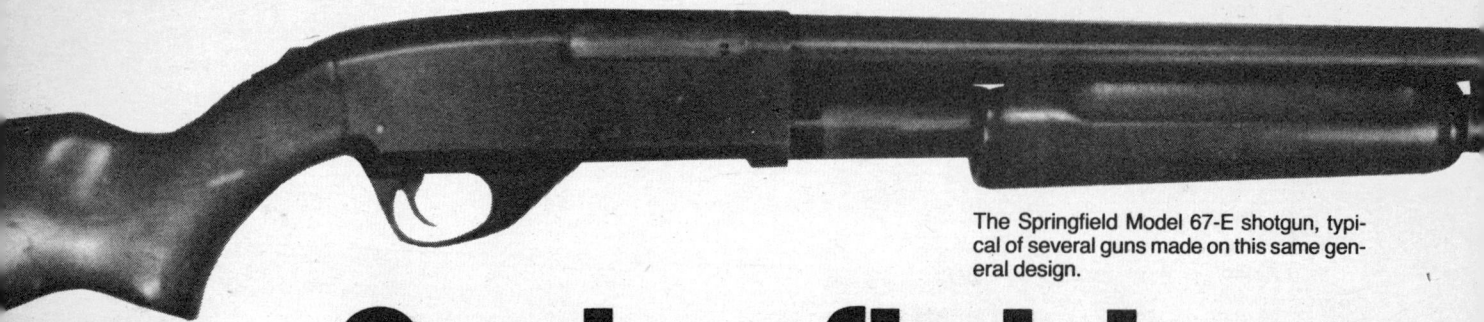

The Springfield Model 67-E shotgun, typical of several guns made on this same general design.

Springfield Model 67 Shotgun

Several guns in the Savage line have been made on this general pattern, a design which made its first appearance around 1954. The Stevens Model 77 and the Savage Model 30 are almost identical in mechanical aspects, and all three guns have feature variations that are designated by suffix letters. The gun shown in our photos, for example, is a Model 67-E.

One of the inherent weaknesses of this design is the mounting of the butt-stock which is attached by a through-bolt that threads into the rear of the trigger group. Made of alloy, the trigger group is retained in the receiver by a cross-screw at the rear and a cross-pin at the front. This arrangement is adequate in regard to recoil force. However, if the stock receives extreme pressure or a heavy blow from the top, the rear tail of the trigger group can be bent or broken, and this will require replacement of the entire group housing. Replacement parts are available for several of the guns in this series, but some of the earlier ones are obsolete, and no parts for these are available.

In the trigger group itself, the slide latch is released, when the gun is fired, by a stud on the left side of the hammer which contacts the hook-shaped end of a round-wire spring mounted on the latch. The shape of the hook, and its relative angle, are very important to the trigger group's proper operation. If the hook becomes deformed, the latch will fail to release when the hammer falls, and the latch must be manually operated before the action can be opened. Replacement springs are available, but the installation and regulation of this part is not a job for the amateur. It is often possible to reshape a deformed spring to restore its function, but this, too, is best done by a gunsmith.

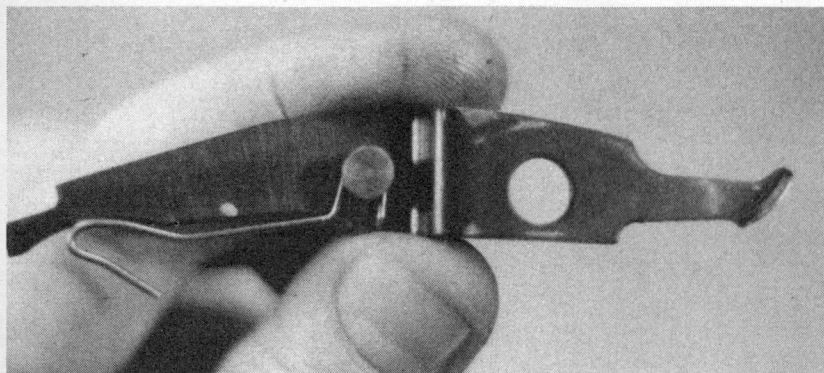

Critical to perfect functioning is the precise shape of the round-wire type release spring mounted on the slide latch. The spring is easily deformed through wear and/or amateur tampering.

The slide latch pivots on a large stud which is integral with the trigger housing, and since the latch is steel and the housing alloy, the stud tends to wear in time. If the wear is severe enough, it can affect the proper engagement and disengagement of the latch. Rather than replacing the entire housing when this occurs, I usually face off the worn pivot stud and drill the housing to take a replacement made of steel, a permanent correction for this problem. The slide latch elevation spring, a round-wire type, is mounted in a small hole on the left side of the housing and bears on the same boss on the latch which retains the release spring. The elevation spring rarely breaks or weakens, but when the latch is removed during complete takedown, nothing retains the little spring, and it is easily lost. Replacements are available, and this spring is also easy to make, as it does not require complicated shaping.

Mounted inside the left wall of the receiver, the ejector is a small rectangular box of steel, which contains a spring-powered plunger that cushions the impact of the ejector against the extracted shell, as the shell is being kicked out of the ejection port. The mounting of this unit is by a single screw which enters from outside the receiver on the left side. The screw will occasionally loosen from repeated impact and should be checked for tightness. If it comes completely loose, the screw will be lost, and the ejector will either drop out the bottom of the receiver or fall into the action, causing a jam. Here again, the ejector unit is available, and there is some interchange possible between the various guns in the series.

The part that is perhaps the most frequently lost through normal use is the shell stop, an irregularly-shaped piece of flat steel on the lower right, inside the receiver. It is retained by a screw from the outside which threads into a slotted nut on the inside, and all three parts have been known to disappear into the tall grass. These parts are on hand at most gun shops, and any good gunsmith will know to use a special tool to immobilize the nut while setting the mounting screw very tight. This is another one that should

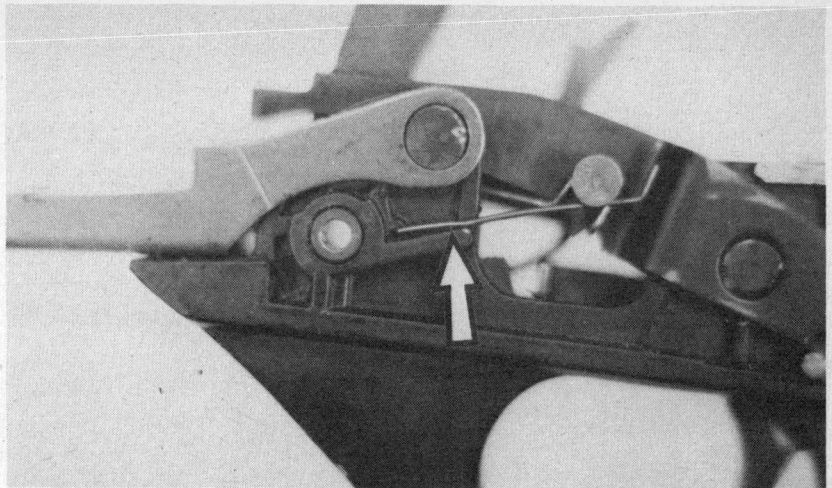

When the slide latch is removed, the slide latch elevation spring (arrow) is easily detached and lost.

Arrow points to the ejector mounting screw, on the left side of the receiver. It should be occasionally checked for tightness—the one shown has been burred by the use of an improperly-sized screwdriver.

The large screw which holds the magazine tube endpiece beneath the barrel is prone to loosening—check it often.

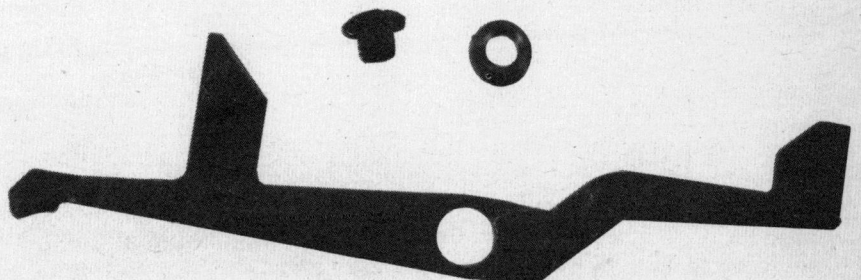

When the shell stop retaining screw loosens too much, the shell stop and its retaining screw and nut can become quickly lost. It is, unfortunately, a common ailment.

be checked with some frequency.

In the same category is the large screw which secures the magazine tube endpiece to its mount below the barrel. In all three screw locations mentioned above, a drop of Loctite on the threads might prevent future difficulty.

U.S. Springfield O3A3 Rifle

The history of the 1903 Springfield Military rifle is well-known to most gun people, so I'll just cite the main dates here. The original 1903 model was adopted to replace the Krag-Jorgensen in that year and was used until 1929, when it was slightly modified to become the 1903A1 model. This gun became our official military rifle until 1936, when the M-1 Garand was adopted. The Springfield was, however, still used by various groups in the military. It was further modified to simplify production, with formed sheet steel parts replacing the carefully machined original type, and became the 03A3 model. This gun, the one covered here, was adopted for military use on May 21, 1942, and 945,846 of them were made by Remington and Smith-Corona.

The Springfield bolt-action is of basic Mauser design with several improvements. Springfield's answer to the famous Mauser third lug (or safety lug) is a large and heavy projection on the right side of the closed bolt, its position being in line with a solid shoulder on the receiver. In the extremely unlikely event that both of the main forward bolt lugs crack, the big lug on the right side, just to the rear of the extractor, would still retain the bolt in the receiver. Like the third lug on the Mauser bolt, it's seldom needed, but it's there, just in case.

A Mauser type, the extractor is tempered to be its own spring and is retained on the outside of the bolt by a ring and T-slot arrangement. Although the extractor on the Springfield bolt is less difficult to remove than some of this same type, it's best to leave it in place unless removing it

Arrow indicates the Springfield version of the third lug, or safety lug, which will retain the bolt if the main forward lugs should fail.

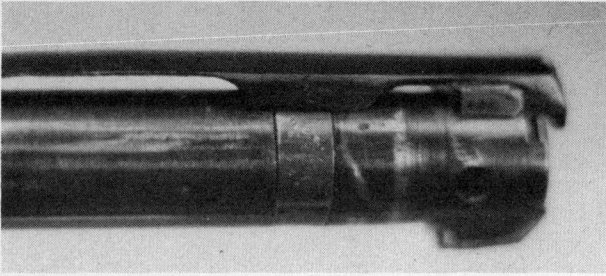

The Springfield uses the Mauser-type extractor, tempered to be its own spring, and retained by a ring surrounding the bolt.

for repair. These extractors rarely break in normal operation, but I have seen several broken during amateur reassembly. Compressing the retaining ring so its flanges will enter the T-slot on the extractor is sometimes tricky and tempts the amateur to use force. Extractors will occasionally weaken, but reshaping and retempering is not difficult. Also, parts are usually available in good quantity, though certain items are in short supply.

In the 03A3 rifle the firing pin and striker arrangement has two advantages over its ancestor, the Mauser. The striker has a knob at the rear, allowing manual recocking without opening the bolt. In case of a misfire, the action is easily recocked for another go at it. In the Mauser, the striker rod and firing pin are a single unit, and the breakage of the firing pin point requires replacement of the whole thing. In the Springfield, the firing pin is detachable from the front of the striker rod and can be replaced separately. The military parts lists, by the way, have interesting names for these two parts. The striker is called the "firing pin rod," a not too ambiguous

designation. There is, however, no firing pin listed. That part is called, of course, the "striker."

At the left rear of the receiver, the Springfield has a combination bolt stop and feeding cutoff. When the lever is flipped upward, showing the stamped word "ON," the bolt has full travel to the rear and will feed the cartridges from the magazine. With the lever turned downward, exposing the word "OFF," the bolt will be stopped short of full travel, and the gun may be single loaded, keeping the rounds in the magazine in reserve. For bolt removal, the cutoff is simply set at the middle position, and the bolt withdrawn to the rear. The cutoff is retained on its spindle by a small set screw, its head visible in the serrated edge of the cutoff. This screw should be checked occasionally for tightness.

The saftey-lever is also akin to the one on the Mauser rifles, but unlike the Model 98 it has only two positions. Over to the right is "safe," and over to the left is the firing position. The lever is plainly marked "SAFE" and "READY," so there is little chance for confusion, even if you are unfamiliar with the gun. Just as on the

Mauser, the safety directly blocks the striker, a very positive system.

While the 03A3 may lack the comparative elegance of the original 1903 rifle with its machined parts, it is an excellent gun, rugged, dependable, and accurate. In one instance, it is also far safer. Most of you will already be familiar with the story of the "low-number" Springfields, but for those who may have joined us late, here are the facts again: Rifles made at Springfield Arsenal and numbered below 800000 and those made at Rock Island Arsenal and numbered below 285506 have receivers of Class "C" steel and have been known to develop dangerous cracks, even with normal loads. If you have an early rifle that falls into this number group, it's best to give it an honored place on your wall and find something else to shoot.

With the combination cutoff and bolt retainer in this position, the bolt can be taken out of the receiver.

Plainly labeled, the Mauser-style safety lever has only two positions—(left) the "safe" position, (right) the "ready" or "fire" position.

Stevens "Crack Shot" Rifle

There were actually several of these little rifles named "Crack Shot," the earlier varieties having a small lever on the side of the receiver which operated the breech block. The later guns, introduced in 1912, have the familiar Stevens under-lever and an entirely different action. These were made until 1939 in regular production, and there was an additional short run of a modified version in 1943. The 1912 to 1939 gun was designated the "Crack Shot Number 26," or "Crack Shot Number 26½;" and, like most of the small Stevens guns, was popular as a "boy's rifle." The "Crack Shot" was the last of the little Stevens lever-action rifles, and its price in 1932 was $6. One of the advantages of this gun (a feature it shared with several similar rifles) was its easy takedown into two compact units by the simple loosening of a large milled knob on the underside of the receiver.

The breech block locking system is simple and effective. The L-shaped breech block is pivoted near the end of its long forward projection and is at-

One of the advantages of this little gun was its easy takedown into two compact units.

tached to the top loop of the lever at the rear. There is a U-shaped cut in the lever, just inside of the frame when closed, which fits over a screw-mounted roller in the receiver. As the action is closed, the upper edge of the angled U-notch rides over the roller, firmly locking the breech face against the rear of the barrel. Firmly, that is, until long use has worn the action. When this is the case, though, it is easily correctable. The main wear points are the breech block pivot screw, the lever link pin, and the locking roller and screw. Replacement of one or more of these parts will usually restore the lockup to original tight-

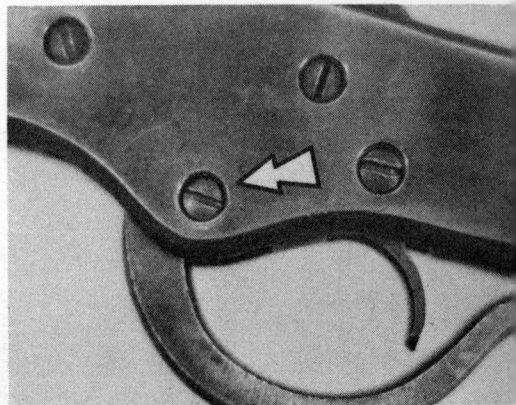

The screw indicated by the arrow passes through a roller which locks the lever in place when the action is closed.

Arrow points to the lever lock roller, a part which is subject to considerable stress and wear.

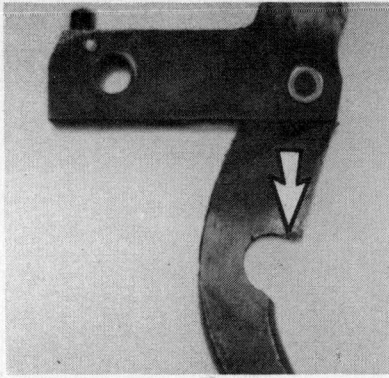

The arrow indicates the area on the lever which locks over the roller in the receiver, a point subject to wear.

The lever lock roller is originally a solid part, but a good substitute is shown here—two concentric tubes which together attain the proper outside diameter.

ness. The screws and the link pin are not difficult to make, and the roller is no problem for any good gunsmith. Also, the used-parts dealers occasionally have some parts for these guns.

Wear is not the only reason for replacement of the locking roller. Perhaps because taking out a single screw drops the roller free, this part is frequently lost. In one recent case, I was temporarily out of the proper size of drill rod to make a replacement roller, and used two concentric tubes to make a sort of "double roller" from a section of a broken auto pistol striker (firing pin) and a half-length of steel roll pin. This combination happened to be exactly the right diameter and worked perfectly.

The firing pin of this gun is rather small and has an offset point, making it somewhat difficult to make when an original can't be found. Most amateurs tend to make replacement firing pins too long, and with these there is a good chance of damaging the ejector when the gun is snapped on an empty chamber. With the point of the pin just inside the breech face, the head of the pin should protrude just a small amount at the rear. If the lowered hammer will not fully meet the rear of the breech block with the chamber empty, the firing pin is too long.

Sliding in a T-slot in the underside of the barrel, the ejector is moved toward the rear by a spring-powered plunger in the forward extension of the breech block as the action is opened. The ejector is rather sturdy and well made, and breakage is rare. More of-

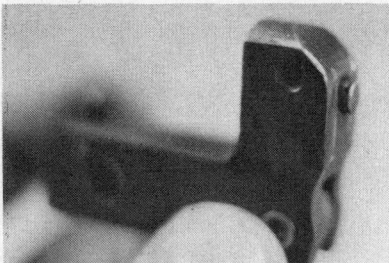

When making a replacement firing pin, care must be taken to make it the proper length. With the point just inside the breech face, the rear head should protrude as shown in this view of the breech block.

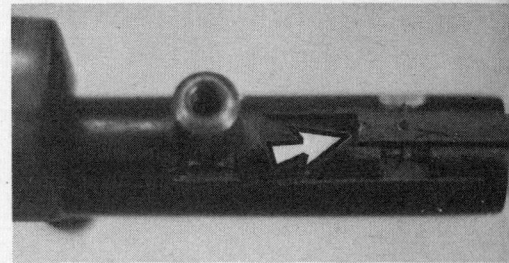

Sliding in a T-slot in the underside of the barrel, the ejector (arrow) is activated by a spring-powered plunger in the forward extension of the breech block.

When deciding whether to restore one of these little rifles, a primary consideration should be the condition of the chamber and the ejector. In the example shown here, both are very good.

ten, the ejector is gouged by an overlong firing pin point, or eaten away by the corrosive qualities of early ammunition. This would be a fairly difficult part to reproduce, but fortunately, a modern reproduction is offered by Triple K. The coil spring which powers the ejector plunger in the breech block will occasionally weaken, but this is easily replaced with any modern coil of proper size and weight.

When deciding whether to restore one of these little rifles, a primary consideration should be the condition of the chamber. As mentioned above,

early ammunition was loaded with blackpowder and corrosive priming, and this combination caused extensive corrosion in the chambers of many of these guns and damage to the barrels as well. When there is severe erosion of the forward part of the chamber, the fired cases will swell into the eroded area, making ejection a matter of prying the cases out. If the gun in question is a family keepsake, justifying the expense, the barrel can be full-length relined, preserving the original exterior. This, of course, should be done by a gunsmith.

Stevens Favorite Rifle

In 1889, when the Stevens company named this little "boy's rifle" the Favorite, they could not have known how appropriate the name would prove to be. For the next 46 years, the gun was indeed the favorite for two generations of young shooters. Most firearms authorities agree that it was the most popular "boy's rifle" ever made. There were five good reasons for this: The gun was simple, rugged, and accurate. It was well-made, and the price was right. In 1908, it could be purchased for the sum of $5.40, and for an additional 25¢, it could be ordered with a special Lyman sight! The Favorite was originally offered in .22, .25, and .32 rimfire chamberings; and, between 1889 and 1915, the internal design of the gun was modified several times. In 1915 it was extensively redesigned, but the main external changes were in the shape of the breech block and forend piece, and the use of a knurled, coin-slotted knob instead of the ring-type barrel retaining screw. Since the early gun is rarely seen outside of collections, it is the Model 1915 that is covered here.

The early guns had blade-type springs powering the hammer and trigger. The flat trigger spring was retained in the Model 1915, but since it is not severely flexed in normal operation, breakage is rare. It does weaken on occasion, but it can usually be reshaped and retempered, or a replacement can be made fairly easily. The hammer spring is rather strongly flexed, and the older blade-type broke with some regularity. In the Model 1915, this was replaced with a well-designed coil spring system, and this arrangement is entirely free of any difficulties.

The ejector of the Model 1915 is centrally located below the chamber, and extends downward to pivot on the lever screw. In the front portion of the ejector, there is a plunger powered by a strong coil spring, the plunger bearing on the underside of the breech block pivot screw. As the action is opened, the ejector is held in place by the plunger until the last fraction of lever movement, and at that time a shoulder on the lever cams it to the rear, snapping the plunger from under the breech block screw giving the empty cartridge case a sharp flick out of the chamber. This system causes no problems, but the location of the ejector in relation to the rim of the cartridge sometimes does, in a roundabout way. In its recess below the chamber, the rim contact portion of the ejector is directly in line with the point of the firing pin. When the ham-

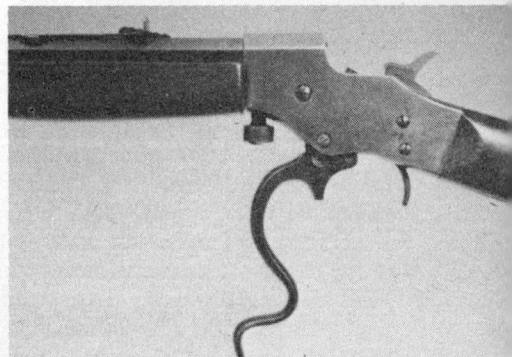

Here's a view of the Model 1915 Favorite with the action fully opened.

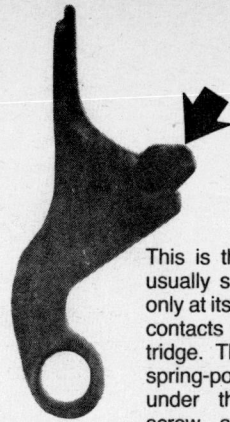

This is the ejector, a part usually subject to damage only at its upper tip, where it contacts the rim of the cartridge. The lug at right is spring-powered, to snap under the breech block screw as the action is opened.

Early guns had a blade-type hammer spring. On the 1915 model, shown here, this was replaced by a helical coil. (The trigger spring was still a blade type.)

When the breech block reaches the fully lowered position, the ejector is snapped rearward out of its recess below the chamber.

mer falls, the firing pin nose actually pinches the cartridge rim against the ejector, rather than against a solid edge of the barrel as in most other rimfire guns.

There is a positive stop shoulder on the original firing pins to prevent the tip from reaching and damaging the ejector if the gun is snapped while empty, but the rather large retaining groove in this firing pin causes it to have a relatively weak rear section, and breakage is not unusual. Based on examination of a large number of these guns over the past 30 years, it would be safe to say that more than 90 percent of the replacement firing pins were handmade by amateurs, using materials most readily available, such as a large nail. Almost invariably, the replacement firing pin was made too long, and the gun snapped frequently with the chamber empty. Before it bent and ceased to function, the over-long tip of the homemade firing pin would usually succeed in severely damaging the top portion of the ejector. I have repaired these by adding steel weld to the top and recutting to shape, but in order to do this, the plunger and spring must be removed from the ejector, and they are stake-mounted in place, in a blind hole. Removal can be very interesting, to say the least. I do not know of any consistent source for the ejector except Dixie Gun Works, and the price is around $9, which is most reasonable. They also have a few other parts for the Favorite, but *no* firing pins. For that, you consult your gunsmith.

The tightness of the finger lever when the breech is closed depends on the proper mating of the breech face and the rear of the barrel, as well as the condition of the various linkage pins in the action. When there is extreme wear, the lever can drop down when the hammer is cocked, allowing the breech to open. There are several ways to cure this, including replacement of worn link pins, setting back the barrel, and so on, but this would come under the heading of extensive rebuilding. Since the second finger is normally gripping the tail of the lever when the gun is held for shooting, correction of this is not absolutely essential, unless the looseness is so severe that excess headspace is allowing the escape of powder gases. As with any rifle of this age, it's best to have it checked by a competent gunsmith before shooting it.

With the cumulative effects of black powder and corrosive priming, the chambers and barrels of early production guns suffered greatly unless they were scrupulously cleaned after every use, and this was seldom the case. If the chamber is badly eroded, the fired case will swell into the eroded areas, and will stick tightly in the chamber. When deciding whether to restore an old Favorite, check the chamber first, then the ejector and firing pin. If all of these are deficient, you may find it more expedient to buy the Savage/Stevens Model 74, a modern recreation of the Favorite.

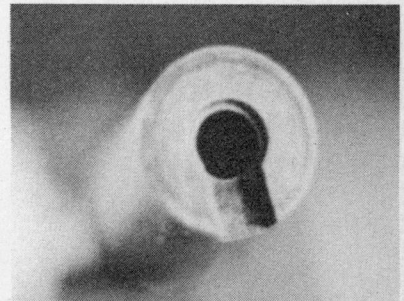

When deciding whether or not to restore an old Stevens Favorite, the condition of the chamber is of primary importance. The one shown here is in excellent condition.

The barrel is retained by a knurled thumb-screw (left) on the 1915 model, its inner tip entering a well (arrow, right) in the underside of the barrel.

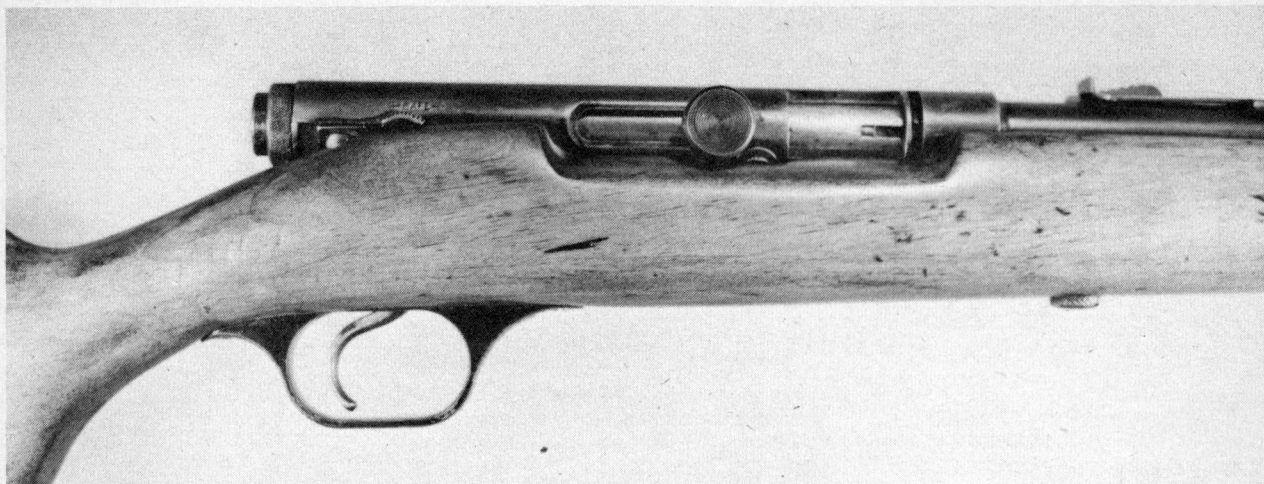

Stevens Model 87-A Rifle

During its long time of production, this rifle has had many names. You may know it as the Savage Model 6A, or the Springfield Model 187, and there are other designations. With slight cosmetic differences, they are all the same basic design. Its most notable feature is a bolt handle that can be pushed in to lock the bolt closed, allowing the gun to be used as a manually-operated bolt-action with Short or Long cartridges, and as a semiautomatic with Long Rifle rounds when the handle is in the extended position.

The disconnector system is of unusual design. During the bolt recoil with the trigger held back, the disconnector catches the bolt and holds it open. On release of the trigger, the disconnector moves downward to free the bolt, and at the same time the sear rises to catch the striker (hammer). When all of the attendant springs have proper tension, and the disconnector and its step on the bolt are sharp, the system works perfectly. The balance of spring tension, though, is critical,

and any variation in the strength of the bolt, striker, or disconnector springs can cause several problems, not the least of which is full-automatic firing. There is no simple cure for this. Straightening out this rather weird system is a job for a competent gunsmith.

The cartridge lifter is another frequent source of difficulty. This part, sometimes called a carrier, is the device that moves the cartridge from the

level of the magazine tube up to the feed lips. Its movement is governed by two lobes on top of its pivot end, and wear of these can cause trouble in two ways. A worn lifter will either fail to depress far enough for a cartridge to enter the magazine guide, or fail to rise far enough to position the round in the feed lips. Replacement of the lifter is the remedy, and fortunately parts are still available from the manufacturer, Savage. A weak lifter

Arrow to the left points to the disconnector. Its external spring also returns the trigger. Center arrow indicates the lifter spring, and the arrow at the right points to the cartridge guide spring.

A new cartridge lifter is shown at the top, while the one below, badly worn, was causing misfeeding.

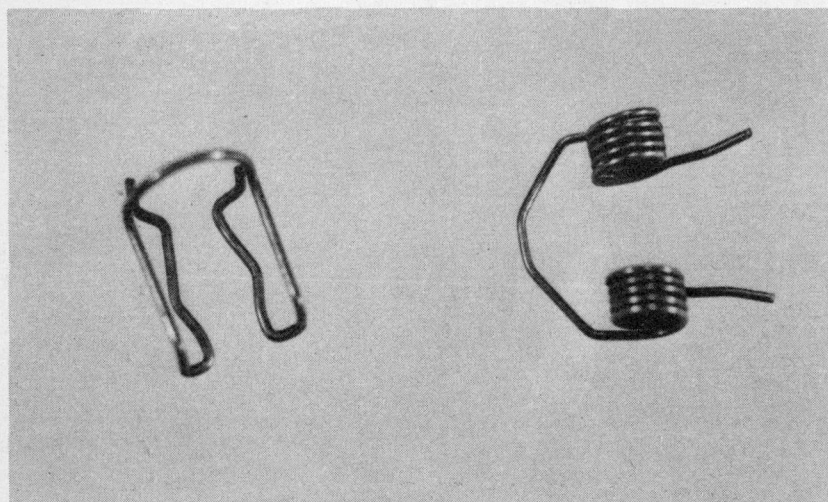
Two important springs in the feed mechanism: The cartridge guide spring is at the left, the carrier spring to the right. The latter one is often found installed backwards.

The cartridge guide is made of formed sheet steel, and the ejector (arrow) is integral with the guide. If the ejector wears, or breaks off, the entire guide must be replaced.

spring can also cause a spectacular jam, but in the many cases that I have examined, the spring is actually not deficient—just installed backwards by an amateur gunsmith.

One of the recurrent troubles of the Model 87-A is breakage or deformation of the cartridge guide spring. This strangely-shaped little unit of tempered wire fits like a saddle on the underside of the cartridge guide and holds the cartridge in position to be picked up by the lifter. When this spring is not right, it can cause jamming that will require complete disassembly of the feed system. Replacements are usually available. If not, this spring can be cold-formed from tempered wire, by someone with a great deal of skill and patience. In later versions of this rifle, the entire cartridge guide system was changed, eliminating this spring.

I have occasionally seen breakage of the ejector, a simple projection from the left feed lip of the cartridge guide. When this occurs, the only cure is replacement of the cartridge guide, as this is a part formed of sheet steel, and there is no feasible way to repair it.

For reasons that will be obvious, most gunsmiths are thoroughly familiar with this rifle.

Stevens Model 1244 Shotgun

This shotgun has fooled many a gun trader. At first glance, it appears to be a semiautomatic, and I have had several of them brought to me for "repair" by new owners who complained that, "It shoots okay, but you have to work the 'danged' thing by hand." Well, that's the way it was designed. Actually, it's a semi-straight-pull bolt-action. When the hammer is cocked, the bolt handle is locked in—its ample diameter entering recesses in the receiver to lock the breech block firmly closed. When the hammer falls, the handle is still blocking the bolt but is no longer locked in. It can then be pulled outward to the right, unlocking the bolt, and pulled back to extract and eject the fired shell. It is then pushed forward, feeding the next round from the magazine, and the handle is pushed back in to lock the bolt.

It may be that this was a somewhat awkward sequence for many shooters, as the production of this gun did not continue for many years. During this brief time, the gun was marketed as the "Stevens Cross-Bolt Repeater," with the designations of "Model 124" and "Model 1244."

In the late 1940s when this gun was produced, the scarcity of walnut for stocks was still being felt, even after the end of WWII. To offset this, the Stevens Company used a plastic called "Tenite" on several of their guns. On their .22 rifles, it worked fairly well, as long as you remembered not to stand the gun too close to

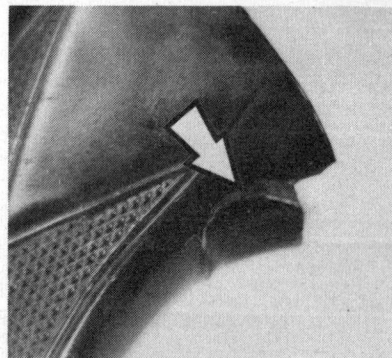

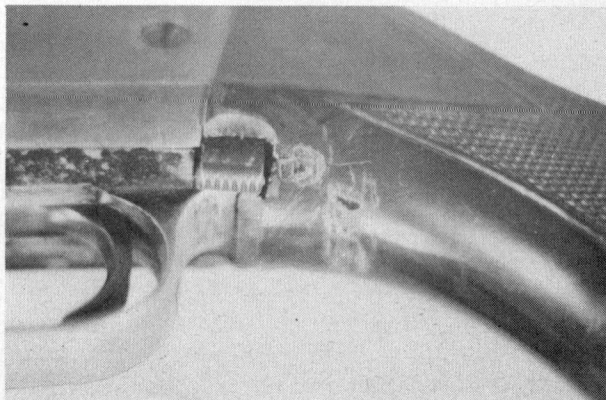

The Stevens Model 1244 features a plastic (Tenite) stock that's subject to breakage. The arrow (top photo) indicates a typical break. In the photo on the right the break in the stock has been "welded" inside and out through the use of a soldering iron— a rough, but effective repair.

a stove, or leave it in the window-rack of your truck in the Texas sun. On shotguns, though, especially in the heavier gauges, the Tenite proved less than satisfactory, to put it mildly. This was an early plastic and lacked the stability of today's materials of this type. Just as extreme heat softened it, very cold temperatures tended to make it brittle, and the pounding of 12-gauge recoil (the only chambering offered in the 1244) was often too much for it.

The stock would usually begin to crack just to the rear of the trigger guard, at the point where the lower edge meets the receiver, and no glue known to man will stick to Tenite plastic. For several of the Tenite-stocked guns, Savage/Stevens can supply a replacement stock of wood with a different mounting bolt. With the 1244, though, you are out of luck, as this one has been obsolete for so long that no parts, including stocks, are available. I recently repaired a broken Tenite stock on a 1244 by "welding" the crack with the tip of a soldering iron, inside and out, and this seems to be a serviceable, though unattractive, method. It held together for several heavy test loads, but I have no doubt that it will break again, eventually.

The feed and firing mechanisms of the Model 1244 are very similar to the ones used in several of the slide-action Savage/Stevens guns, and they

Refitting of the engagement of the interrupter lobe on the bolt handle release (arrow) is often necessary.

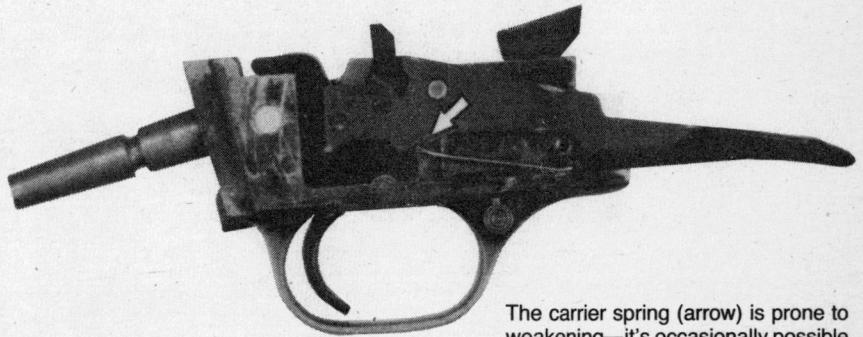

The carrier spring (arrow) is prone to weakening—it's occasionally possible to reshape it without replacing the entire part.

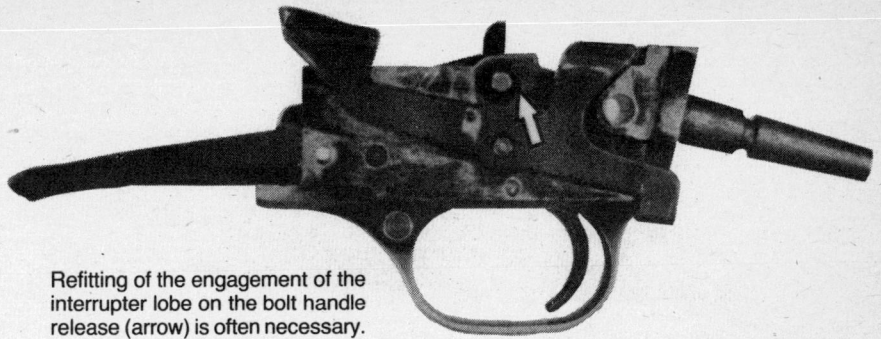

One of the 1244's more critical parts is the bolt handle latch release spring (arrow)—check it for deformation or breakage.

share some of the same ailments. There is a stud on the left side of the hammer which contacts a hook-shaped spring on the bolt lock, drawing the lock down and out of engagement as the hammer falls. This spring is subject to both breakage and deformation, and replacing it is not a fun project. It will have to be made, and its shape and length must be exactly right for proper operation.

Also a round-wire type, the carrier spring is located on the right side of the trigger group and looks deceptively simple. This one rarely breaks but is prone to weakening. Here, again, the length of the spring and its engagement with the lobe on the carrier are quite critical. There is one bright note here—the carrier spring for the slide-action Model 77 series gun—still available—will usually interchange.

There is an interrupter lobe on the bolt handle latch which contacts a large stud on the upper left side of the hammer, preventing the hammer from dropping before the bolt is locked in place. With extreme wear, or amateur alteration of the sear or sear step on the hammer, this lobe can make improper contact and make operation of the manual bolt release difficult, if not impossible. In this case, any good gunsmith can alter the mating of the lobe with the stud on the hammer and can correct the problem without replacement of parts—if, indeed, any parts could be found. Considering the problems, if you own one of these guns in good condition, it might be best to just put it away for the future time when such a limited-production Stevens gun might have some collector value.

This particular Swedish Husqvarna is a pre-WWII gun that features a tapered forend and fixed rear sight.

Swedish Husqvarna Rifle

The Husqvarna Vapenfabriks Aktie Bolag has been around since 1689, and over the years has produced all types of arms for the Swedish Military forces. In more recent times, they have been famous for the production of fine sporting rifles, many of which have been previously imported into this country. For the past 4 or 5 years they have been unavailable, having no U.S. importer. These were well-made guns of typical Mauser pattern and were offered in a wide range of chamberings, including several magnum calibers.

Made before WWII, the particular gun covered here is a European-style sporter which is chambered for the 9.3 × 57mm round. This is a fairly common hunting cartridge in Europe but is not too well-known on this side of the ocean. It was formerly available in a Norma loading but was dropped from the U.S. list some time ago. For those who are looking for various odd foreign rounds in shoot-able modern loads, I can highly recommend the custom loader where I get mine: Ballistek, P.O. Box 1813, Kearney, NB 68847.

This gun's bolt system is of early Mauser pattern with twin opposed lugs at the forward end, but lacking the "extra" lug near the bolt handle found on the Mauser Model 98. Even so, the strength is more than adequate for the original chambering. Husqvarna has always used only the best steel, and they've been learning about heat

Done in the style of pre-war Husqvarnas, the barrel markings not only denote the name of the maker but the cartridge for which the gun is chambered. (Postwar guns were made for a wide range of more popular cartridges.)

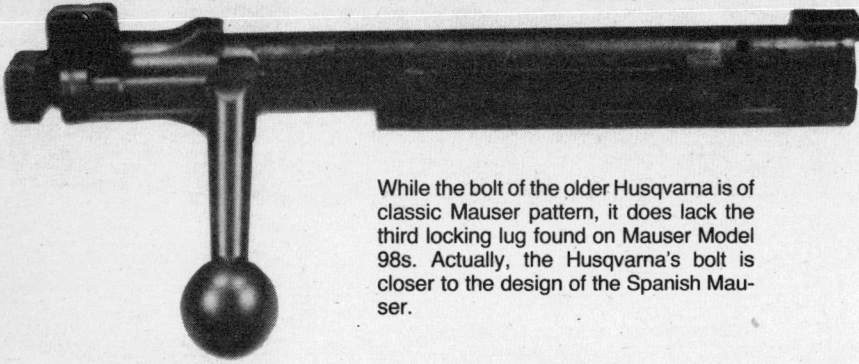

While the bolt of the older Husqvarna is of classic Mauser pattern, it does lack the third locking lug found on Mauser Model 98s. Actually, the Husqvarna's bolt is closer to the design of the Spanish Mauser.

The safety lever, shown in the vertical "on-safe" position, is the familiar Mauser-style "flipper"—in this case nicely knurled.

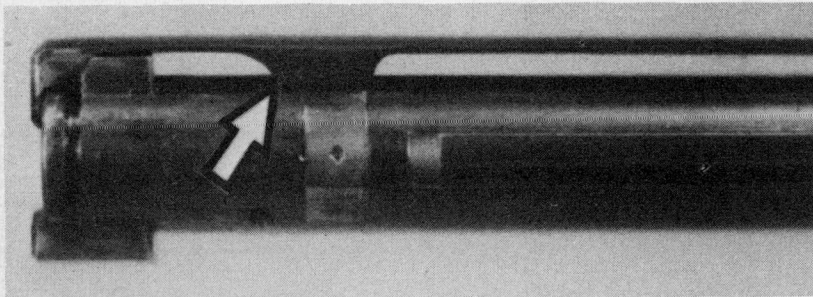

Breakage of the Husqvarna's Mauser-style extractor is rare, even though it's tempered to be its own spring. Arrow points to the extractor's attachment base.

treatment for nearly 300 years. The thing to remember about this action, and others of its type, is to avoid using any warmed-up loads, and never re-barrel or rechamber the gun for any cartridge that would create breech pressure in excess of the original chambering.

The familiar Mauser-type flip-over safety lever directly blocks the striker, and both the safety and the angled end of the striker knob are knurled. The striker and its firing pin point are heavy, strong parts, and breakage is unlikely. In the event that some part does let go, you may have some difficulty, since there is no current importer. Both Tradewinds and Stoeger have imported these guns in the past and may have some parts in stock for the more recent models. However, for one of the older guns, it may be necessary to have a gunsmith make whatever is needed if it can't be located among the used-parts dealers.

The extractor on this gun is the standard long Mauser type, mounted on a pivot ring which encircles the bolt body. The extractor is tempered to be its own spring, but breakage is rare. I have occasionally seen these with a chipped beak, but this can be built up with weld and recut to shape, and if it's done properly, the tail will not lose its temper. This can be done by covering the rear portion of the extractor with welder's clay or a wet cloth while working on the beak.

Like most Mauser-based bolt-actions, these rifles will usually just go on working forever. In addition to good design, they have the advantage of Husqvarna quality.

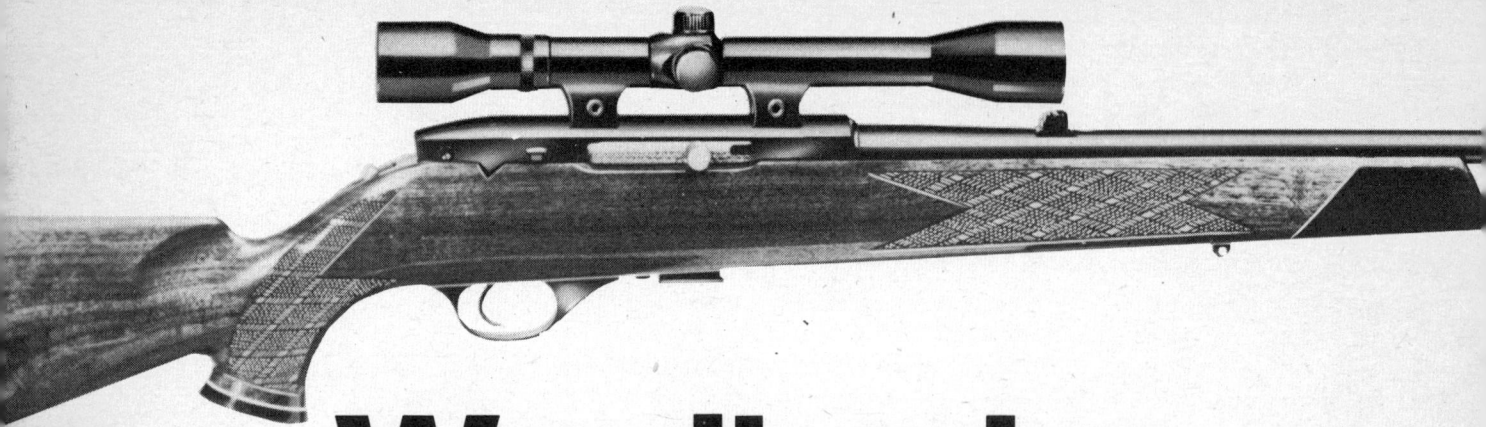

Weatherby Mark XXII Rifle

Like all of the guns bearing the Weatherby name, the Mark XXII rifle is elegant in appearance. The external fit and finish are superb, and this same attention to detail is apparent in the design of the internal mechanism. As in most modern rifles, there are some formed steel and alloy parts, but where these are used, they are heavier than usual, with ample allowance for strength.

The trigger group is particularly well-designed, and has no potential trouble spots. The two-part cartridge

The two-part cartridge guide of the Mark XXII is a nicely machined, solid steel casting. Note the sturdy ejector lug, an integral part of the left feed lip.

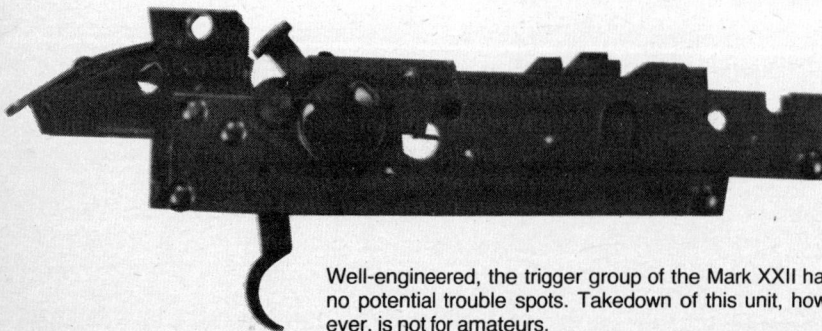

Well-engineered, the trigger group of the Mark XXII has no potential trouble spots. Takedown of this unit, however, is not for amateurs.

guide is a heavy cast assembly, and the raised portion of the left feed lip which forms the ejector looks as if it will last forever. On the left side of the trigger housing there is an aperture allowing visual inspection of the engagement of the sear and hammer without disassembly. Takedown of the trigger group, by the way, is not for amateurs, as there is an interde-

On the left side of the trigger housing, there is an aperture (arrow) through which the engagement of the hammer and sear may be seen.

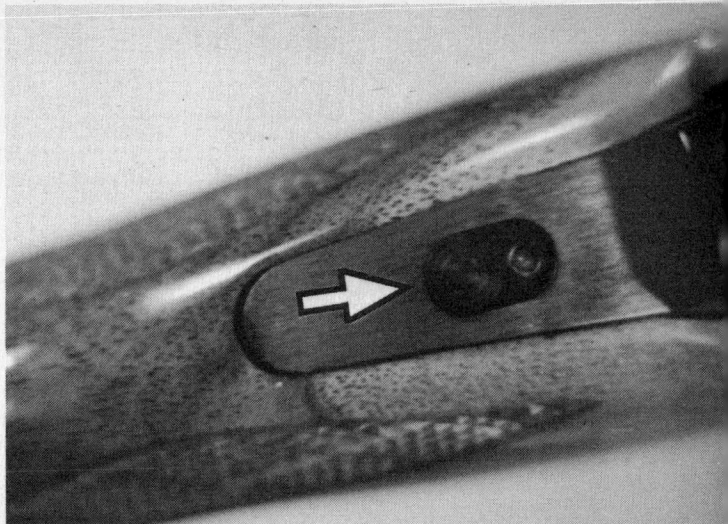

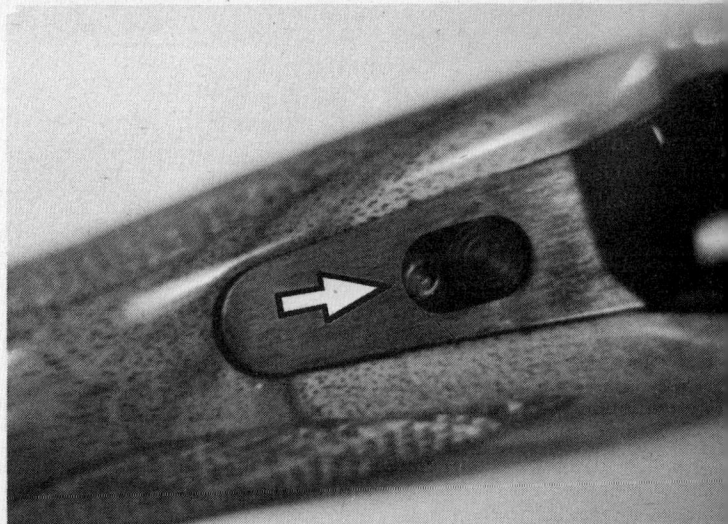

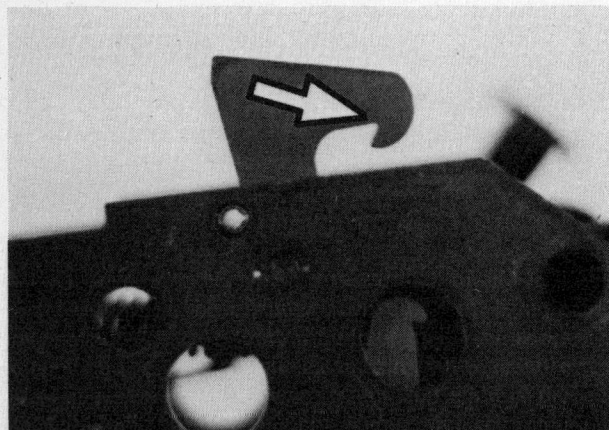

The sear beak of the hammer is at the top rear (arrow) giving good leverage and a crisp trigger pull. A sear system of this type is not tolerant of amateur alteration.

The thumb-operated safety catch, located conveniently on the upper tang, is shown in the on-safe (top) and off-safe (bottom) positions.

pendence of parts that could give the nonprofessional a lot of difficulty.

The sear contact beak of the hammer is at the top rear of that part, giving good leverage which contributes to a crisp trigger pull. It should be noted that a sear system of this type is not tolerant of amateur alteration. The factory pull is excellent, though, and I doubt that many will try to change it. The safety catch is conveniently located on the upper tang, just to the rear of the receiver and is pushed forward to off-safe position.

The Mark XXII has two unique features. One is a quick-takedown arrangement, in which a large spring-retained cross-pin at the rear of the receiver is pushed out to the left, allowing the entire action to be lifted from the stock for cleaning. The most notable innovation, though, is a selector which permits regular semi-auto or single-shot firing. The selector lever is located on the right side of the receiver, in a position where many .22 rifles have a safety. When rocked to the rear, beside the word "AUTO" on the receiver, the rifle fires in regular semi-auto fashion. When the selector is pushed forward, to align with the letters "SS," the bolt will remain open after each shot and will close to chamber the next round only when the

selector is pushed further forward to release it. This is a handy feature, especially when teaching a beginner to shoot with this gun—a situation in which a semi-auto would normally be the last choice. The selector accomplishes this mode of firing by means of a spring-powered hook on its lever-plate, which is raised to catch the bolt each time when the selector is in forward position. The hook is under some stress when catching the bolt, but it appears to be well-shaped and strong, and I think breakage is unlikely.

There is, in fact, only one part on the rifle that I believe might be prone

161

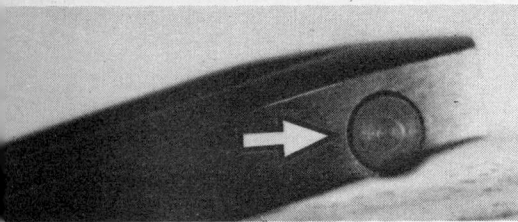

When removed from the left, a large spring-retained cross-pin (arrow) at the rear of the receiver allows for easy removal of the action from the stock.

to damage, and it has nothing to do with the feed or firing mechanisms. The Mark XXII is fitted with a rear sight that is similar in principle to the ones used on some of the older British sporting rifles. It has a fixed base with a notch for closer range shooting, and two pivoting leaves marked for the longer ranges. The pivot loops of the two leaves are each offset, to utilize the same cross-pin, and this results in the rear leaf having a long projection to the left, and the front leaf a similar extension to the right. If either of these unsupported projections suffered a blow of sufficient force, they could be deformed or broken off. If only deformed (and this might not be noticed), accuracy might be affected. This is no great detraction, though, as the receiver has provision for mounting a scope sight, and these days, nine times out of ten, a scope is used rather than iron sights.

In the unlikely event that some routine replacement, such as a firing pin, might eventually be needed, parts are readily available. If anything is unavailable locally, Weatherby gives good direct service.

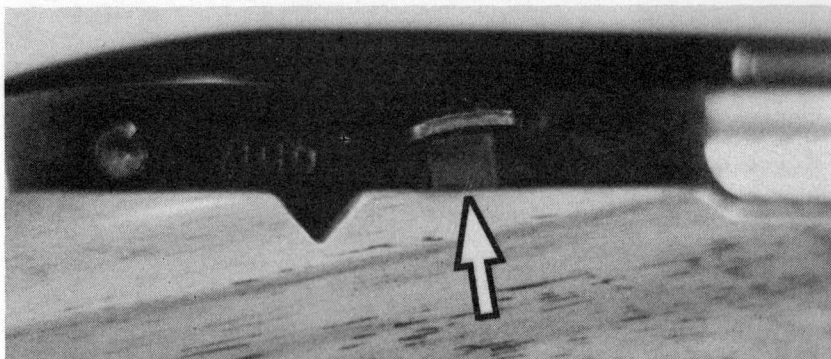

The selector (arrow), located on the right side of the receiver, is shown in the semi-auto (top) and single-shot (bottom) positions.

Here the arrow points to the hook on the selector lever-plate, which catches the bolt during single-shot firing.

While the two-leaf folding rear sight is an ingenious design, it's susceptible to deformation or breakage if struck sharply.

Winchester Model 61 Rifle

This fine little rifle was made from 1932 to 1963, and toward the end of production, in 1960, it was slightly redesigned and offered in .22 Magnum chambering, in addition to the regular .22 version. One element of its excellent cartridge feeding system was recently brought back in the internal design of the lever-action Model 9422 rifle. There is an extractor-like part at the lower edge of the bolt face which grips the cartridge as it leaves the magazine, plus a T-slot in the bolt face which guides the cartridge rim as the round is lifted by the carrier. When a Model 61 is in good working order, there is no such thing as misfeeding since the cartridge is firmly guided through the entire sequence.

All of the springs in this gun are round-wire type, either helical coil or torsion, according to function, and there is ample allowance for age weakening. The only part which occasionally causes trouble is the cartridge cutoff, located in a cylindrical housing at the rear mouth of the magazine. The cutoff is a simple, flat part, pivot-mounted with a single pin, and has two lobes at the rear. One lobe contacts the cartridge rim, to keep the round in the magazine until the action is cycled. The other lobe bears on the action slide bar, and a shoulder on the bar cams the cutoff inward as the action bar is moved, preventing the feeding of more than one round each time. The cartridge contact lobe, which touches only the brass of the cases, is not subject to much wear. The other, however, is eventually worn to some degree by the action bar; and, when this wear is severe enough, the inner lobe will have insufficient protrusion to properly stop the cartridges. Replacement of the cutoff is the obvious cure for this problem; and, although this is an obsolete model, many gun shops still have parts on hand, and some may still be available from the factory. If not, the cutoff is not difficult to make. Installation, however, is somewhat more than a routine job and should be done by a gunsmith.

I have made a few other repairs over the years to the Model 61, but none of these could be considered chronic ailments. The slide lock, made of formed sheet steel, has a

In this view through the bottom of the receiver, the arrow indicates the cartridge cutoff, the one part in the Model 61 most likely to cause difficulty.

In this view, the arrow points to the turned-over shelf on the slide lock, which is the contact point for the left lug of the hammer. Here the hammer is cocked, the slide lock is elevated.

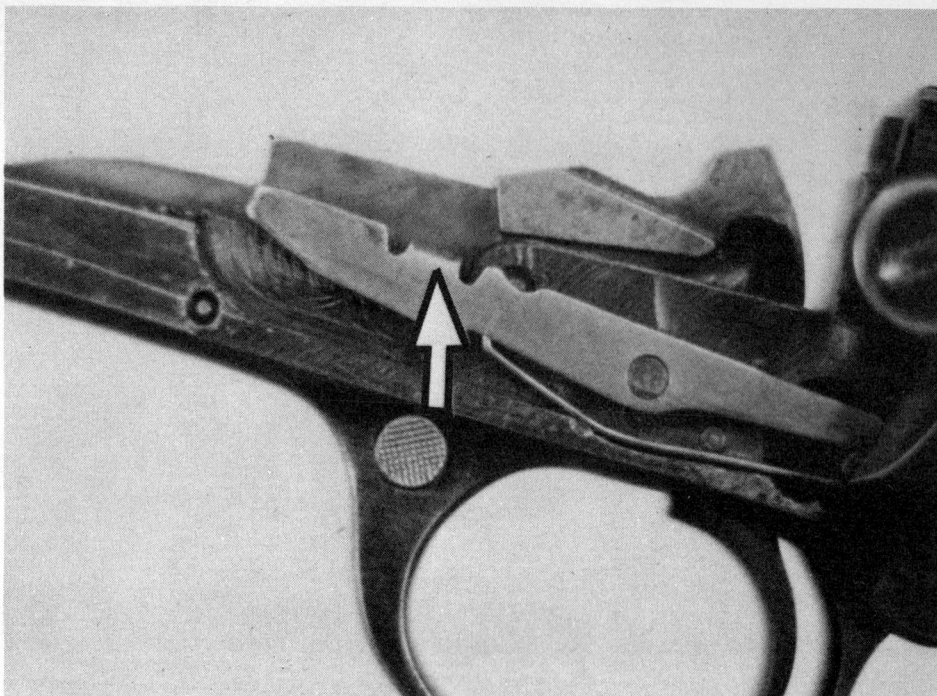

The arrow indicates the engagement of the left lug of the hammer with the slide lock. In this view, the hammer is down, the slide lock depressed.

turned-over shelf at its forward end that is struck by a lug on the left side of the hammer each time the hammer falls, to unlock the action. I have seen one case in which the shelf broke away from the slide lock, and since the factory no longer has this part, it was repaired by welding.

The ejector is a long, slim part which lies in a slot on the upper left side of the breech block, and these will occasionally break, usually at the point where they are narrowed to accommodate the ejector return spring. If this part is unavailable, it is easily made, but must be properly hardened,

The lower extractor (left arrow) grips the cartridge as it is fed from the magazine. The ejector (right arrow) and its spring lie in a slot on the upper left side of the breech block.

On the right side of the breech block (bolt), the arrow points to the firing pin stop pin, which not only retains the firing pin but also compresses the firing pin return spring.

as it is subject to quite a bit of impact in normal use.

The firing pin retaining pin is unusual, fitting tightly in the firing pin, and extending outward on each side to the sides of the breech block. On the left side, it rides in an oblong cut in the bolt. On the right, its end acts as a compressor of the firing pin return spring. This pin will break every so often, but making a replacement is so easy that looking for an original Winchester replacement is hardly worth the trouble.

The Model 61 has no other serious quirks, and many thousands of them are still in everyday use. The main problem these days is finding one, as collectors are vying with shooters for the few remaining on the market.

Winchester Model 70 Rifle

The original version of this rifle was made from 1936 to 1963. In 1964, in an effort to keep the price at a reasonable level in spite of rising costs, the gun was redesigned, and several manufacturing shortcuts were used—an expedient that brought cries of anguish from those who were accustomed to Winchester quality. The company was listening, and in 1972 the gun was up-graded to a better standard, but retained several of the good innovations that were introduced in 1964. The price, of course, was increased, but most shooters would rather pay a little more and have a quality firearm. In many ways, the present Model 70 is actually better in certain respects than the original.

For example, the original had a long Mauser-type extractor, ring-mounted on the outside of the bolt. The currently-made gun has a small sliding extractor, powered by a spring-and-plunger, mounted in a T-slot in one of the bolt lugs. Because of its diminutive size, some may think that the present system is weaker. In actuality, it is stronger. The ejector in the new gun is a plunger type, powered by a coil spring and is mounted in the bolt face. The original ejector was a flat steel part mounted at the rear of the receiver. Neither of these is subject to wear or breakage, but I have heard several complaints of "sleepy" ejection in the new guns. In two recent cases, I replaced the original coil spring with one having considerably more strength. The ejection was improved but still not equal to the solid flip given the cases by the old fixed ejector. This is not to say, of course, that the ejector of the new model doesn't work properly—it does. In fact, those who handload often prefer soft ejection, as it makes recovery of the brass easier.

Covered here is the currently-made Model 70, and its trigger and sear system, much like the original, is extremely simple. There is an adjustment for spring tension and over-travel at the rear of the trigger by

The small extractor is mounted in a T-slot in the bolt lug; and, although it is tiny, it is well-supported and does not often break.

In this view of the bolt face, the extractor is at the left, and ejector at lower right.

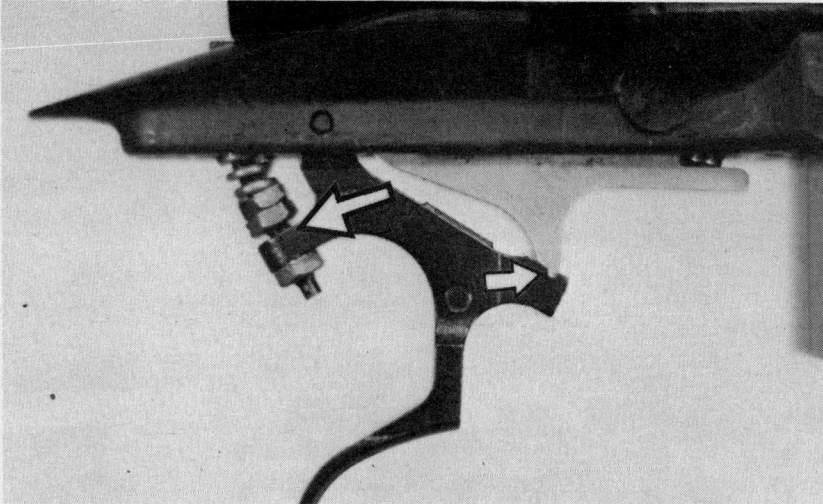

Trigger spring tension and over-travel are adjustable by means of three lock nuts (left arrow). The right arrow indicates the engagement of the trigger and the sear, which should be altered only by a professional.

means of three lock nuts. It is possible for the knowledgeable amateur to adjust this system by trial and error, but unless you are familiar with this sort of thing it's best left to a professional. In regard to alteration of the engagement of trigger and sear, this is definitely a job for a gunsmith, unless you have an endless supply of triggers and sears, and just like to experiment.

The bolt stop of the Model 70 is located in the usual position, at the left rear of the receiver, and is pushed forward and downward to release the bolt for removal. Disassembly of the bolt is much the same as in the original pre-1964 guns, but removal of the striker/firing pin combination is not quite as easy, as the new guns have a split-ring type retainer for the spring, while the older guns had a large sleeve with serrations for easy grasping. On the new guns, it may be best to leave bolt disassembly to a gunsmith, as the small retainer and its back-up washer can travel quite a distance if your fingers should slip.

Since the ejector quirk mentioned earlier should not be considered an ailment, the Model 70 can be considered to be free of any chronic troubles. In the event of some routine breakage over the years, such as an extractor or firing pin, all parts are available. Note, however, that the design has been changed twice since 1936, so when obtaining parts be sure to give the serial number of your gun.

During its long period of production, the Model 70 has been offered in a number of special versions and submodels. At the present time, collector interest in the pre-1964 guns has reached such proportions that in some cases they have become almost too valuable to shoot.

The bolt stop (arrow) is much less obtrusive than the old Mauser type used on many other bolt-action guns. It is pushed down and forward to allow bolt removal.

The bolt sleeve lock (arrow) is not only the key to bolt disassembly, but also locks the sleeve in position when the bolt is opened.

The Winchester Model 75 rifle shown is the target version—the most commonly encountered type.

Winchester Model 75 Rifle

This gun was originally designed to be a lower-priced version of the Model 52 rifle, but it soon had an ardent following of its own, some of whom actually preferred it to the more expensive gun. Like the Model 52, it was offered in both sporting and target versions, the latter coming out a year before the other, in 1938. The Model 75 had several features of the Model 52, including a speed-lock firing mechanism. It lacks a fully adjustable trigger, but does have an adjustment for the trigger spring tension. The Model 75 proved many times that it could compete on an even basis with target rifles costing much more, and today's collectors and shooters often bid against each other for the few guns remaining in circulation. In the WWII era, the U.S. Government bought large quantities of the Model 75 for training purposes, and many of these will be found bearing the "U.S. Property" marking.

A well-designed rifle, trouble spots on the Model 75 are at a minimum. The magazine system is good opera-

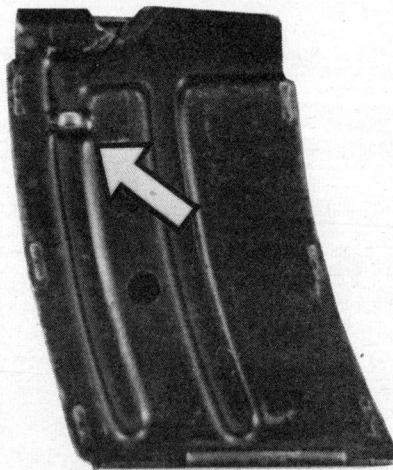

Arrow indicates the catch stud on the magazine, a raised portion of the magazine wall. These will occasionally wear and cause misfeeding.

tionally, but has one quirk which appears after long use. The magazine catch is a formed, tempered piece of flat steel, located on the right side of the receiver, and is activated by a push-button on the left side of the

stock. The catch is its own blade-type spring, but it is not flexed severely, and rarely breaks. An opening in the catch snaps over a protrusion on the right side of the magazine to hold it in place, and the catch protrusion is merely a pushed-out portion of the magazine wall. The sharp edges tend to wear, and the catch will then fail to hold the magazine securely. This can sometimes be repaired by reforming the catch protrusion outward, but if the wear is severe, this may not work. The Model 75 is long out of production (1958), and new replacement magazines and other parts are often difficult to find. The only certain source for magazines is Walter Lodewick, whose address appears in the listing of parts dealers.

The Model 75 has a particularly good safety system, with a pivoting lever on the right side of the receiver which slides a steel bar forward to fill the space between the forward arm of the trigger and a shelf on the trigger spring housing—a very positive arrangement. The bar is retained on the

An accessory to the target model rifle was the single-shot adapter shown at the bottom.

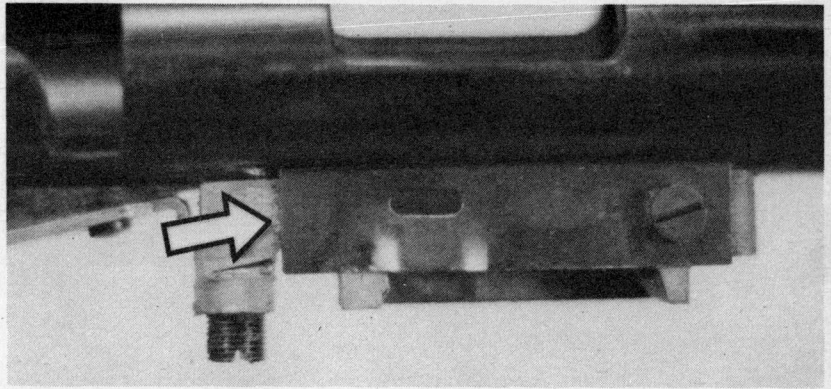

Arrow indicates the magazine catch, a formed and tempered piece of sheet steel. It is not flexed to a great degree and does not break often.

The arrow points to the engagement step of the safety bar. The parts are shown in the off-safe position and just below the arrow is the trigger spring adjustment screw.

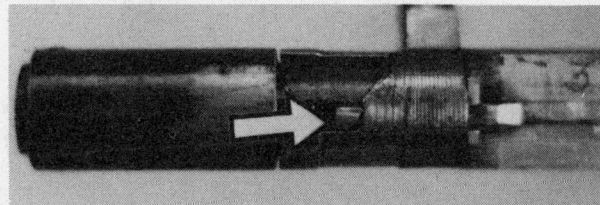

Arrow points to the cocking lug on the combination striker and firing pin. This is the site of occasional breakage.

trigger by a single screw, and this should be checked occasionally to be sure that it hasn't loosened.

On the 75 the cocking lug for the combined striker and firing pin is at the extreme rear of that part, and these will occasionally break off. If a replacement can't be found, this is a flat part and is not too difficult to reproduce. At the rear of the bolt is an end piece which appears to be a screw, but definitely isn't. The cross-slot is simply a reassembly aid, to help in aligning the end piece for insertion of the cross-pin. Takedown of the bolt should *not* be attempted by the non-professional.

The barrel band screw is tapered for easy reinsertion through the large hole in the band, and this screw should not be turned in as far as it will go. Just centering it in the stock will hold the band properly.

The target version of the Model 75 was originally supplied either without sights, for those who wished to select their own, or with a Redfield aperture sight at the rear and a Winchester

105A front sight. The gun photographed for this section had an elaborate set of Lyman sights, front and rear, and scope base blocks that appeared to be factory original.

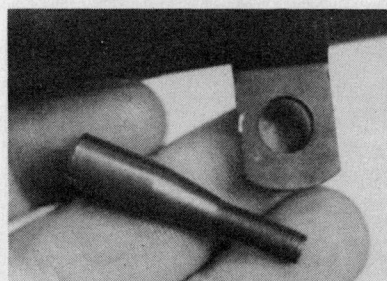

Here's a rare sight—an undamaged bolt end piece. The rear end piece of the bolt appears to be a screw, but it isn't. The screw slot is a reassembly aid.

The barrel band screw is tapered for easy reassembly.

Winchester Model 1890 Rifle

The arrow at the lower left of the picture below points toward the blade-type hammer spring which is severely flexed—it breaks with some frequency. The arrow at upper right indicates the location of the carrier spring, another blade-type spring which frequently breaks.

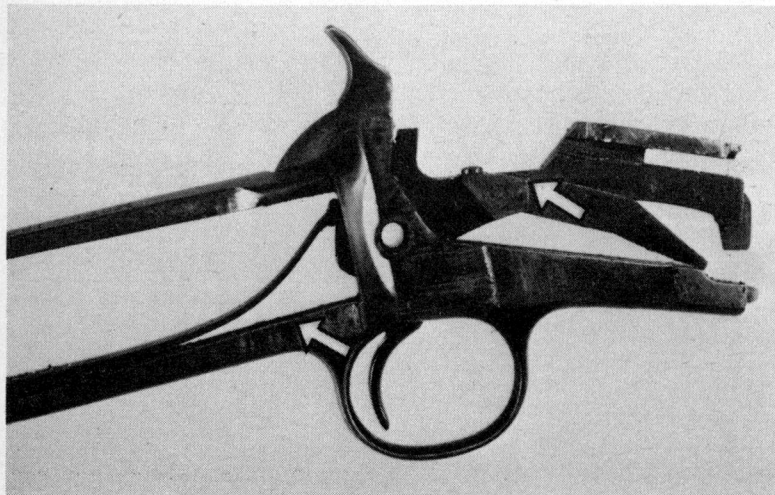

For many people, including this writer, this gun is remembered as the first rifle they ever fired. In my case, the venerable octagon-barreled Model 90 was in the .22 Short chambering, but during its years of production it was also made in .22 Long, .22 Long Rifle, and .22 W.R.F. models, separately. The gun was designed for Winchester by John M. Browning, and as with most of his designs, these rifles seem to go on working forever.

Like most of the early guns, the Model 90 is full of blade-type springs, and some of these are flexed rather severely. There are five main trouble spots: the hammer and trigger springs, the extractor, the carrier lever spring, and the breech block lock. The flat hammer spring breaks occasionally, the trigger spring less often. Replacement of either of these is not difficult, and original parts are usually available from the used-parts dealers. If these can't be found, either of these springs can be duplicated in doubled round wire (piano wire).

The extractor is tempered to be its own spring, and in addition to extraction it also functions as a cartridge mover. The breech block is tilted upward at the time a cartridge is chambered, and there is a projection on the extractor, just to the rear of the beak, that pushes the round from the carrier into the chamber. When age has weakened the extractor, or there is

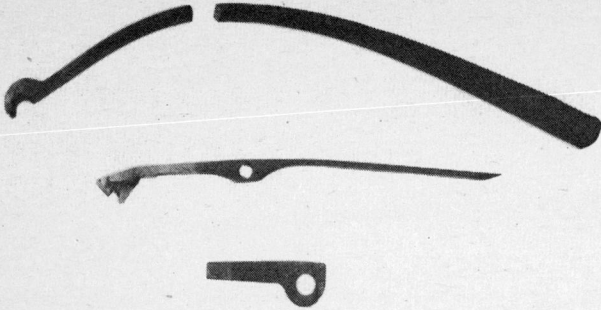

While the Model 1890 is a solid gun, there are three springs that are commonly replaced. They are, from top to bottom: the hammer spring (this one broken); the extractor (which is tempered to be its own spring); and the small carrier lever spring—the two bottom springs are intact.

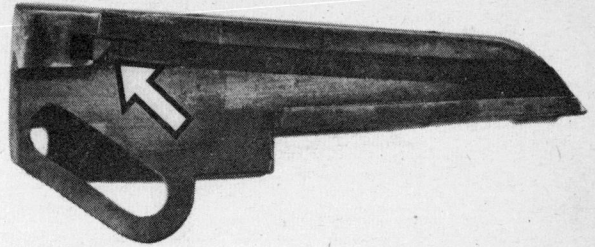

Arrow points to the bolt locking lug, an integral part of the firing pin. These rarely break, but wear in the locking recess inside the receiver can cause looseness.

resistance from dirt or a peened chamber edge, the forward portion of the extractor will often snap off. Used replacements can usually be found.

The only thing that could be called a chronic ailment is weakness or breakage of the carrier lever spring. This little curved blade is retained on the right side of the carrier by a small screw and bears on a lever which keeps the carrier positioned during the closing of the breech. The carrier is lifted into position by the opening movement of the breech block, but if the lever spring is weak or broken, the carrier will drop during the closing cycle and cause a misfeed. If a used replacement spring is unavailable, this one, also, can be replaced with round wire.

There is another trouble spot which can occur after many years of hard use. The breech block is locked in closed position by a projection on the forward left side of the firing pin which latches into a recess inside the receiver. The locking projection is harder than the receiver wall, and the recess edges will wear in time. It is sometimes possible to tighten the latching by careful peening of the upper edge of the latch recess, but if the wear is serious, it will require spot welding and recutting to restore tightness.

The firing pin of the Model 90 is a large, heavy part and seldom breaks. Occasionally the point will snap off, but this is easily replaced. The firing pin is retained in the breech block by a long, narrow bar of steel which is held in place by two tiny screws, and removal requires extreme care. It

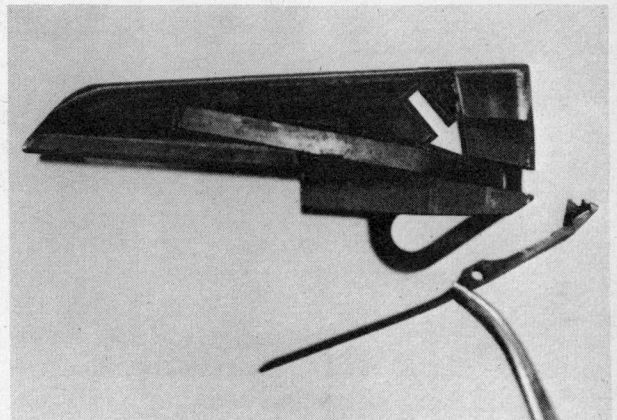

Still in place on the breech block is a broken extractor (arrow). The forceps hold a replacement.

should be slid out toward the rear of the breech block, as any attempt to pry it toward the side will break the bar at one of the screw holes.

In 1908, Winchester added an automatically-adjusting cartridge stop to the carrier, allowing the use of .22 Short, Long, or Long Rifle rounds, interchangeably. Other design changes were made in 1932, resulting in the Model 62, replaced in 1938 by the Model 62-A. When the Model 62-A was discontinued several years ago, the design refused to die. It was reproduced by the Rossi Company in Brazil and is currently available. Among all of the models, including the Rossi version, some parts are interchangeable, but this is not always possible.

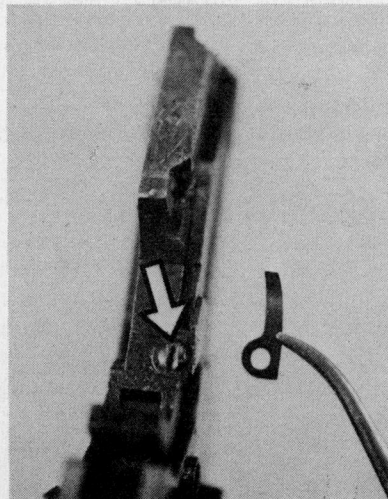

As mentioned, the carrier lever spring is subject to breakage. The arrow indicates a broken carrier lever spring, still in place, while the forceps hold a replacement.

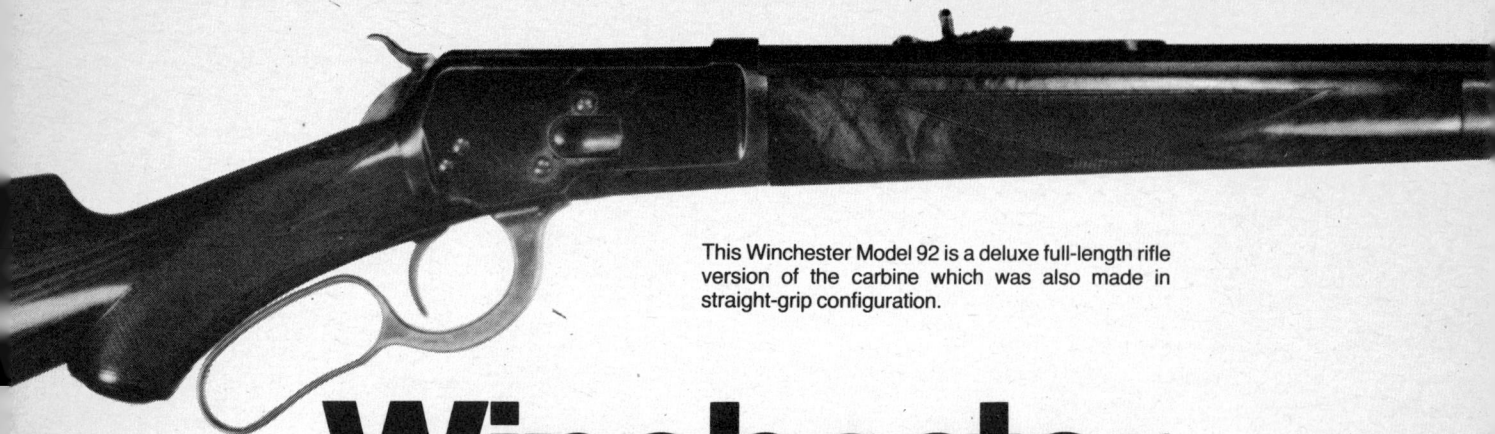

This Winchester Model 92 is a deluxe full-length rifle version of the carbine which was also made in straight-grip configuration.

Winchester Model 92 Rifle

Caliber designation will usually be found clearly marked on top of the barrel, just forward of the receiver. The oval marks are the Winchester proof.

In 1892, John M. Browning scaled down his design of the big Model 1886 Winchester, and chambered the smaller gun for the .25-20, .32-20, .38-40, and .44-40 cartridges. The latter two rounds were also common to the Colt Single Action revolver, and the westerner in remote locations could standardize his ammunition for rifle and handgun. For this reason, and several others, the Winchester Model 1892 became immensely popular. Although its cartridges were rather weak by today's standards, the rifle remained in production until 1932, and the carbine version was made until 1941. Between 1924 and 1932 a half-magazine gun with a redesigned forearm was offered, and designated the Model 53. In recent years, quite a few of the Model 92 guns in the .32-20 chambering have been converted to .357 Magnum, but this is not a simple alteration.

For the cartridges of its original chamberings, the Model 92 was an excellent design. As with most Browning-designed guns, there is

ample margin for strength in all parts, and breakage of any major component is quite unusual. There are a number of flat springs in the gun, and some of these may occasionally let go, or weaken with age. The hammer spring is a heavy blade, with a double hook and stirrup connection at the hammer. This one is rather difficult to reproduce, but replacement parts are often

available from the used-parts dealers because over a million of these guns were made. The loading gate has a tempered tail, supplying its own spring power, and even though this one is severely flexed in loading, it rarely breaks. The extractor is its own spring, and also seems immune to breakage, but is often found to be weakened, slipping off the rim of the

Loading gate (right arrow) is mounted in the receiver by a single screw (left arrow). This should be checked occasionally for tightness.

The long extractor (arrow) is tempered to be its own spring. Breakage is rare, but there may be some weakening with age and long use.

fired case and leaving it in the chamber. It is not too difficult to reshape and retemper the extractor, restoring the proper tension, but this should be done by a gunsmith.

The cartridge stop spring and trigger spring are also blade-types, but neither of these is severely flexed in normal operation. Even if one of these should break, they are simple to reproduce in any good gun shop. The top of the hammer face and the cocking surface on the underside of the breech block are susceptible to wear, and if it is severe enough, the hammer will fail to stay cocked when the action is cycled. To avoid affecting the heat treatment of these parts by welding, I usually repair this by drilling a small hole in the underside of the bolt at the cocking point, and installing a tapered hard steel pin, driven into place, to take up the wear.

Occasionally, a deformed lever or extreme wear in the area of the locking bolt pin will prevent the locking blocks from rising all the way to the top of their normal position in the receiver. Since the locking of the breech block depends on their full bearing surfaces, it is possible that any appreciable reduction of this might make the gun unsafe to fire. If you have a gun in which the tops of the locking blocks are not protruding slightly above the top edge of the receiver, even with the top curve of the bolt, it would be best to have it checked by a gunsmith before shooting it.

The Model 92 is not a complicated gun, and there is very little that can go wrong. The Winchester collectors are now trying to talk the shooters out of their pet Model 92 guns, usually with little success. A large number of these guns are still in everyday use.

Cocking of the hammer by the rear movement of the breech block occurs at the point indicated by the arrow. Extreme wear of either part at this location will result in a failure to cock when the action is cycled.

If the twin locking blocks do not rise to the level shown, because of a deformed lever or some other malfunction, the gun may not be safe to fire.

Winchester Model 94 Carbine

The famed John Moses Browning was the designer of the Winchester Model 1894 carbine and rifle, and with this in mind, it is no great surprise that the gun has been in continuous production with no basic changes for more than 80 years. Someone once ventured the opinion that more deer had been taken with this gun than any other—it's probably true. At the present time, more than 3 million Model 94 guns have been made. As might be expected with any design that has gone unchanged for this length of time, the Model 94 seldom needs repair. There are, however, a few things that may need attention, especially on the older guns that have seen a lot of use.

For a time in the mid-to-late '60's, Winchester experimented with a cartridge carrier made of formed sheet steel, and aside from having a cheap appearance, they were also susceptible to deformation or breakage, depending on the level of heat treatment they received. After numerous complaints, the factory (in recent years) has returned to using the old-style solid steel carrier. The long extractor, visible on top of the breech block, is tempered to be its own spring. This is a heavy part, and I can't recall ever seeing one of them broken. On older

The long extractor of the Model 94 (arrow) is tempered to be its own spring. Breakage is rare, but they occasionally weaken after many years of use.

guns, they do occasionally become a little weak, the beak slipping off the cartridge rim and leaving the fired case in the chamber. When this occurs, it is usually possible to reshape and retemper the extractor. Or, it can simply be replaced, as all parts are readily available.

A massive locking bolt rises behind the breech block when the action is closed, and it contains a short striker which connects the hammer with the firing pin. If there is some malfunc-

Winchester, for a time, experimented with a carrier made of formed sheet steel, but soon returned to the solid machined part shown.

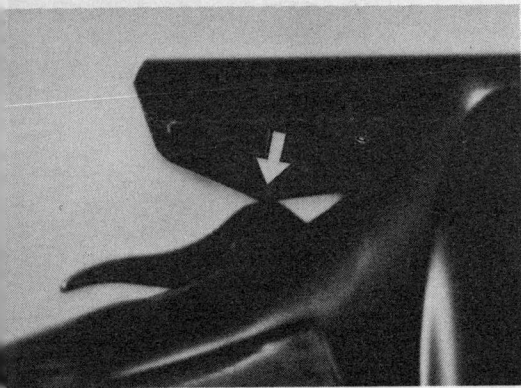

On older guns, extreme wear of breech block or hammer at the point indicated by the arrow will cause cocking failure when the action is cycled.

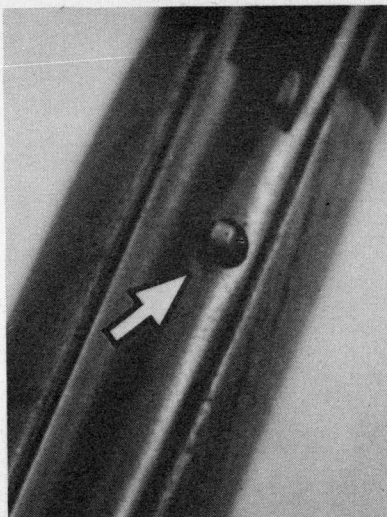

The safety catch (arrow), located on the lower tang, blocks trigger movement until the lever is fully closed.

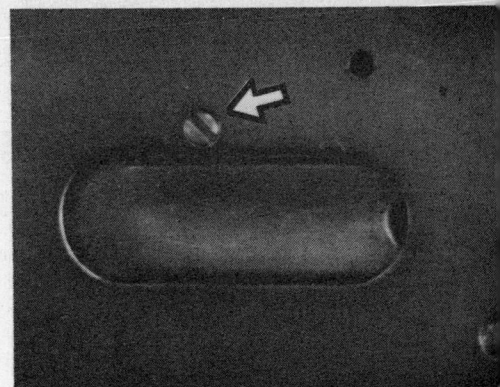

Internal cartridge guides are mounted in the receiver by a single external screw (arrow) on each side. These should be checked occasionally for tightness.

The loading gate is mounted by a single screw (arrow) which threads directly into its spring-tempered tail.

tion that prevents the locking bolt from rising to the top level of the receiver to properly lock the breech (an unlikely occurrence), the separate striker would not align with the firing pin, and the gun could not be fired.

On older guns, there is often considerable wear at the top of the hammer and on the underside of the breech block at the rear. If the wear is severe enough, the opening of the action will fail to depress the hammer enough for proper sear engagement, and the hammer will fail to cock, following the breech block forward as it closes. There are several ways to correct this, including the installation of a new hammer, or, in extreme cases, a new breech block as well. Adding steel by welding is unwise, as it will affect the factory heat treatment of the parts. I have often repaired this condition by drilling the top of the hammer and force-fitting a slightly tapered hard steel pin, then trimming it off until the hammer is depressed to the proper level.

In the lower tang, just to the rear of the trigger, there is a small protruding button that is an extension of a part which Winchester calls the safety catch. It is actually a trigger block, preventing movement of the trigger until the button is depressed by a flat surface of the lever. This system insures that if the finger should bump the trigger during operation of the lever, the hammer will not be released. On some Model 94 guns, especially those of very recent manufacture, the spring that powers this part is *very*

strong, and in some extreme cases, a conscious effort is required to keep the lever squeezed tightly enough to free the trigger. The problem is not as serious as it sounds, since any gunsmith can slightly weaken the spring. In this same area, I have received several questions over the years regarding the "looseness" of the Model 94 trigger when the gun is not cocked. This is a normal and harmless feature of the gun, but if it causes concern, it is not too difficult to make a replacement for the combination sear and safety spring that has an altered shape on the sear side thus eliminating the "loose trigger" syndrome. Before you ask—no, I don't know of anyone who makes the spring commercially.

The internal cartridge guides, one on each side, are mounted in the receiver by a single external screw, one for each guide, the one on the right being just above the loading gate. These screws should be checked for tightness every so often, and this same advice applies to the loading gate screw, located to the rear of the loading gate. The tail of the loading gate (into which this screw is threaded) is tempered to be the loading gate spring. Here, again, they seldom break but will often weaken with age. The cures are the same as described in reference to the extractor—either replace the part, or have a gunsmith reshape and retemper the tail to re-

store its tension.

I can recall, over a long period of time, replacing one broken ejector, and one broken carrier spring, but these were isolated cases and do not indicate any chronic weakness in those parts. In obtaining or ordering any replacement parts for the Model 94, it should be noted that some parts, such as the ejector mentioned above, have been changed very slightly over the years, and you should *always* give the serial number of your gun when ordering.

Shown here is the carbine version of the Winchester Model 100.

Winchester Model 100 Rifle

Made from 1960 to 1974, the Model 100 may have been dropped from the Winchester line because it became too expensive to manufacture while keeping the price within reason. It was a well-designed and well-made gun. Its gas system was a particularly good feature, as it had an expansion chamber which allowed a gradual buildup of gas pressure and expansion against the piston. Because of this, the Model 100 would operate with loads of different levels without adjustment; and, within reasonable pressure ranges, handloads would function with no problem—a situation found in few semi-auto rifles.

The Model 100 has a three-lug bolt head which turns to lock on closing. The turning is governed by a large cross-pin riding in helical open tracks in the bolt sleeve. The bolt is actually a three-piece system, consisting of the bolt head, bolt sleeve, and the main body of the bolt. (Winchester refers to these as the bolt, bolt sleeve lock, and bolt sleeve, respectively.) I think the

When the action is removed from the stock, the trigger group is retained only by a tiny pin at its forward end, and care should be taken that the group isn't damaged.

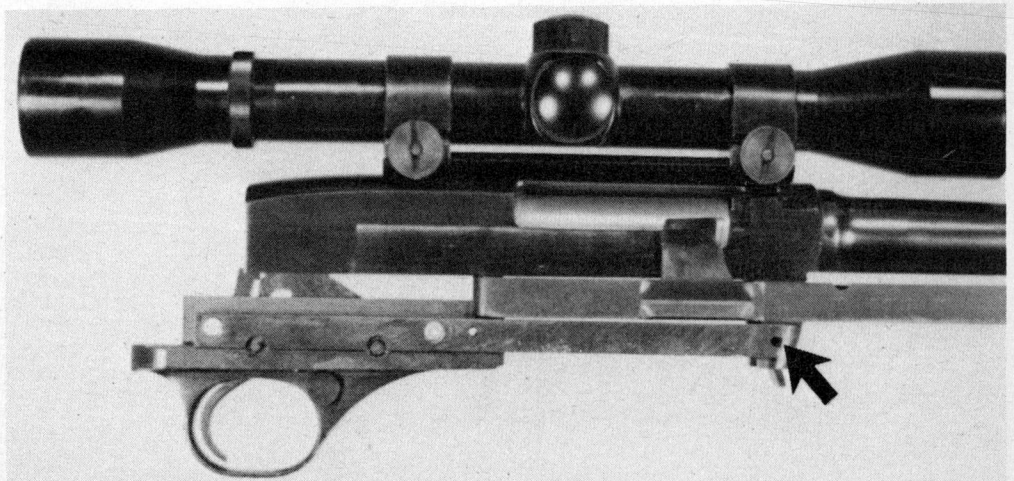

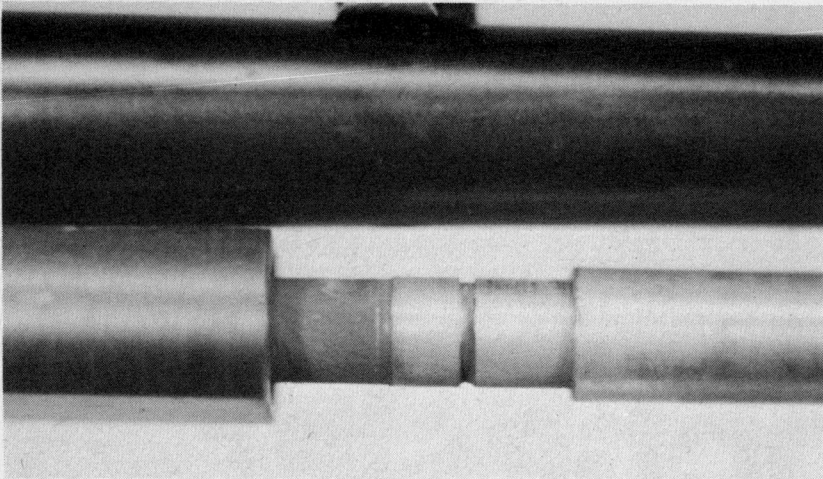

Here's the gas piston of the Model 100, shown with the operating slide retracted. Note the buildup of powder residue on the piston.

amateur should be discouraged from disassembling this unit, as there is a way to put it back together wrong, and it will go back into the gun that way. No danger, it just won't work. So, unless you are very familiar with the inner workings of this gun, it's best to leave takedown of the bolt to a professional.

The extractor of this gun is very similar in design to the one used in the new Model 70 rifle and is set into a T-slot in one of the bolt lugs. It's a tiny thing, but the stress pattern is well-engineered, and breakage should not be common. If one should break, installing a replacement is not difficult, and parts are, of course, available. This gun has a double ejector, twin plunger-types, and ejection is very positive.

Because of its passage through the bolt sleeve lock pin, and its retention by the bolt sleeve pin, the firing pin has a rather slim forward section, with a rebated area behind its retention collar. I have seen several cases of breakage at this point, but not in sufficient quantity to call this a chronic ailment. When it does happen, though, the bad thing about it is that the broken off rear portion of the firing pin can come out the rear of the bolt and jam the action. If this happens during the firing cycle, there can be damage to other parts.

Just as in most gas-operated guns, the piston of the Model 100 will, in time, accumulate powder-gas residue, and this should be removed every so often. If not, the buildup can retard the proper operation of the system. This should be done by a gunsmith, as there is a possibility of damage during

amateur disassembly of the gas assembly. I can usually tell when a Model 100 has been disassembled by a non-gunsmith—the little spring retainer for the gas cylinder cap will almost invariably be installed on top of the cap, next to the barrel. Apparently, some like doing things the hard way.

When the action is removed from the stock, the trigger housing is retained on the receiver only by a small pin at its forward end. If the action is dropped while out of the stock, or the trigger group struck sharply against some unyielding object, the forward side bars of the housing can be deformed, creating a whole set of problems. They can be straightened, but this will require the attention of a professional. Just as with the bolt, leave general takedown to a gunsmith.

The gas cylinder cap retainer (arrow) can be installed as shown without harm but is difficult to remove in this position. It is supposed to clip on from below.

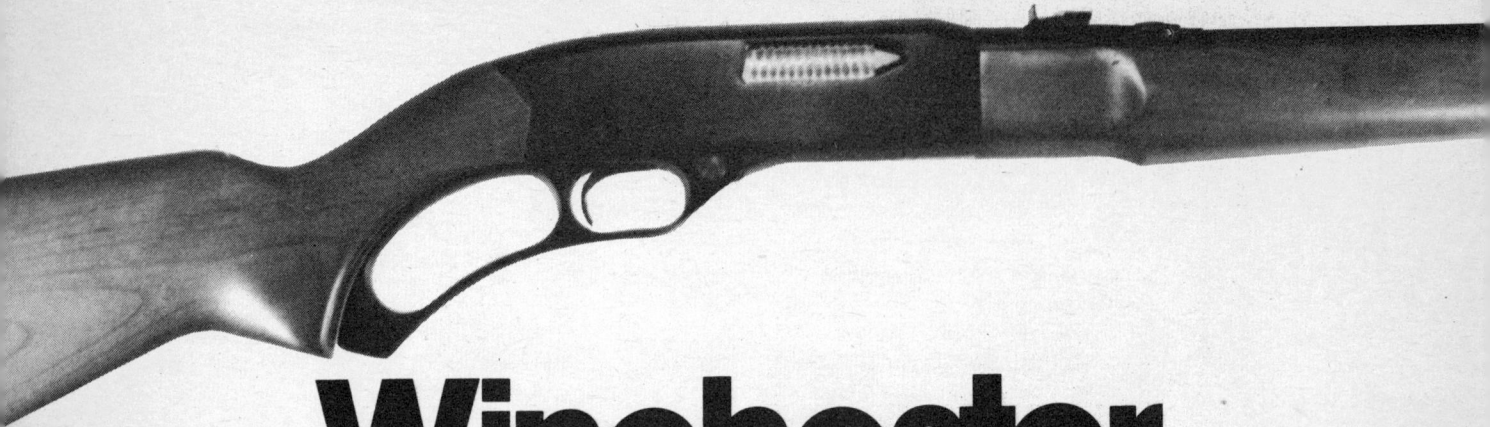

Winchester Model 250 Rifle

Among .22 lever-action rifles, the "hammerless" types have never enjoyed wide popularity. There have been models by Remington, Mossberg, Marlin, Noble and Winchester, and all were made for a relatively short time and then discontinued. The last to go, just a few years ago, was the Winchester Model 250. The rifle looked good and handled well, and one outstanding feature of the design was the mounting of the trigger in the lever unit, traveling with the lever when the action is operated. If the trigger should be pressed when the lever is closed, a disconnector prevents firing until the trigger is released and pulled again. With no need to remove the trigger finger when working the lever, subsequent aimed shots can be delivered quickly. And, there is no chance of pinching the trigger finger, as can happen with guns having a receiver-mounted trigger.

The arrow points to the engagement of the lever arm with the stud on the bolt locking plate. All of the tension of bolt movement and locking is centered on this small pin.

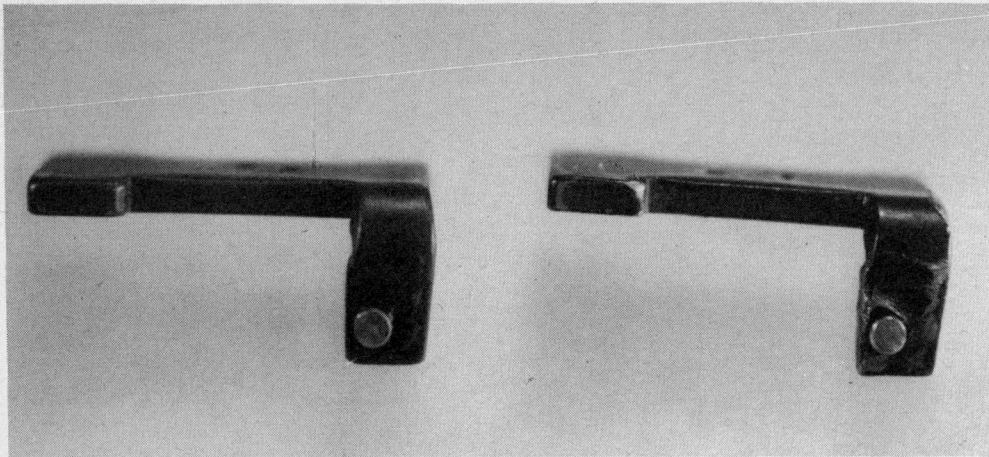

On the left is a new locking plate. To the right is one that has been well used—note how the contact stud has loosened and deformed the lower end of the plate arm.

There were a couple of mechanical factors that may have contributed to the demise of the Model 250. The bolt locking plate is recessed into the top of the bolt and tilts up at the rear to lock against a shoulder inside the top of the receiver. The receiver is made of aluminum alloy, and the locking plate is steel. After some time, the locking shoulder in the receiver will begin to peen over and wear, creating a condition that might "charitably" be described as slight excess headspace. The first indication of this will be bulging of the case heads, and when it reaches certain proportions, the gun will begin to misfire. This condition can be repaired by installing angled steel pins in the top of the receiver, to supply a new shoulder for the locking plate.

The locking plate has an arm which extends down the left side of the bolt, with a small riveted pin at the forward lower edge of the arm. This pin contacts an L-shaped open track in the upper extension of the lever, serving to move the bolt and cam the locking plate upward in the final movement of the lever. The pin is under great strain and is located very near the edge of the arm. In time, it works loose, enlarges its hole in the arm, and deforms the edge. Parts are available, for the time being, and replacement of the locking plate will correct the problem. If no replacement can be found conveniently, a spot of weld can be used to stabilize the pin, after correction of any deformation that may have occurred. Late in the production of this rifle, Winchester redesigned the lockplate, eliminating this problem.

The sear and disconnector system of this gun has a fairly delicate engagement, but this seems to produce no problems unless an amateur gunsmith attempts to "adjust" the trigger pull. Any alteration of the parts in this system is usually not repairable, and will require replacement of the entire unit. The cartridge feed guide is of very lightweight steel, and here, again, any "adjustment" will likely produce the need for a new part.

The safety, a cross-bolt type, is also the pivot for the lever, and once again we have the situation of a steel part in an alloy assembly. After long years of use, the cross-tunnel can become "washed out," and the safety will begin to wobble. Also, the safety is positioned by one tail of the hammer spring, and any weakening of this spring can allow an indefinite positioning of the safety.

If the rifle is used infrequently—say, once a year during squirrel season—it may be several years before any of the problems described make an appearance. As an every-weekend plinking gun, though, it's not the best choice.

Winchester Model 9422 Rifle

It was intended to be a small-caliber companion to the popular Model 94 carbine, so its close external resemblance to that excellent gun is no accident. The Model 9422 is available in two chamberings—regular .22 (it handles Short, Long, and Long Rifle interchangeably), and .22 Magnum. Introduced in 1972, this gun is one of the currently-made *high-quality* Winchester products, and goes a long way toward making up for some of the .22 rifles they produced between 1963 and 1972. I have found only one part in the gun that is not solid steel—the plastic magazine follower, a part that is under no great stress. Even in places where others cheat a little with alloy, such as the barrel bands, the Model 9422 has steel. It's a relatively expensive .22 rifle, but it's worth the price.

Removal of a single large coin-slotted screw which crosses the rear of the receiver allows separation of the front and rear sections of the gun, but this is intended for thorough cleaning or repair, not casual takedown or transportation. Removal of the buttstock and receiver sub-frame frees the bolt and bolt slide, and there are certain small parts which can be lost or damaged through careless handling while the gun is taken down. The bolt cam pin, for example, is free to fall out when the bolt is taken out and separated from the bolt slide, and if the

A single, large, coin-slotted screw (arrow) allows the separation of the firing mechanism and buttstock from the receiver.

bolt is dropped, the ejector and its spring are easily damaged.

The bolt itself should not be disassembled by the nonprofessional, but if for some reason this has to be done, it should be noted that the piece of tempered round-wire at the lower left edge of the bolt is not the spring for the carrier pawl, it is just the retainer. The spring is a tiny coil, located inside the round pawl-piece, and might be overlooked and lost unless you are aware that it's there.

The cartridge feed system of the Model 9422 is very similar to one used in an earlier Winchester design, the Model 61, and this is the reason for its reliability. When the cartridge leaves the magazine, its rim is gripped by an extractor-like part at the lower right edge of the bolt. As the cartridge is lifted upward by the carrier, its rim is sliding in a T-slot on the front face of the bolt. When it gets to the top, it is gripped by two extractors, right and left. At no time during the feeding process is the cartridge free, and there is no chance for misfeeding. The car-

Upper arrow points to the bolt cam pin which is free to fall out when the bolt is removed from the receiver—it's easily lost. The ejector and its spring (lower arrow) are occasionally subject to damage.

The carrier pawl (arrow) is not powered by the tempered round wire that crosses it, but has its own internal coil spring.

Because of the two-piece bolt assembly—the bolt and the bolt slide at the rear—the firing pin system is also a two-part arrangement. A flat firing pin striker is located at the rear in the bolt slide, and the firing pin is up forward, in the bolt. Neither part appears to have any weak points that might lead to eventual breakage. When the action is cycled, the bolt tips downward at the rear to unlock, and when this occurs the striker is no longer aligned with the firing pin. Thus, if the trigger is touched and the hammer falls when the action is partly open, the gun won't fire.

With the exception of the disassembly cautions mentioned earlier, the gun has no other quirks, and *no* trouble spots. The Winchester Model 9422 is one of the *very good* ones.

tridge cutoff of the Model 61 was sometimes a source of difficulty, but the one in the 9422 is of entirely different design, and has ample allowance for wear.

The spring which keeps the finger lever snug when not in operation is a flat type, but it is not severely flexed in normal operation, and I can see little chance for breakage. It might weaken slightly after long and hard use, but it could easily be reshaped and retempered, or simply replaced—all parts are available, and will be for a good long while.

The cartridge cutoff (left arrow) is designed to preclude breakage or wear. The lever arm (right arrow) is a separate part. If it is damaged, the lever does not have to be replaced.

Here's the bolt shown in locked position, with the bolt slide piece attached. Note the angled track in the slide piece which controls the vertical movement of the bolt.

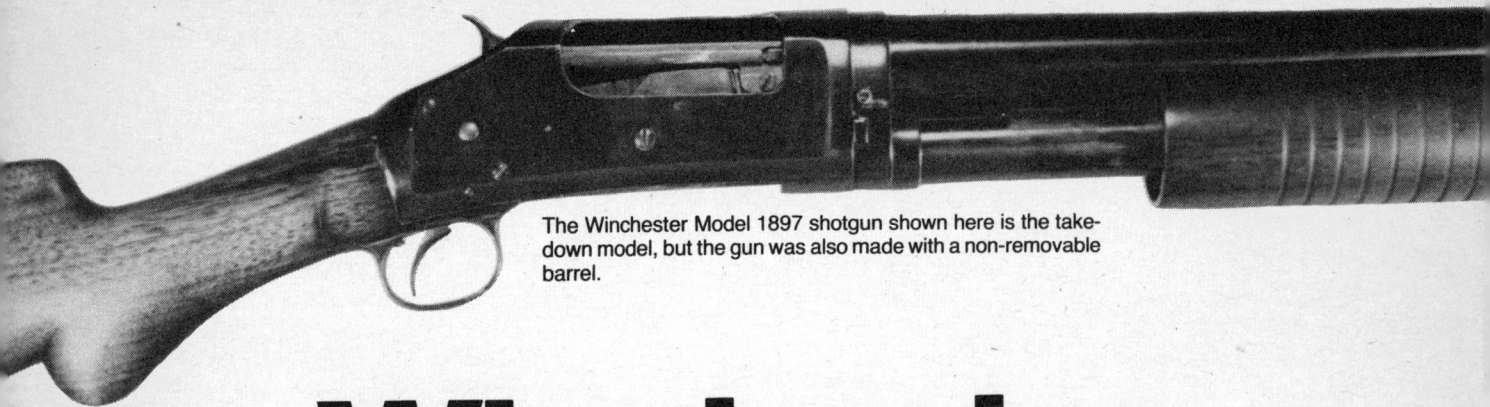

The Winchester Model 1897 shotgun shown here is the take-down model, but the gun was also made with a non-removable barrel.

Winchester Model 1897 Shotgun

In these days of the sleek, modern slide-action shotgun, a surprising number of hunters—and they're not all old-timers—insist on using a gun designed more than 80 years ago. The Winchester 97's only real advantage is an external hammer—its heavy carrier and poor mechanical advantage result in an action cycle that requires a very strong arm. In spite of this, many owners of the old 97s will not even consider trading them in for a more modern gun. Perhaps one reason is its bank vault bolt locking system. When that massive carrier swings up to lock behind the bolt face, it gives a feeling of security. John Moses Browning designed it to be tough, and through years of hard use, the 97 has demonstrated this well.

The Model 1897 has its ailments, of course, but most of them show up only after many of those "years of hard use" mentioned above. The ejector breaks with some frequency. This part is a small piece of formed spring steel only .025-inch in thickness, and it receives a sharp blow from the shell rim each time the action is opened. It is backed up by a solid steel block, but breakage is common enough that it's a good idea to keep an extra one on hand. Two items of good news on this: First, the part has been reproduced in modern times and is readily available; second, the part can be replaced without stripping the gun since the ejector is retained by an external screw, its tip entering a hole in the receiver.

The gun was made in both takedown and solid-frame types, the latter being made in smaller quantity. In the takedown model, wear of the helical locking lugs (interrupted threads) on the magazine tube can allow the tube to slip out of the receiver on the forward stroke of the action slide. There are several ways to repair this. The most frequently seen *wrong* way is to add bronze weld to the worn lugs. The heat will almost always warp the tube out of round, interfering with feeding. One repair method that will work is to install two or three very short screws in the sides and bottom of the re-ceiver, extending into the tube, their tips faced off to clear the shells. Also, the magazine tube hanger screws and their spacer can be (if necessary) shortened, allowing the hanger to clamp the magazine and barrel tight-ly, helping to ease the strain on the added screws. With this method you no longer have the easy takedown sys-tem, but in some ways that's good, as it will prevent further wear in the bar-rel-mounting area.

The carrier is locked in place by a laterally-pivoted narrow bar of steel which lies in a recess on the left side of the carrier. If the locking well in-side the receiver becomes worn, or the lock bar spring weakens, the car-rier, which is also the bolt block, can fail to lock in place when the action is closed. When this condition occurs, amateur gunsmiths will often attempt to cold bend the lock bar outward for better contact without removing it from the carrier. The lock bar is ex-tremely hard, and when this is tried, it will always break. The proper way is to remove the bar from the carrier,

On the takedown model, extreme wear of the magazine mounting threads (arrow) can cause the entire assembly to pull loose on the forward stroke of the action.

When the slide-lock bar (arrow) or its seat inside the receiver become worn, the gun will fail to lock closed when the action is run forward.

Extreme wear of the upper surface of the bolt guide channels (arrow) can cause the hammer to miss reaching full-cock when the action is cycled.

heat it to the right color, and bend it just enough to give improved contact. It should then be rehardened, of course. It's a job for your gunsmith.

When a Model 97 is well-worn from years of use, it may fail to cock when the action is cycled, the hammer coming down when the action closes. Usually, this is due to wear of the bolt tracks in the receiver, the bolt tipping upward at its rear limit of travel and failing to depress the hammer enough for sear engagement. This can be corrected in several ways. A very small spot of steel weld on the upper surface of each bolt track in the receiver, recut to fit, will cure it. Or, a hard steel pin installed on each side in the same location works. A less fancy way is to peen the edge of each track, at the rear, inside. In each of these methods, the idea is to lower the bolt and minimize tipping, so that it will depress the hammer enough for engagement of the sear.

The Model 97 was discontinued on January 1, 1957, and by that time nearly a million had been made. They still bring down the game and command good prices on the used-gun market. It takes a long, long time for a Browning design to die.

The Model 1897's ejector (arrow) is externally mounted on the left side of the receiver and is easy to replace.

This is the ejector, a simple piece of spring steel with a screw loop—replacements are readily available.

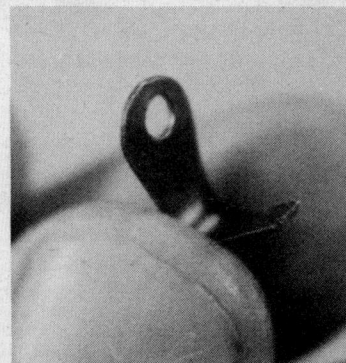

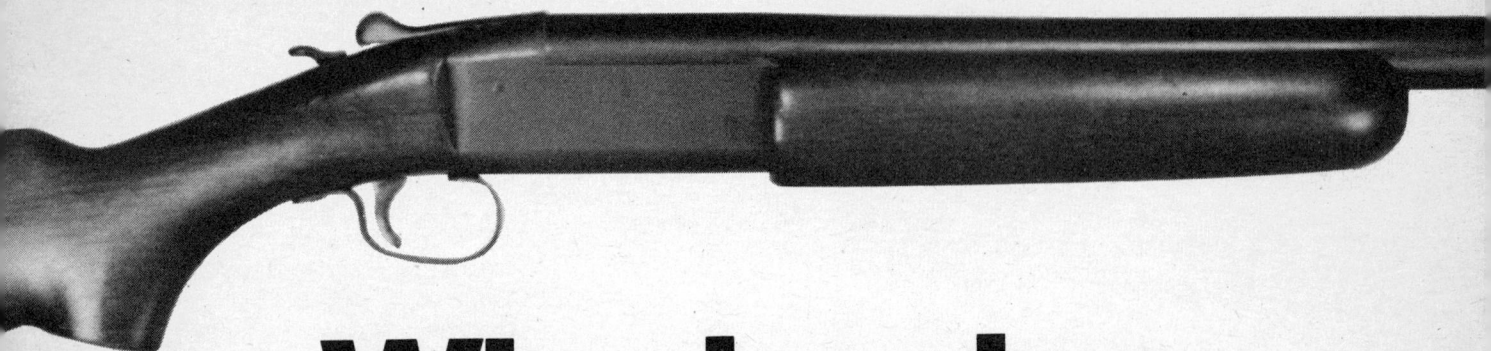

Winchester Model 37 Shotgun

Winchester's first top-break single-barrel shotgun was the Model 37, made from 1936 to 1963. In 1968, a completely redesigned version was offered, designated the Model 370. Then, in 1973, the basic Model 370 was altered to become the Model

A poorly-made foreign copy of this gun was imported a few years ago, but the true Model 37 guns are deeply marked in this manner on the bottom of the receiver.

The narrow ejector, an automatic trip-catch type, is prone to breakage.

37A, and this one is still in production. Mechanically, there is very little similarity between the Model 37A and its ancestor, the Model 37. The Model 370 and Model 37A, for example, have a true pivoting hammer and a firing pin mounted in the receiver.

In the Model 37, the part behind the barrel latch lever that appears to be a hammer is actually a cocking lever, directly attached to a combination firing pin and striker. The firing pin/striker is divided at the rear to admit the unthreaded shank of a small screw which enters from the topstrap of the frame, and this screw shank forms the base for the heavy spring which surrounds the striker. When the gun is cocked, the compression of the spring puts considerable stress on the unsup-

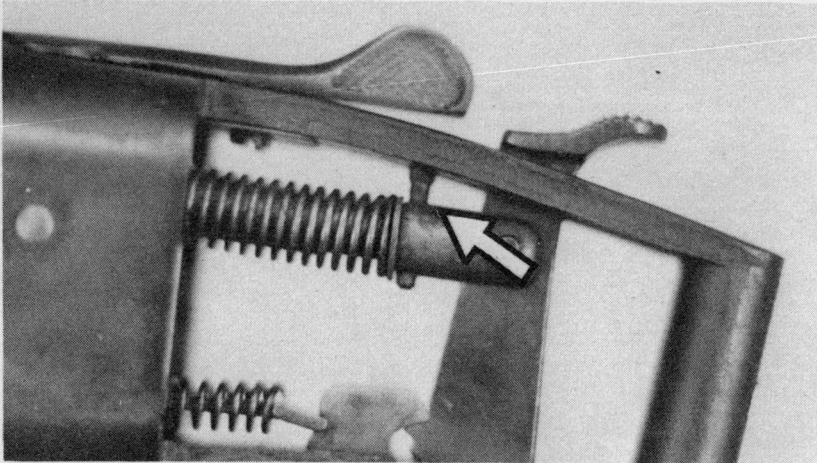

When the gun is cocked, the lower extension of a small screw (arrow) supports the considerable tension of the striker spring. This was not one of Winchester's better ideas.

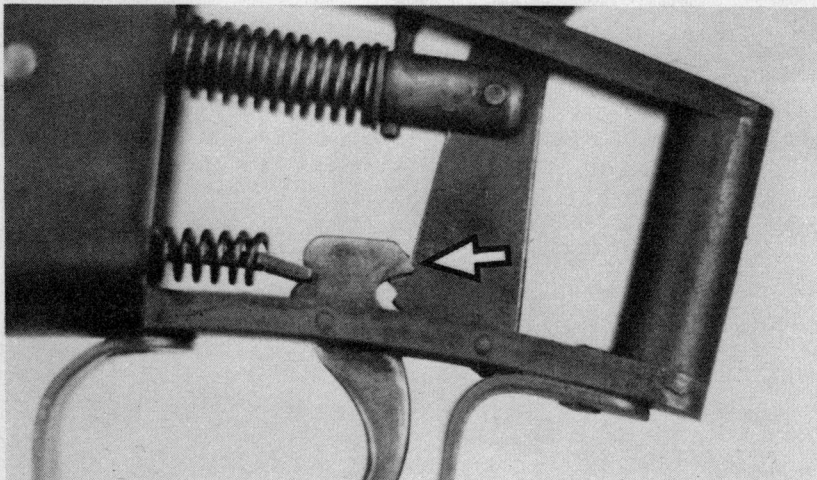

In this view, the cocking lever is in the safety position. The arrow indicates the contact point of the sear beak and the safety step on the lever.

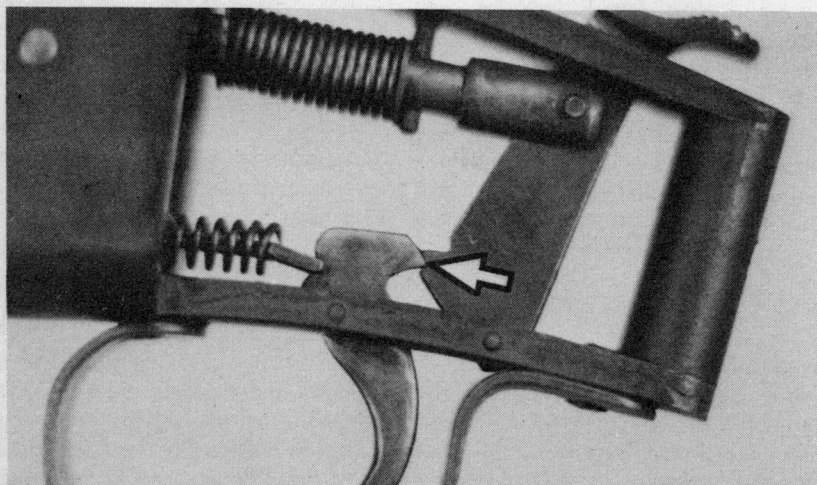

Here, the arrow points to the engagement of the hammer-like cocking lever and the sear beak on the trigger. In this view, the gun is cocked.

ported shank of the screw, and bending and breakage are a frequent problem. This system was not one of Winchester's better ideas, and it was wisely abandoned in the two models which followed.

The hammer-like cocking lever is pivoted and retained by a very small cross-pin through the lower tang of the receiver, and the size of this pin is often not equal to the stress. Breakage and bending are not uncommon. At the lower front edge of the striker lever is a projection that contacts the sear beak, an integral part of the trigger. There are two notches, one for full-cock and one for a safety step. It should be noted that a direct blow on the cocking lever spur may break the pivot pin, and if this happens, there is nothing to prevent its being driven forward to fire a chambered shell.

The Model 37 has an automatic trip-catch type ejector, which snaps out as the action is fully opened to kick the fired shell clear of the chamber. The ejector is quite narrow, made from flat stock, and is deeply cut near its forward end for the beak of the ejector sear. At this point, it often breaks. The factory may still have some parts for the Model 37, but I can tell you one certain thing—they have no ejectors in 12, 20, or .410 gauge. If a replacement can't be found among the used-parts dealers, the only alternatives are to repair the broken ejector by welding, or have a gunsmith make a replacement. Here, again, in the design of the Models 370 and 37A, the ejector is of a much more sturdy pattern.

A final note about the little screw that serves as the base for the striker spring (the factory designation is the "firing pin spring stop screw"): I have, on several occasions, replaced these with a slightly heavier part, a block of steel cut to fit the slot in the striker and retained by two screws through the topstrap, one of them using the original hole for the stop screw. This solves the problem for good, but comes under the heading of custom alterations and is not really practical for a low-priced single-barrel shotgun. Trading for a Model 37A is a much better idea.

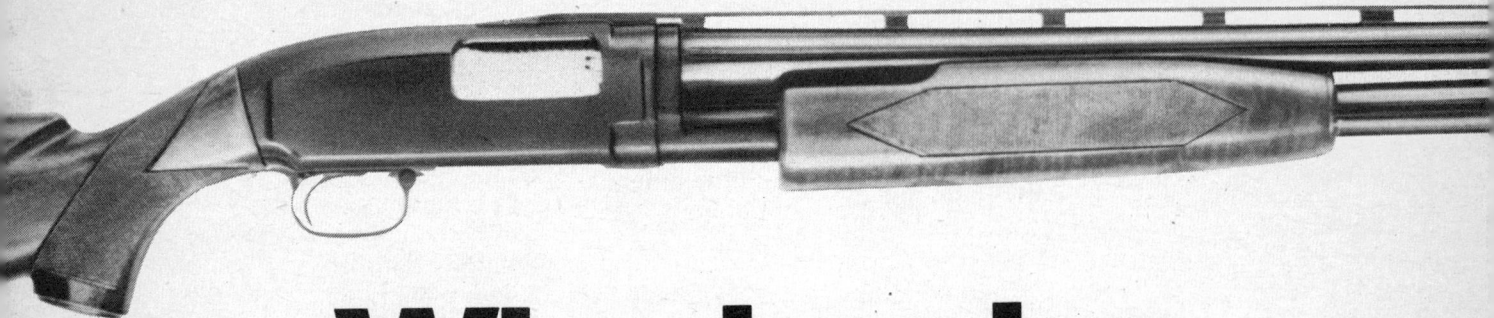

Winchester Model 12 Shotgun

Winchester's first enclosed-hammer slide-action shotgun was originally called the Model 1912 and was designed by Thomas C. Johnson. It was first offered only in 20 gauge, and in 1914 became available in 12- and 16-gauge chamberings. A 28-gauge version was added in 1934. During its time of production, the gun was made in a great variety of styles and barrel

Not as sturdy as the primary extractor on the right, the left extractor (left arrow) is more susceptible to breakage. The firing pin retractor (right arrow) is often left out during amateur reassembly of the bolt. The gun will work without it, but there is a possibility of accidental firing.

The action slide lock is activated by two straight round-wire springs which contact a lug on the left side of the hammer. The top spring is visible here, indicated by the arrow.

lengths, including models for field, trap, Skeet, and the military. The original design was so good that very few changes in the basic mechanism have been made over the years. The number of guns produced passed the 1 million mark in 1943, and when the Model 12 was discontinued in 1965, it was still so wanted by both shooters and collectors that prices soon rose to ridiculous levels. Because of this demand, Winchester resumed production of the gun in 1972, and a deluxe trap version is still being made.

As indicated by its popularity and long manufacturing time, the Model 12 is unusually dependable, with few chronic ailments. One of the very few weak points in the mechanical design is the system used for locking and release of the slide lock, which is activated by two straight round-wire springs which contact a lug on the left side of the hammer. These springs are riveted in place in recesses on the inside face of the slide lock, the upper spring lifting the lock when the hammer is cocked, and the lower one

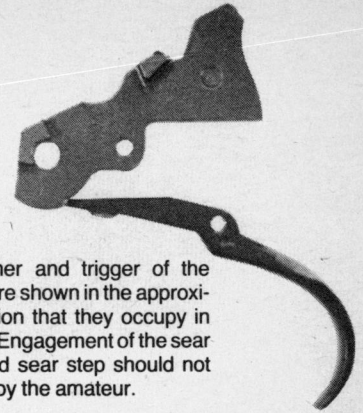

With long use, there may be wear on the disconnector arm of the slide lock at its contact point with the hammer (arrow). Repair of this condition should be left to the gunsmith.

The hammer and trigger of the Model 12 are shown in the approximate position that they occupy in the action. Engagement of the sear surface and sear step should not be altered by the amateur.

When tightened, the carrier pivot screw (arrow) *must* be turned to the left as it has a left-hand thread.

moving the lock downward when the hammer falls. When one of these little springs breaks—and they do, eventually—replacement is not a simple job. The springs are mounted at two levels, one atop the other, and it is usually the innermost one that goes, requiring that the unbroken outer spring be unstaked to replace it. There is, however, one bit of good news. If original Winchester parts are not available locally, the springs are easily made from round-wire spring stock of a suitable diameter. Replacement of these springs is most definitely a job for a competent gunsmith.

The primary extractor, on the right side of the breech block, is well-made, and sturdy, and breakage is unusual. The left extractor, however, is not as strong, because it is not subject to as much direct stress. These do break occasionally, the fracture usually occurring between the pivot point and the forward beak. All parts for the Model 12 are usually readily available, and installation is not difficult.

The firing pin retractor, located in a slot in the top of the breech block, has been known to break at its narrowest point, just behind the pivot. Some amateur gunsmiths, finding that the gun will work without it, just leave it out during reassembly. This is unwise, as the heavy firing pin will then make the gun prone to inertial firing, setting the scene for an accident.

The narrow ejector, free-mounted in a recess in the left inside wall of the receiver, has a delicate appearance, but breakage is unusual. It is powered by a slightly curved blade-type spring which is staked to its base, and the spring will occasionally succumb to fatigue, either breaking or losing tension. Replacement is not difficult, and

if original parts are not at hand it is easily made.

With long use, there may be wear of the disconnector arm of the slide lock at is contact point with the lug on the hammer. It is often possible for a gunsmith to recut the beak of the arm to correct this, but in extreme cases the entire slide lock must be replaced. A badly worn beak can be built up with weld, but this necessitates removal of the two springs mentioned earlier, to prevent damage from the welding heat.

The sear of the Model 12 is an integral part of the forward extension of the trigger, and its engagement with the sear step on the hammer should not be altered by the amateur. It is possible to alter the trigger pull of this gun, but this should be done only by a professional.

There are numerous screws on the Model 12 that should be checked occasionally for tightness, and one of these, the carrier pivot screw, has a left-hand thread. To tighten it, it is turned toward the *left*, and care should be taken against its loss. The carrier plunger screw, on the opposite side, is staked in place and should not be disturbed during routine disassembly. It is not likely to loosen in normal use.

The magazine band bushing screws and the magazine plug screws should also be kept tight to prevent loss. In the case of a very loose magazine band, there is a method of tightening this by removing a very small portion of the band screw tips and an equal amount from the surface ends of the bushing, but this is an operation best left to your gunsmith.

The shell stop, or "cartridge cutoff," as Winchester calls it, is of good design, and it is not susceptible to wear or breakage. I know of one case in which the lower rear edge of the breech block sheared off, at the contact point of the action slide bar, but I think this could be viewed as a freak occurrence. In spite of the quirks which can appear with age and long use, the Model 12 is one of the very good ones.

The carrier plunger screw (arrow) is staked in place for good reason. It should not be removed during routine disassembly.

Winchester Model 190 Rifle

This is Winchester's low-priced .22 semi-auto, and it has a "deluxe" counterpart, the Model 290, which has a checkered stock and forend plus other refinements. The mechanical details are the same. Their latest semi-auto gun, the Model 490, has a different mechanism.

On the Model 190 the weakest point in the design is the combination sear/disconnector unit. Made of thin formed steel, this unit is pivoted at the rear, and its top forward projection is struck by the rear edge of the bolt as it cycles—an arrangement that is not mechanically efficient. At its forward tip, the disconnector arm has a small projection that is right-angled into a large hole in the trigger group to limit its upward travel. The little limiting projection breaks off with some frequency and requires replacement of the entire unit. These units are readily available and inexpensive, and installation is not difficult. It is also possible to install a limit-pin in the disconnector arm to replace the broken tip, and this will cure the problem without parts replacement.

The cartridge guide, which holds the round picked up from the magazine in position for feeding into the chamber, is of rather lightweight formed steel. In normal use, it will usually cause no difficulty. With any improper disassembly or reassembly, or other tampering, however, it is easily deformed. If the cartridge guide does become deformed, it can often be straightened, or easily replaced.

The bolt cocking handle of the Model 190 has always reminded me of an old-fashioned electric lamp switch, and is not the sort of thing

The arrow points to the forward tip of the disconnector where a small projection is right-angled into a hole in the trigger group. Unfortunately, breakage of the tip is frequent.

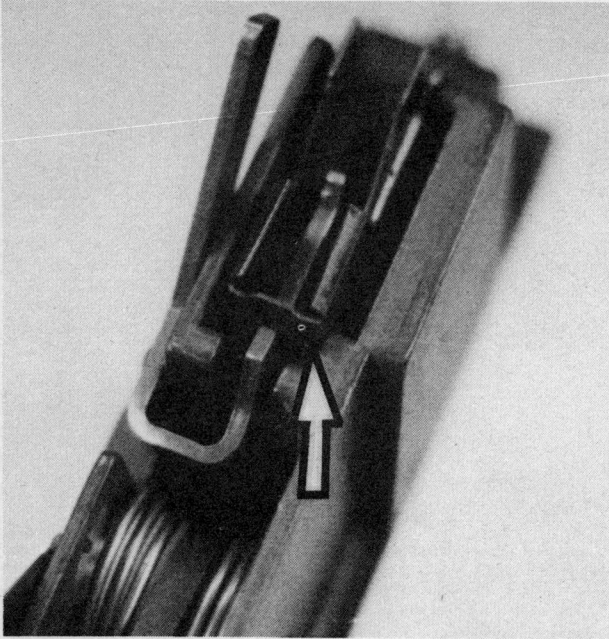

CAUTION: Don't tamper with the cartridge guide (arrow). It's made of rather lightweight formed steel and will, if abused, become deformed.

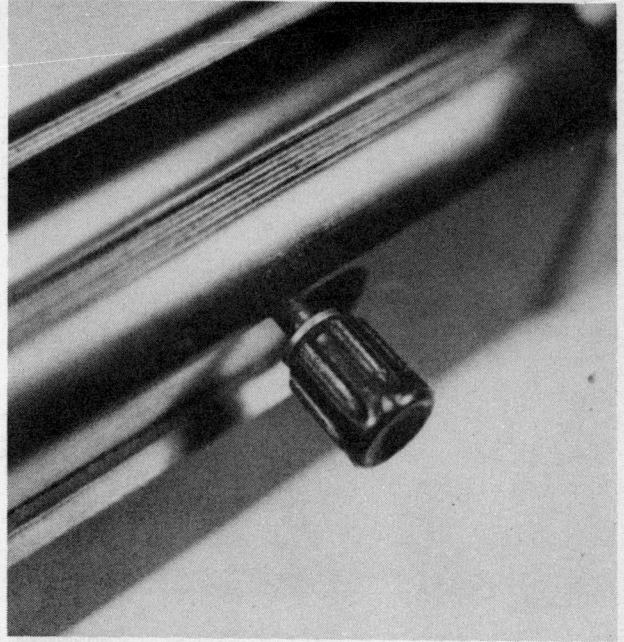

Treat the Model 190's cocking handle with some degree of care. The handle itself is a ridged plastic knob on a small-diameter steel shaft—a few cases of shaft bending and/or knob breakage have been observed.

you'd expect to find on a Winchester. It consists of a ridged plastic knob on a steel shaft of relatively small diameter, and a few cases of broken knobs and bent shafts have been seen. On several occasions I have made solid steel replacements with necks of slightly larger diameter, and any gunsmith could do the same. Original replacements are available at low cost.

On very early guns, the magazine tube hanger and lock system were of plastic, as was the rear sight—there was frequent breakage. On later guns (like this one), these parts were made out of steel.

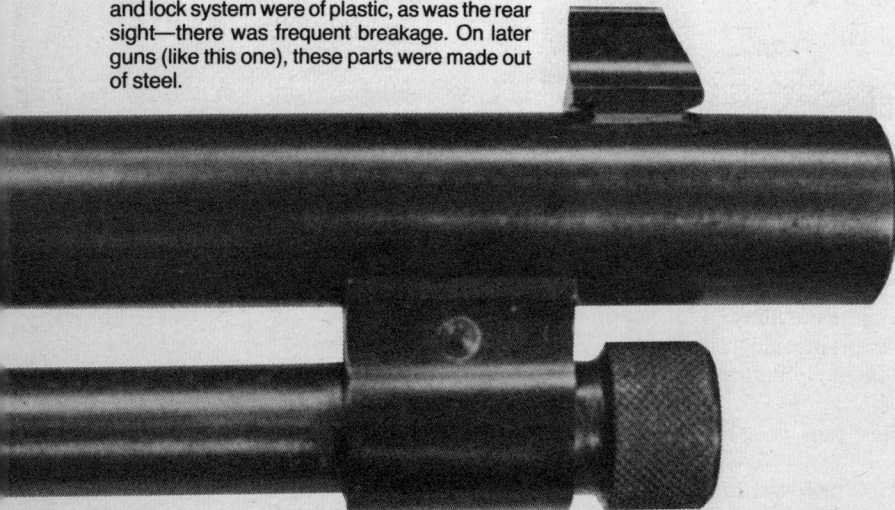

The trigger group, the sub-frame which contains the feed and firing mechanisms, is retained at the front by a plug which enters a hole inside the receiver and at the rear by a cross-pin made of plastic. This pin is tough and rarely breaks, but with frequent takedown it can become "shaved" to the point that it is a loose fit in the receiver. Here, again, I have often made replacements of steel, but original plastic pins are so inexpensive that it would make sense to just keep a couple of spares on hand.

On very early Model 190 guns, the magazine tube hanger and lock system were of plastic, and the rear sight was also of this material. Breakage was frequent, and replacement of a broken magazine hanger was not a simple matter. This was later corrected, and guns of current production have these parts made of steel. If you have one of the early ones, these plastic parts are available, and your gunsmith can replace those that are broken. Unfortunately, the new steel parts are not adaptable to the older guns, as the barrel is of a different configuration.

The sear, trigger and hammer engagement of this gun is rather delicate and will not tolerate any attempts to alter it to accomplish a trigger pull adjustment. The amateur will often try to change the sear step on the hammer, the most accessible part, and the result is almost always disastrous. It is possible to make this adjustment and achieve a smoother trigger pull, but this is definitely a job for your gunsmith.

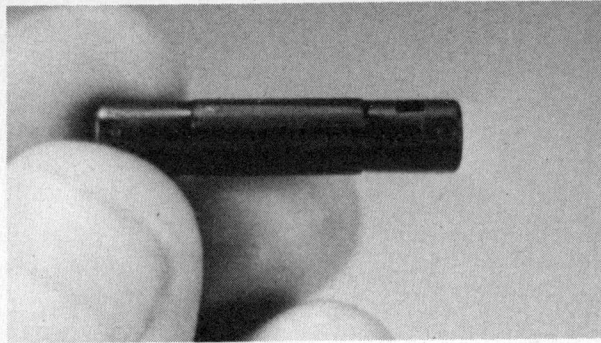

The 190's trigger group is retained at the front by a plug which enters a hole inside the receiver, and at the rear by this cross-pin. While these pins do not break, they are made of plastic—frequent takedown can shave them into looseness.

Sear, trigger and hammer engagement on the 190 is *very* delicate. Those who attempt to "adjust" the trigger pull by altering the sear step on the hammer (arrow) are inviting trouble.

Made of nylon, the hammer pivot bushing (which supports the hammer spring) never breaks. It can however, be damaged by amateur disassembly and reassembly.

The hammer pivot bushing, which Winchester calls the hammer spring support, is made of white nylon and is practically immune to breakage. It is frequently damaged, though, by amateur reassembly, as the hammer pin has a flat side which fits a corresponding surface inside the nylon piece, and it is possible to force the pin through misaligned. In the same area, one tail of the hammer spring is the positioning detent for the safety button, and during reassembly it is possible to leave this outside its proper slot, making the safety inoperative and deforming the spring.

This gun was introduced during Winchester's "cheap" period, and will probably be dropped in time.

Manufacturers and Importers

Some of the firms listed have been in business for many years, and have also produced several of the older guns listed in the book. Parts for these long-discontinued arms were exhausted many years ago. Trying to obtain them from the manufacturer will waste a lot of time—both yours and theirs. In this case it's best to go directly to the used or surplus parts dealers. When you do write the parts folks be sure to mark your letter, "Attention: Parts Department." For the older parts, check the listing of used-parts dealers in this book.

In regard to the older guns, some of the manufacturers can supply certain information, such as when a particular gun left the factory, where it was shipped, the original finish and so on. A small research fee is usually charged for this service.

Browning Arms Company
Route 4, Box 624-B
Arnold, MO 63010

Charter Arms Corp.
430 Sniffens Lane
Stratford, CT 06497

Colt Firearms
150 Huyshope Avenue
Hartford, CT 06102
(Sauer)

Harrington & Richardson
Industrial Rowe
Gardner, MA 01440

High Standard Mfg. Co.
31 Prestige Park Circle
East Hartford, CT 06108

Interarms, Ltd.
10 Prince Street
Alexandria, VA 22313

Ithaca Gun Company
Ithaca, NY 14850

Iver Johnson Arms, Inc.
P.O. Box 251
Middlesex, NJ 08846

Marlin Firearms Co.
100 Kenna Drive
North Haven, CT 06473

Bob Meece Co., Inc.
1602 Stemmons, Suite C
Carrollton, TX 75006
("Snake-Charmer")

O.F. Mossberg & Sons, Inc.
7 Grasso Street
North Haven, CT 06473

Navy Arms Company
689 Bergen Boulevard
Ridgefield, NJ 07657

Remington Arms Company
Bridgeport, CT 06602

Savage Arms Corporation
Westfield, MA 01085

Sears, Roebuck & Company
825 South St. Louis
Chicago, IL 60607

Smith & Wesson
2100 Roosevelt Avenue
Springfield, MA 01101

Stoeger Arms Company
55 Ruta Court
S. Hackensack, NJ 07606

Sturm, Ruger & Company
Southport, CT 06490

Tradewinds, Inc.
P.O. Box 1191
Tacoma, WA 98401

Weatherby's
2781 Firestone Blvd.
South Gate, CA 90280

Wilkinson Arms
803 N. Glendora Avenue
Covina, CA 91724
(Terry Carbine)

Winchester Repeating Arms
New Haven, CT 06504

Parts Suppliers Directory

Don Butcher   *(1890 & 1906 Winchester parts)*
1006 Country Club Dr.
Hays, KS 67601

Walter Lodewick   *(Winchester parts)*
2816 N.E. Halsey St.
Portland, OR 97232

Numrich Arms Corporation   *(A general dealer)*
West Hurley, NY 12491

Sarco, Incorporated   *(Surplus military & general*
192 Central Avenue   *parts)*
Stirling, NJ 07890

Martin B. Retting   *(A general dealer, some older*
11029 Washington Blvd.   *parts)*
Culver City, CA 90230

Sherwood Distributors   *(Surplus military & general parts,*
18714 Parthenia Street   *also currently reproduced parts)*
Northridge, CA 91324

Triple K Mfg. Company   *(Replacement magazines & re-*
568 Sixth Avenue   *produced parts, some surplus)*
San Diego, CA 92101

Fenwick's Gun Annex   *(A general dealer)*
P.O. Box 38
White Hall, MD 21161

Traders Den   *(A general dealer)*
1011 Excelsior Ave. W.
Hopkins, MN 55343

Ozzie's Gun Parts   *(A general dealer)*
P.O. Box 274
Mineral, IL 61344

Bob's Gun Shop   *(A general dealer, specializing in*
P.O. Box 2332   *parts for modern imported guns)*
Hot Springs, AR 71901

W.C. Wolff Company   *(Gun springs)*
P.O. Box 232
Ardmore, PA 19003

E.C. Bishop & Son, Inc.   *(Stocks)*
Box 7
Warsaw, MO 65355

Reinhart Fajen   *(Stocks)*
Box 338
Warsaw, MO 65355

Dixie Gun Works   *(Primarily for muzzleloaders, but*
Gunpowder Lane   *many parts for early cartridge*
Union City, TN 38261   *guns as well)*